my
thinning
years

"*My Thinning Years* is the story of all of us as we come to terms with who we are. It takes courage to tell your story, to come out, to remove yourself from an abusive relationship. These pages help usher in our more tolerant present and our ever-evolving hearts."

—Will Dailey, award-winning singer/songwriter

"A fantastic and harrowing story, told deeply and honestly . . . an emotional read . . . a generous, hopeful book I dearly hope gets into the hands of the many people who face similar hardships and desperately need to hear Jon Derek Croteau's story." —Randy Harrison, actor, *Queer as Folk*

"A heady mixture of raw emotion, pathos, and humor are everywhere in evidence in this powerful journey from self-hatred to self-affirmation and healing. *My Thinning Years* is an inspiring story of one man's struggle with anorexia, with sexual identity, and with finding himself."

—Betsy Lerner, author of *Food and Loathing*

"*My Thinning Years* is a powerful story about overcoming adversity. Jon Derek Croteau's courage, honesty, and unfailing passion are sure to both inspire and keep the pages turning!"

—Jenni Schaefer, coauthor of *Almost Anorexic* and author of *Life Without Ed* and *Goodbye Ed, Hello Me*

"*My Thinning Years* is not just a labor of love but a love letter to those who are struggling silently and suffering deeply with an eating disorder. Jon Derek Croteau sheds incredible insight and a heartfelt vision for surviving and thriving in your life."

—Jess Weiner, author, strategist, and self-esteem expert

"*My Thinning Years* is an emotional journey through Jon Derek Croteau's struggle with eating disorders and accepting his identity as a gay man. In his struggle to accept his sexuality, Croteau attempts to erase his pain through trying to erase himself. This is an honest, powerful, and raw insight into the self-punishing, self-harming, and consuming force of eating disorders." —Grace Bowman, author of *Thin*

my thinning years

Starving the Gay Within

Jon Derek Croteau

HAZELDEN®

Hazelden
Center City, Minnesota 55012
hazelden.org

ISBN: 978-1-61649-509-1

Editor's note
Some names, details, and circumstances have been changed to
protect the privacy of those mentioned in this publication.

This publication is not intended as a substitute for the advice of
health care professionals.

18 17 16 15 14   1 2 3 4 5 6

Cover design: Jon Valk
Interior design: Trina Christensen / Terri Kinne
Typesetting: BookMobile Design and Digital Publisher Services

For my mother, who saved me from disappearing,
and for my husband, who found me at the right time.

contents

preface

When my mother died in 2009, I finally accepted my own resilience. Just as I thought I'd never be able to survive living in my father's house, or to move past my disordered eating, or to make it through Outward Bound, or to navigate living in Europe on my own, I was convinced I would never be able to survive my mother's death—the death of my greatest champion and ally. I didn't realize it at the time, but she inspired me, and gave me the skills—the gift—to endure, through any challenge. She made sure that I had the heart to not only survive, but thrive.

My Thinning Years has been a story thirty-eight years in the making. For many reasons, I held back on sharing my story. Perhaps it was fear of being rejected. Maybe it was the shame of being different. Or the guilt over facing some hard truths about myself. Probably all of it. In recent years, however, I've felt compelled, more as time goes on, to share these "thinning years." If my honesty—about the darkness that once overshadowed my life and that, years of hard work later, has transformed into something brighter—can save just one life, then I'll know it will have been worth it.

I seem to hear horrifying stories more than ever about people facing hardships similar to mine: a young college student, taking his life because being gay felt too hard to live with; a twelve-year-old constantly being bullied at school because she's a bit taller than the other girls; a young man starving himself to numb the pain of his home life. I was all of these people, but something inside of me, something deep inside, made me, even in my worst moments of despair, in the deepest of doldrums, decide to let hope in. There were special people in my life who stood up for me and made me believe it would get better.

Every time I hear of another life lost, I wish anew that my story might be an inspiration for others who need some hope in their lives.

I feel as if even in death my mother has been encouraging me to tell my story. Maybe she's run into all the young people up in heaven who left us too soon. Maybe she wants me to try to inspire other people to keep holding on like I did. She taught me to be giving and loving, even when I stood to get nothing in return, even when it was risky. Writing *My Thinning Years* has been risky. But believing that I can help others helps me to broach that intimacy, to be brave enough to reveal my innermost thoughts. After everything I've seen, my mission is nothing less than to help others.

I hope to reach teens, young adults, and adults alike who have suffered in their lives, or are still suffering, because of their sexual orientation or some other perceived difference, and show them that they can heal. A struggling young person, a suffering adult, a begrudging parent—I want to show them that they are all worth it.

I should know. I suffered a long war against myself. I thought the self-hatred, the suicidal thoughts, the obsession with dieting and exercise, the internalized homophobia would never lift. But there were turning points, key moments in my life that tugged at my heart and convinced me to strive on. And it *was* worth it. Although nothing is perfect and every day still has its challenges, I am living proof that no matter how hopeless life can seem at times, with hard work and the support of loved ones, things really can, and do, get better.

In *The Stories We Live By,* Northwestern University professor Dan P. McAdams describes how we come to understand ourselves, psychologically and emotionally, by talking about and writing about our personal stories. This is the story *I live by.* This is my introspective perspective based on the recollection of my memories and my truth as I experienced it. Certainly, others who have been intimately involved in my life may have a different perspective and interpretation of an event, a period in history, a conversation, or a moment in time. How we all remember things and interpret them is uniquely individual. Therefore, I've changed the names of the people and many of the places in this book to protect others' anonymity. The only exception is my husband, Justin, who insisted upon sharing this journey with me openly.

I have written this from my heart and my mind to yours, hoping it moves you to embrace a child you have abandoned, or encourages you to stop punishing yourself for just being who you are, or inspires you to open your heart to someone who is different from you.

These are my "thinning years" that I share with you.

prologue

In my mind, there was this glob of fat making its way around my digestive system, looking for a place on my body to deposit itself, and it had to be stopped.

I was alternately speed walking and lightly jogging around Boston in the wee hours of the morning, obsessing over what I'd done. (I would have been full-out running if I weren't still in my khakis, button-down shirt, and loafers from the evening before.) *Oh my God,* I thought, *I can't believe I gave in. My life is over. I'm disgusting. I hate myself. And for all I know, semen has as many grams of fat as CREAM CHEESE. I need to burn this off now!*

For a while I'd been limiting myself to a maximum of five grams of fat a day, but I felt more at ease, safer, when I kept it closer to zero. Consume more than that, and I wouldn't be able to stand myself, like how I felt right then, frantically wandering around Boston in the early morning light. I vowed to run again, more heavily, when I returned home to Andover later that day. Maybe I'd keep it up for two hours this time and really sweat. Anything to keep that fat glob from finding a home on my belly.

It was seven in the morning, and after rehashing the graver implications of my previous evening's transgressions for a solid hour, I'd moved on to berating myself for the dietary consequences of my actions. When I'd woken, startled, at six, with my skin literally sticking to Paul's naked body, I could no longer escape the ugly truth: At nineteen, in the wake of my first sexual encounter ever, I was now without question what my father had most feared and strictly forbidden—a *faggot.* If he found out—*when he found out*—he was going to kick my ass.

I was paralyzed, haunted by the paranoid fantasy that my father—big, imposing, a volunteer athletic coach in my hometown—was somehow there in the room with us, perhaps under the bed. Or outside in the hallway. Maybe in the lobby. Of course I knew, in my head, that he was safely in his bed thirty minutes away, at home in Andover and obviously not anywhere near the neighborhood of the college I was visiting. I knew it, but I still didn't trust it.

Surely my father could telepathically detect that his youngest son had finally succumbed to the impure, un-Catholic urges he'd resisted for so long. At any instant, Dad might burst into the room, breaking the door off its hinges as he had at our house one night in a fit of rage. "You disgusting little faggot!" he'd shout before slugging me or dragging me away from Paul's bed by my hair. He'd be sure to throw in a verbal dig about my physique. "Nice tire around your waist, you fairy. Now give me a hundred push-ups!"

My father stood about five feet eleven, with a sizable belly. He held most of his weight in his torso. He was a meaty guy, of Italian descent, with chunky hands that always frightened me. He kept his fingernails impeccably manicured, though, which I thought strange for a "man's man" like him, along with the flashy pinky ring he wore—gold with diamonds. He wore two gold chains that he never took off, one that was snug around his thick lower neck, and another that hung to the middle of his chest that held two gold pendants. You could hear the Jesus Christ medal hitting the cross when he moved, mean and fast.

He was meticulous about his clothes, too, and his thinning light brown hair, which was always perfectly combed over. Honestly, I hated the mere sight of him. I would look in the mirror and pray that I would not see his pronounced nose or his double chin on my face.

The fantasy horror scene of my father barging into Paul's room flickered before my eyes as I lay there, staring at the ceiling. I replayed it again and again; I even checked under the bed a few times to make sure. When it was clear my heart was not about to stop racing, I threw on my clothes and bolted, leaving Paul as he slept. On the way out, I caught a glimpse of myself in the full-length mirror behind his door. I still looked the same—same preppy, medium-height guy with a strawberry blond Buster Brown haircut and a faint glow from tanning. But inside, I was completely changed.

It would be a couple of hours before I could reasonably tiptoe back into the dorm room of my close friend from high school, Bianca. I was supposed to be visiting her for a college weekend tour. It was supposed to be all so innocent, so normal. *What happened? How did I allow myself to succumb to what is surely a mortal sin? I'm going straight to hell.*

I focused on the fat globule. I just kept moving, weaving in and out of one street then another, alternately walking and jogging, obsessing about burning it, getting rid of the indiscretion that I felt was now somehow sitting in my stomach. *It has to go,* I said to myself, *and sooner or later, so do I.*

✳

Chapter 1

Sex Change for a Preschooler?

I loved the way my mom looked and smelled, even after she had just smoked a cigarette. She often wore red fitted sweaters that accentuated her slim frame, which she accessorized with a crinkled pack of Winston Red 100's. I'd always gravitated toward my mom and loved everything about her. She and I seemed to be connected from as early as I can remember.

My father, on the other hand, was oil to my water. I found him repellant. Just a whiff of the Vitalis tonic he used in his thinning hair made me want to run. My earliest memories of him are entangled with fear and anxiety. I think he resented how close I was with my mother. Or he was afraid of it. He blamed her for everything I appeared to be and was to become.

Most mornings before afternoon preschool, Mom and I went to Mary and Ted's restaurant in the center of town, where we'd sit in the same booth every time. I had a cheese omelet and she had Frosted Flakes with whole milk and an English muffin smothered with butter and grape jelly. From the picture window beside our booth, I could see the kids from my school's morning session playing in the church's yard. I never went outside during recess and wondered what it was like to play on the swings and to climb on the tires.

Our breakfasts were some of my favorite times while living in Hudson, Ohio. Everyone at Mary and Ted's knew us by our first names, and my mom would chat with Jo, our waitress, about the tornado sightings from the spring before and about the chill in the air, signs of the coming winter.

After our late morning feasts, Mom and I would climb in her over-sized brown Chevy station wagon. Every time we got into that wagon, I insisted that I sit on the "hump," the armrest in between the driver and passenger seats, and she let me. (What a different world then; no mandatory car seats strapped in with seatbelts.) The car seemed giant to me and felt like it could fit dozens of people. On many hot summer days, when I didn't have school, we would load the wagon full of towels, chairs, tennis rackets, and our neighbors, the Vildans, and go to the Redwood Swim Club.

Around noontime on school days, she'd drive me across the town green to the church, and I would jump out after receiving a Winston 100–scented, maroon lipstick kiss on my cheek. I spent the rest of the afternoon at Hudson Country Day.

Hudson Country Day was located in the basement of a very small church in the center of town. The building's white paint had been rotted by many midwestern downpours. It had green doors and a bell tower with a working bell that rang every day at noon. The floor's concrete was covered with a worn blue industrial rug, and the room had oversized chests overflowing with toys, games, costumes, Etch A Sketches, and abacuses. Scattered throughout were beanbags, pillows, and metal folding chairs.

In one corner of the classroom, there was an old cherry wood vanity. It had a mirror that had been stained with rust and six drawers on either side of the pushed-in chair. Next to it was a floor-to-ceiling mirror. In the drawers were faux pearls and diamonds, hair clips, brooches, pins, feathered hats, boas, scarves, dresses, and other dress-up items. Draped on the mirror were faux-fur stoles and old-fashioned umbrellas and yellowed, white lace parasols. Not many of the boys in my class were drawn to the vanity—but I was. Whenever Miss Turley read to us, I'd imagine myself over by the vanity coming up with the next outfit for the girls to wear. At recess, the boys would run outside to play on the hard top, but I'd run to the vanity.

My mom picked me up every afternoon at three o'clock, after the end-of-day snacks—graham crackers and pint-sized milk cartons—

and story time. Once or maybe twice, when my father wasn't away on business, my mom and dad would pick me up together in his fancy company car.

The company for which my dad worked gave him a new Buick, and because it was a company car, we were rarely allowed to go in it. It was brown with a beige imitation-convertible top, and it had silver spoke wheels. The interior dash and doors were covered in shiny wood, and the seats were made of crushed amber velour. I loved stroking the seats in the back with my hand, changing the color from dark to light, depending on which way I rubbed them.

One of the rare occasions when my dad joined my mom in picking me up had been a movie day at school. I'd stuffed myself with two bags of yellow buttered movie popcorn, so I didn't feel very well. I didn't say anything at first. My dad didn't like it when I "whined like a girl." When I came to the car, I groveled to sit on the soft hump, like I always did. "Okay," my mother said. "It's a special occasion." We were going out for dinner to a nice restaurant in Cleveland, as a family. Jared and Julie were getting ready at home, and we were on our way to pick them up.

My mom was already dressed for dinner, and she looked beautiful. She had on a black dress, ruby earrings, and a matching ruby and gold necklace. She was also wearing her diamond pinky ring, the one she wore on the same hand as her wedding and engagement rings, when she dressed in out-to-dinner clothes. Because it was late fall and our first frost was due that evening, my mom had on her rabbit fur coat. I was enamored with her coat of many colors—white, brown, gold, and gray. The fur was so silky; I would bury my face in it and move my hands all over it when given the chance. It smelled like her and her Charlie perfume. Sometimes when my dad was away, my mom would let me wrap myself in it and walk around the house. She'd laugh with me as I'd pretend to be a king or a queen.

I was mesmerized by my mother's loveliness. People said she looked like a taller, thinner Geraldine Ferraro, the first female candidate for U.S. vice president. Her hair was perfectly frosted, her figure was fit, and her face had many wrinkles, an acknowledgment of her absorbing the sun's rays most of her life without sunblock. I never liked it when my father told her that her wrinkles embarrassed him. I found them to be glamorous.

I remember many nights when they'd come home from business dinners and he'd yell at her, screaming that she made a fool of herself and of him, and that her wrinkles were ugly. He'd say that she should get a facelift because her wrinkles were so bad from smoking so many cigarettes. Her smoking bothered me, too, but it was something that I grew accustomed to. Her everyday clothes smelled like a mixture of her perfume and stale smoke, a scent that told me she was near, even if she wasn't in the room.

I also knew she was close by when I'd hear her snapping her Wrigley's Spearmint gum, which she'd buy by the fat pack and chew on one stick after another, sometimes while she smoked. The frosty mint smell of the many open packs of gum wafted from her pocketbook on car rides. Dad would snap back at her, "Judy, would you stop snapping that gum!" I think she did it just to drive him crazy.

As my father pulled out of the school's driveway and began to accelerate, my stomach lurched. "I don't feel very well," I reluctantly moaned. I was convinced I had to throw up. He immediately pulled over and pushed me out of my mom's side of the car. I leaned over on the side of the road for about five minutes until the cramping in my bloated belly passed. "You sure you're okay now?" he asked. "Because I don't want you getting sick in this car." I got back on the hump of the car and my dad accelerated once again. Suddenly, I was overwhelmed with nausea, worse than before, and I began to cry, "I'm going to throw up," I warned him. "I'm going to puke!" It was Bit-O-Honey brown and had what appeared to be popcorn kernels in it. It came up so fast, I hurled all over my mom's fur coat and my dad's prized Buick.

My dad had barely finished pulling over the car before he started screaming at me. "What the Christ did you do?" I didn't know what to say; I was just four years old, and I didn't mean to do it. I also thought it was obvious. He turned red. "You are so stupid, Jon. Do you know how much it is going to cost me to get this fixed? Do you? Do you?" My mom was visibly upset, but she didn't yell at me. She urged him to hurry home so they could clean up. It wasn't going to be easy; it was everywhere. My father sped through our tiny town like a madman. My mom appeared overtaken by the heavy stench of the vomit. She rolled down the window, but it didn't make a difference. We pulled into our driveway, the car bouncing over the bump at the end.

I wanted to help clean up the mess, but my father yelled at me and told me to go to my room and not to come out until he said so. "You ruined the night, you ruined everything!" I didn't get dinner that night and cried myself to sleep. I didn't get to come out of my room until the next morning, despite my whining, which enraged Dad more.

A few weeks later, my friend Katie and I found ourselves giddily playing at recess, donning flowing scarves and clip-on earrings, play-spraying empty bottles of perfume onto ourselves when I heard laughter. I looked over and there was a circle of mostly boys and a few girls pointing at my outfit. "Sissy!" they took turns saying. My dad had angrily called me that once, so I knew it wasn't a good thing. I looked at Katie, and she didn't seem to care about what they were saying. She linked her arm into mine and pulled me closer to the vanity's mirror. Looking at our reflection, she said, "I think you look pretty, Jon."

Even though I agreed with Katie and thought the high-heeled shoes I had on were perfect with the red hat on my head, I was bothered by the kids laughing at me. I took off the hat and put it back into the chest that I'd pulled it from. Slowly, I removed the earrings, the necklaces, and the scarves that had made a perfect wrap-like dress. I slid out of the shoes and looked downward, feeling so plain in my tube socks, corduroy shorts, and polo shirt. I asked Miss Turley if I could be excused to use the bathroom, and she obliged. When I closed the door, I locked it and checked it. I turned toward the sink and the mirror above it and looked at myself and wondered why I was different than the other boys. They made me feel so bad. I grabbed a bunch of toilet paper and stopped my running nose and sat on top of the toilet's cover until Miss Turley knocked on the door. "You okay in there, Jon? Come on out now."

My mom noticed something different when she picked me up that day (or maybe Miss Turley had called her). "You seem sad, Jon, did something happen today?"

"Nope," I said with assurance.

"You know you can tell me anything, right? We don't have secrets, remember?" she continued.

"No secrets," I agreed. I didn't know enough at that age to tell her that the boys were laughing at me. She didn't know I never went outside on the playground because I was desperate to find the newest article of clothing in the vanity that had come in from the local thrift store. I had dressed up before when I was even younger, and I'd put on her Candies mules and a few of her necklaces. I would sing "You Light Up My Life" in front of some of my parents' dinner guests. Everyone laughed and clapped, except my dad. He'd just look disgusted and would order my mom to get me out of the room. Later, after the guests would leave and I was lying in my bed, I could hear him yelling at her.

"It's your fault Jon is like that," he screamed. "This is because you baby him, Judy!"

"You're ridiculous!" she shouted back. "He's just a little boy. He's playing."

"You're going to make him a sissy!" my dad insisted, not letting up.

I wanted to tell her everything, but I was scared. I wanted to tell her my secret about how when she was in the shower sometimes, I would sneak into her jewelry box and put on her rings; I would put one on every finger. It excited me. I loved the way the jewels sparkled in the lamp light. I did the same in my sister's jewelry box when she was at school, although her jewels were not as nice as my mom's. Sometimes, I would pull all of my mom's long scarves out of her bureau drawers and drape them all around me. I loved the way the soft silk felt on my neck and face. It made me feel special and fancy. I didn't tell her or anyone else because I was afraid of my dad finding out. The fear, which I didn't understand at the time, was almost instinctual.

After asking ten different times if I was okay after the incident at school, my mom changed the subject, and we drove to our home on Victoria Parkway. That night, as I lay in bed, I felt guilty for keeping a secret from my mom. I thought about getting up and walking into her room to tell her what had happened that day at school, but my dad was home, not away on business, and I couldn't tell her when he was around. I fell asleep praying that my dad would go away again soon, but promised myself that I wouldn't play at the vanity in the meantime.

A week later, after sitting in a corner at recess by myself, Katie asked me if I wanted to try on a new dress that she had found deep in the bottom drawer of the vanity. It was champagne colored and had lace around the neck. She said it would fit me perfectly. "Not today," I said sadly.

"What's wrong, Jon?" I didn't want to talk about it. "I'm just not feeling good," I said.

"Really?" Katie asked. "You look fine to me. Well, if you change your mind, I have a really fun game we can play." I watched her playing with a few other girls from my corner and felt like I was missing out on something important. Perhaps it was a royal ball or a dinner at a palace. What if she was having a gathering at her estate? I jumped up and ran toward them and told the girls that I was ready to play.

That night I woke up shortly after my mom had put me to bed. The setting red Ohio sun was still igniting the sky. My heart pounded. I didn't want to keep secrets from my mom. I didn't know why I thought this was a secret, but I did, and she had always told me that I could tell her anything.

The first time I remembered her saying that was months before, when she got the impression I was keeping a secret from her. My friend Quince from down the street and I would often play in their finished basement. It was one of those cool basements with a pool table and lots of games and toys. For months, I'd been sneaking in to the family room when my mom was watching soap operas on days that I didn't have school. On occasion she'd see me standing there, but I was in there more than she knew, and I saw lots of kissing—the dramatic soap opera, movie kind of kissing.

One day, in Quince's basement, I'd somehow convinced him to play along with mimicking one of those kissing scenes. I told him to lie down flat on the ground and then I lay down on top of him. Our bodies awkwardly together, I pursed my lips tight and pressed them against his. They were wet and sticky from the lollipops we each just had upstairs with his mom. I instructed him to twist and turn his head fast and in circles, just like I had seen on TV. We giggled in between our fumbling kisses. Suddenly, Quince's mom rushed down the stairs screaming, "What are you two doing? Get off him, Jon!" She pulled me off Quince and carried me by my shirt all the way to my house, three houses down and across the street. She knocked on our front door and my mom answered. She told her what we had been up to, and my mom looked at me disappointed. She politely thanked Quince's mom for walking me home and closed the door behind her. I was scared to death. But Mom didn't freak out. "Jon, I hope you know you can always tell me anything, no matter what it is. No secrets. Now go on up to your room and get ready for dinner."

I didn't completely understand what it was that I was supposed to say. I was just having fun with Quince reenacting things that I had seen her watching on TV. I didn't get why Quince's mom got so upset, but it would certainly be something I'd never forget. I still don't know if my mom told my dad, but given what was to come, she must have.

That night after I'd played dress-up again at school, I lay sweating in my sheets, my stomach in knots. Unable to fall asleep, I arose and walked down the long staircase and into the kitchen where my mom was washing dishes in the sink, looking out into the large, open, flat backyard. My father was sitting in the family room, reading the sports section while listening to John Chancellor deliver the *NBC*

Nightly News on the television set. I pulled my mother's hand and walked her into the family room with me.

For some reason, I felt like I had to tell her, like I had been told to do in confession at church, to shed my sins. I couldn't hide it any longer. So I told them both at the same time. "I play dress-up and put on girl clothes at school," I said. "I just wanted you to know how much fun it is and it is so fun to play with the other girls. I mean it is fun and we play castle and shop and it is just fun."

"WHAT?" my father shouted. My mother looked down as my father stood up and became loud and large. "Upstairs, Mister," he bellowed. "Turn around and upstairs to your room!" He pointed with one hand out of the family room and whacked my butt with his other. I ran away from him and scurried up the stairs, my tiny feet moving as fast as they would. Once in my room, I jumped onto my bed and curled into a ball.

I heard my father's loud, heavy steps slowly coming up the stairs. The shadow of his huge frame appeared in my doorway before he did. He turned the corner into my room and slammed the door behind him. He removed his belt from his waist, furiously, the skinny black leather making ticking noises as it passed each belt loop.

"What you do at school is disgusting to me," he said. "Do you know that? Disgusting! I should whip you for that." Intimidating me, he positioned the belt in front of his chest and cracked it as the leather smacked itself. His threatening stance made me quiver. I was sure I'd get the belt, so I pulled up the covers and got myself under them. He continued on his tirade. "Do you know what they call boys who dress up like girls? Fags. That's what. Do you want to be a girl? Huh? Or do you want to be a boy?" I sat there, unable to answer. "Well, you have one night to figure that out, Mister! I'm not letting you out of this room until you decide." He opened my closet and threw all my little pants and jackets on the floor. "We'll take all of these clothes and sell them to boys who want to be boys and buy you all new girl clothes. Is that what you want? You can go to the hospital and change—do you know that?"

He didn't stop there. "You don't get breakfast or lunch, and you are NOT going to that school. Never again! And you'd better make the right decision! I want an answer by the time I get home from work tomorrow." He marched out and slammed the door. I broke into sobs. It was so much for a child to take in—the threat of being hit by the belt that had lined my legs with swollen stripes many instances before. Or the fear of being spanked again by his massive hands that left ring marks on my bottom. Was I sick so I had to go to the hospital? Is that what he meant? *What's wrong with me?* His sharp, cutting words pierced my heart. I was confused about why something that was so much fun was being treated as if it were something so bad.

Dad banished me to my room without meals until dinner the following night. The next day, after whining to my mom through my bedroom door's crack, she showed up at my door with a grilled cheese cut up in squares and a plastic cup of strawberry milk. She sat with me on my bed as the toasty bread and gooey yellow cheese comforted my aching belly. She fixed my hair with her long burgundy nails. She didn't say much, but she didn't have to.

I dreaded the moment when Dad would ask me for my answer. I was chewing my fingernails to stubs at the kitchen table as Jared and Julie ate Mom's rich chicken divan. Dad was watching a ball game on TV alone in the family room. He never sat at the table. After it was clear Dad wasn't ever going to ask for my answer, I shoveled my food in, fearing it could be a while until I'd eat again.

Suddenly he called out, "Jon, I'm signing you up for basketball tomorrow. You're going to learn how to play a real sport and learn how to be a real man. Enough of this sissy stuff."

The next morning, after my father had really calmed and deflated, I was released from my grounding. Mom called me down to the kitchen. She had toasted some frozen waffles and smothered them in butter and syrup. We didn't go to Mary and Ted's that morning. Instead she said she was taking me to a new school, where I was to be one of the morning kids.

On the way out of our driveway, I looked at our basketball hoop from the hump of Mom's car. The idea of throwing a ball into a basket didn't excite me, and I knew that I would stink at it and dreaded it.

After she finished all of the paperwork in the school office, she kissed me good-bye and walked out the door waving with a half smile that didn't activate the laugh lines around her eyes. As I turned to go play with the girls at my new school, my teacher directed me toward the trucks and the Nerf basketball and the short hoop and told me that I was to play with the boys.

I never saw Katie or the inside of Hudson Country Day again.

＊

Chapter 2

Take Me Out of the Ball Game

"Ready? Set? Hut, hut, hike!" I ran at the quarterback as fast as I could with all of the heavy gear on me and scooped the ball in between my flimsy arms. I huddled it close to my body just as I was instructed. Tommy and Sam tackled me just across the line of scrimmage. I'd barely gained a yard.

My faceguard was mashed into the field's grass and muck, sinking into the soggy, chilly earth. The helmet smelled like a mixture of adolescent boys, sweat-filled locker rooms, moldy kitchen towels, and now, horse manure. *Yuck!* The stench was enough to make me want to run away from the field, not to mention my groaning teammates, their slimy, drool-filled mouth guards, and the monotonous plays we had to practice over and over.

What could possibly be fun, I wondered, *about smashing into one another and trying to run the ball into a make-believe, magic area?* I had no idea. And I had no fun. Even though I begged, I wasn't allowed to quit, most of all because my dad was one of the coaches.

I hadn't volunteered to play football; I had no choice. My dad thought that a contact sport would make me "tougher" and would get me into better shape. "It's good for you," he'd say. "It'll make you a real man." He said I was the right body type because I was "chunky and big-boned," but I could also run fast. I was the perfect fullback, he said, and maybe I could get a scholarship to Notre Dame some day. I was in fifth grade; I barely knew what Notre Dame was. All I remembered about it was that when we lived in Ohio, we drove forever to get to Indiana, where we got to run on Notre Dame's football field. It didn't leave much of an impression on me. My attention was probably focused on the marching band practice.

Sports were at the core of my father's identity as a "real man." In his mind, you couldn't be a real man if you didn't play and watch sports. He wanted his two sons to grow up to be real men. He'd already pushed Jared into sports to great success. Jared was a gifted athlete. He was good at any sport that centered around a ball. For me, sports were always a source of stress.

My sister was pushed into activities that were more traditionally acceptable for girls. So she did ballet and figure skating and cheerleading. As the youngest, I got to learn what activities I gravitated toward by first observing my older siblings participating in all of theirs. If it were up to me, I would've picked ballet or figure skating, but it wasn't. None of us had a choice in anything we did. My father continued to push me into the three sports he considered manliest: basketball, baseball, and, worst of all, football.

I was terrible at football, as I was at most sports. What's more, I hated it. I dreaded going to practices and games. I tried groveling to my mom. "Please, Mom," I begged, sobbing, one day before another hideous practice. "Don't make me have to play!" But neither of us had the power to overrule my dad. "It's just not a battle worth waging, Jon," my mother said, sounding defeated. I don't remember many battles that she thought were.

I would get sick to my stomach on the days when there was a game. The mere thought of the field made me queasy. I tried to come up with an illness or a condition that could get me out for the entire season, but I just wasn't clever or dishonest enough to come up with something believable. So, I prayed every night for something, anything to get me out of it.

Even though I was just a wimpy elementary school kid, I was forced to play against the heavier, taller kids who were in the sixth, seventh, and eighth grades. I never understood why at every practice the coaches made the A-team—the starters and the older kids—scrimmage against the B-team—the younger, scrawnier, less experienced kids. I was so little, the helmet was too heavy for my flimsy neck to hold up in place. Maybe pummeling the B-team gave the A-team more confidence. I dreaded those scrimmages. I dreaded running into Eric Greenspan's massiveness.

For me, there was only one upside to our football games and practices: the cheerleaders. Samantha and Kendra were the captains. They were my best friends. We'd met in Mrs. Winter's second grade class when I first moved to Andover from Hudson. No one really talked to me because I came in the middle of November, and everyone already had their friends. But Samantha talked to me. She and I grew closer and closer; we were like Vada and Thomas J. from the movie *My Girl*. Kendra, on the other hand, initially became my friend because our parents went to high school together. But over the years we became close and found the same things funny, often laughing hysterically together. She brought out the best of my sense of humor.

The coaches and my teammates yelled at me during practices because I always moved late after the snap. I was too busy watching Samantha and the other girls practice their cheers. I thought of myself somewhat as a cheerleading connoisseur. My sister was a cheerleader for most of her teenage years and made her way to being captain of the squads in both Hudson and in Andover. I attended many of her practices with my mom. I loved watching them do all the synchronized, choreographed moves to their loud, odd lyrics. "Let's get a little bit rowdy, R-O-W-D-Y!" Or "Unite . . . tonight . . . and prove without a doubt . . . that the *Warriors* are number one . . . so shout it out!" All the while they would move their arms like windmills and do "Russians" or spread-eagles. I think I could do half of the cheers myself by the time I was ten. I never did them in public, only in my room in front of the mirror, mouthing the words silently so my father couldn't hear.

Our second game of the season was against the Colts. It was an unusually warm fall day, around seventy-eight degrees, with the bright sun beating down on the field. Bumblebees and yellow jackets were out in full force, scavenging their last specks of flower pollen to store in their hives for the winter.

Typically, the A-team would play the first two and the fourth quarters, while the B-team only played the third quarter. That was fine with me; I only had to endure one quarter, and I'd count down the seconds until it would end.

I spent the first two quarters of that game against the Colts running away from the many bees drawn to our benches because of the orange slices' and Gatorade's sweet smell. When I wasn't running from the bees, I spent most of my time watching Samantha and Kendra and the Redskins' cheerleaders. Their halftime show was a choreographed dance to Janet Jackson's "Rhythm Nation." Samantha's sister was their coach, and she'd done a good job choreographing. I wished I could have done it with them, but instead I was supposed to be listening to my father and Coach Bailey explain to us all the things the A-team did wrong in the first two quarters, which was probably why we were losing 13 to 7.

When the Colts' cheerleaders finished their halftime routine, I knew the fun was over and I was going to have to play in a few minutes. The head referee blew his whistle and called the game back on.

We got the ball on the thirty-yard line and had to trudge a distant seventy yards to score a touchdown. It wasn't going to happen, but there we were in the huddle, squeezed butt to butt, and our quarterback called the play. The play was a hand off to me, and I was to find a hole between two of the linemen. *Oh, shit,* I thought. I hated when the play starred me. My heart began to race. "Ready; break!" All of us clapped at the same time as we dispersed from our circle. Everyone made it to the line, and I was further back in the field, to the right of the quarterback. As I crouched down into my uncomfortable three-point stance (I did not understand why we couldn't just stand there waiting for the hike), my hand touching the dry, dead grass and dirt, I glanced to my left toward the benches. Out of the corner of my left eye, I saw the cheerleaders doing the cheer "Big G, Little O, Go, Go." They started moving into formation for a mount. I couldn't help but watch as Samantha made her way to the top of the pyramid and then, suddenly, she lost her footing and slipped down to the bottom.

Luckily, she was fine, but I wasn't! When I turned my head to get back in the game, I discovered the ball had already been snapped and I was too late for the hand off. Mike, our quarterback, got sacked, and I heard my father scream from the sidelines. "Get your head in the game, Jon! For Christ's sake!"

The ball was kept away from me as much as possible for a few yards, but soon it was another second down. The same exact play was called—for me to do the hand off and run-through-the-hole thing. I concentrated and kept my head on straight. I did not dare look to my left at the girls. The ball was snapped and I ran toward Mike, just like I was supposed to. I snagged the ball and kept it close to my body like I was supposed to. I ran through the hole that the linemen created for me like I was supposed to. And I saw openness and I ran for it just like I was supposed to, my feet circling one after the other with all the speed and energy of a locomotive. I thought I was running faster than I ever had before. I was determined to silence my dad and make him proud of me. I kept running and it felt like I had left everyone in the dust. The end zone was in view and I actually imagined myself crossing into it, people cheering, my teammates putting me on their shoulders, my dad smacking my helmet with joy.

Then, something hit me from behind like a bulldozer, crushing me violently to the ground. My left leg was planted into the turf like a figure skater's toe pick before a Lutz, while the rest of my body continued to move forward until it crashed to the ground. The defensive player who tackled me collapsed with all of his weight onto my left hip. I heard a crack inside my body and instantly screamed.

I thought my leg was forced out of my hip joint. I was in agony. I'd never felt physical pain like that before. There I was, lying on the ground, nearly paralyzed with pain. All the coaches from both sidelines rushed to my aid, even the coaches from the other team. I looked around above me, all of these faces asking if I was okay, and none of them looked familiar. In the distance, though, I could hear my father's voice coming toward me. "Get up, you sissy," he yelled. "Stop faking it, you baby. Get up! Get up!" I grabbed my hip with my hand and turned my head so that I did not have to see that familiar spitting face in the distance and I sobbed, not just because of the pain in my hip.

Several hours in Lawrence General Hospital's Emergency Room and several X-rays later, it was determined that I wasn't at all faking it. The growth plate in my left hip shattered when the Colts' tackle fell on me. I was to be out for the rest of the season with intense physical therapy. *Thank you, God.*

I got a pair of crutches and a sticker for being brave. My mom, who had traveled behind the ambulance and never left my side at the hospital, pushed me in a wheelchair out onto the emergency room's circular driveway. After she got me situated in the front seat of her station wagon, she said, "Let's get you to McDonald's. You deserve a Quarter Pounder with cheese and some fries." She took my hand and held it, promising that I would be okay. I smiled at her because she knew exactly how to make me feel better. (Sadly, it wasn't her home cooking.) I looked up at her and asked, "Mom, do you believe that God can hear us when we pray to Him?" She looked at me curiously, squeezed my hand, and said, "He listened to me when I prayed for a son just like you, didn't He?"

■ ■ ■

Up until that football game, it seemed God hadn't heard many of my prayers. For years, on a daily basis, my father unrelentingly drilled me, my brother, and my sister like a sergeant. "Did you do your push-ups? Sit-ups? Jump rope? Sprints? Did you shoot your baskets? How many? Did you swing the Bratt Bat? Did you do your squats?"

Sometimes, when my brother and I were studying later in the night in our bedrooms, Dad would sound off his signature, loud whistle. EEAWEET. EEAWEET. The high-pitched shriek that he'd make from his mouth was a call we knew not to disobey. We'd run downstairs and into the family room at attention like the Von Trapp family kids from *The Sound of Music* obediently awaiting orders from the Captain.

In our family room was this odd, wooden footstool that looked like a large turtle, about eight inches high. It had legs, a head, and a tail, and an orange carpet shell. Once we got downstairs from our bedrooms, my father would make us jump over it in front of him. He'd set his watch for sixty seconds and make us jump over it side to side at first. The next sixty seconds we had to jump over it from front to back. If we touched the turtle's back, which I did, again and again, we had to start over. There were nights I reached the point of almost vomiting from the number of times I would have to start over.

Every day after school, Dad would interrogate me, asking whether I'd been practicing and exercising. Exhausted mostly from his questioning, sometimes I'd make up my answers, but then he'd catch me in my lies. I think he set traps, too, placing the basketball or the baseball bat just so and checking later to see whether either of them had been moved. When he busted me, I'd pay the price, either with the belt, or being grounded, or getting banished to my room without food or television.

We weren't allowed to watch TV on school nights anyway, so I never really missed that. But I spent many nights with red lines from his belt on my thighs and butt, or with my stomach growling with hunger.

Food in our house was never treated as fuel. Instead, it was used for either punishment or reward. Consumption ran to extremes. Food was continually watched, scrutinized, and restricted, or it was flowing abundantly during holiday feasts—charades before the eyes of extended family and friends—that later turned disastrous in private. Sugared cereals, like Froot Loops and Apple Jacks, were banned. Oreos and Chips Ahoy! were not treats; they were *the enemy*. If I was hungry and Dad was in the family room when I wanted a snack, I'd tiptoe around the kitchen attempting to forage undetected. Without fail, he'd sense me there, get up, and see what I'd grabbed from the pantry or the fridge. "You know," he'd remark, "that crap is going to make you pudgier."

To complicate matters, my mom wasn't a gourmet cook by any

stretch of the imagination, except for a few Italian dishes that my dad's mother had taught her to make. I remember earlier in my childhood, my mom tried to always have dinner on a nicely set table. On most of those nights, my father would complain that she'd dried out the chicken or seared the steak too long. Or he'd yell at one of us kids for doing something less than perfectly, like getting a B on a spelling test or having our shirt untucked. Frustrated, she'd throw the dishes in the sink, sometimes breaking them. "Why don't you do the cooking yourself?" she'd ask. "And leave your kids alone." He'd quickly put her in her place, though. "You wouldn't have any food to ruin, not to mention this nice house, if I weren't sacrificing for you all every day," he'd say, his finger pointing in her face. "Remember that!"

Eventually, Mom stopped trying. She gave up cooking meals and stopped setting the table, especially when my father wasn't on a business trip. Ironically, when he was away, the four of us would enjoy a relaxed meal at the kitchen table, laughing and joking about our days. She'd also let each of us pick out a box of our favorite sugared cereal as long as it would be gone by the time he got back from his trip.

Most meals were microwaved or warmed in the oven. Frozen chicken fingers or crunchy fish sticks with macaroni and cheese or packaged fettuccine Alfredo became the staples through my high school years, along with takeout pizza, McDonald's, or roast beef sandwiches made at Harrison's, a local deli. Despite there not being much junk food in the house, and not being allowed chips and other salty or sugary snacks, we were not exactly the poster family for eating healthy. How could we be when Mom herself was known to live on soda, potato chips, and cigarettes and still somehow remained rail thin?

On some Saturdays and on holidays, Dad would allow Mom to break all the rules and fill the house with cold cuts and pizza bought from an Italian deli in the neighboring city of Lawrence. She'd also make her sauce and meatballs. Jared would invite his best jock friends over, and we'd gorge on the food after morning practices or games. Dad loved it when those guys were over. Ironically, my father would indulge more than anyone. He'd stuff his face and chew his food at warp speed—something that grossed out all of us. I am sure the food comforted him the way it comforts so many of us. But I wondered whether, in light of his many rules and judgments about food, if it also made him feel guilty afterward. He couldn't have been comfortable in his own skin. He had a double chin and had gained considerable weight over the years of working long hours to provide for us, as he always reminded us. I never saw him exercise, despite being the dictatorial coach that he was. And he was always angry.

■ ■ ■

As with football and basketball, I was forced to play baseball, too. I began my baseball career back in Hudson, in T-ball at age five, but only after screaming and crying in the front seat of my mom's station wagon, pleading to not have to play. And while a broken growth plate in my hip in fifth grade gave my mother the leverage to help me escape the horrors of football for good, a broken eye socket, a shattered carpal navicular bone in my left wrist, and sixteen weeks of casts, splints, and physical therapy weren't enough for my father to let me ditch the baseball field.

I would have preferred doing just about anything other than sliding in the dirt and getting my perfectly white uniform dirty. I'd just discovered I had a pretty good voice, and got into singers like Tracy Chapman and Whitney Houston. I didn't understand why I should waste time on the baseball field when I could be in my room, singing (or lip synching when Dad was home) popular hits like "Fast Car" and "How Will I Know?"

But the more I resisted playing, the more my father dug in and became determined to make me. I wasn't going to win that way. By the end of the first season, I realized the only way I could avoid having my father yell at me constantly for sucking so bad was to improve. By the time I was twelve, I ended up actually *earning* the spot on the Red Sox Little League team. (I'd made the team when I was ten, but only because my father was the coach.)

Begrudgingly, I discovered that I had a bit of talent when it came to baseball. I could hit and I could run, and when I was an infielder, I could field ground balls and make double plays from second base. Even though my father was a tyrant on the diamond, I actually didn't loathe baseball the way I despised playing football or basketball— that is until he became obsessed with making me a catcher.

At twelve, as I got to prepubescence and began filling out more, my father decided that I was roomy enough to become a great catcher like him. I had been playing second base, but thanks to the combination of my evolving and growing a catcher's build, and one of my father's practice line drives getting lost in the sun at Chandler Field and having hit my eye socket, cracking my orbital bone, my father moved me behind the plate.

My father always told us that he played for the Yankees as a catcher. He insisted that if not for a blowout injury when a player slid into him at home base with metal cleats and tore his knee apart, he would have had a long career in the major leagues. I'd tell my friends in elementary school that my father played for the Yankees, and they all must have thought I was crazy. As I got older, I learned that many of my father's stories were lies.

There was nothing I hated more than catching: the mask smelled like the football fields I loathed and it made me sweat. Even worse, it gave me zits. The pads were heavy and uncomfortable, not to mention the jock strap and cup that were required. My job was to, at any cost, catch a speeding baseball tossed by the pitcher, even if it was flying high above my head or heading straight for the dirt. From the dugout, my father would yell at me, "Turn your glove . . . put your face into the dirt. . . . Jesus Christ, Jon, lean into it. What, are you afraid of it?" Actually, I was. I thought anyone would be afraid of a baseball flying at him at fifty miles per hour, especially when he had already broken his eye socket. Many times I could hear our assistant coach, Mr. Lombardi, say, "Let up on him, Jimmy, you're going to drive the kid nuts!"

He didn't let up, though. Not in public and certainly not in private.

On drives home, he would drench me with his spittle in his burgundy Cadillac Fleetwood Brougham, the leather in which carried the scent of his breath mixed with his green Polo cologne. Once in the car, he would tell me how much I embarrassed him in front of everyone at the game. He had no problem telling me how terrible I was, not only as a catcher, but also as a hitter.

In one game, I struck out all four times I got to bat. I knew I'd get it on the way home. I tried to get my mom's attention so I could ride home with her, but she had already made her way to her car.

I was waiting in the passenger seat of the car while Dad finished up his postgame debriefing with Mr. Lombardi. He slid into the driver's seat and the car wobbled to his side. He slammed the door, his anger visible already on his reddened face, but waited to pull out of the parking lot to even utter a word. As soon as his blinker clicked off from the right-hand turn onto Chandler Road, he snapped, raising his voice, "How could you embarrass yourself like that? Do you know how much of a fool you made of me, too? You are a disgrace, an absolute disgrace. And it's because you are lazy. L-A-Z-Y capital letters lazy!"

I decided to just take it and not say anything. That turned out to have been the wrong move, setting him off even more. "What are you going to do, just sit there and be a pussy about it and not say anything? Be a man!" His anger turned from rage to a hatred I'd seen only a couple of times before, but would sadly get to know better in the years to come. He was so far out of control, he had to pull the car over to the side of the street. He jammed on the brakes and threw the car into park before it even came to a complete stop. All just so he could unleash his rage on me. Looking back, it couldn't have been just about striking out, but I certainly didn't know that at the time. His spit was all over my face and I didn't dare to wipe it off. I could smell it under my nose, and despite its stench, I didn't move a muscle. I felt one wrong move would send me to the hospital.

He didn't touch me that time, but he did warn me not to tell my mother when I got home, "or else." He said my complaints to her about the way he treated me—a way he believed was normal—caused the two of them to fight constantly. "Do you want us to get divorced? Huh? Do you?"

"No," I said, barely breathing.

"Then don't mention this to your mother. I will make you a man one of these days!"

When we got home, he ordered me out of my uniform and to shower up. I was to go to my room without dinner.

Soon, I began striking out every time I was at bat, and I also got worse as a catcher. My father would harp on me, on the field and off. It didn't make a difference, which just pissed him off even more. Maybe that was my unconscious battle strategy, to be so horrible he'd have to bench me. But I'd underestimated my father's determination.

Over the years to come, he dedicated his energy toward coercing me to get good at baseball. He sent me to baseball camps, clinics, and trainings, even in the winters. He put up tees and soft toss stations in our basement, and hung a baseball on a rubber band that was fastened to the ceiling and held down by a cinder block. He demanded that I take at least a hundred swings at that ball every night, sometimes more.

I quickly lost any remaining interest or enjoyment I had gotten from the sport. Why would I want to keep doing something I was told I was so terrible at, day in and day out? I didn't care to get any better at baseball because no matter what I tried, no matter how well I did, it was never good enough for my father. So when I was supposed to be taking my one hundred swings at night in the basement, I'd make sure my dad was two floors up watching TV in his room or taking one of his epic baths while snacking on Cheez-Its (we were allowed to have his favorite snack in the house) and reading the sports section. When I knew it was safe, I'd go to the other side of our basement where there was a kid's den with a couch, a couple of chairs, a television, and a stereo. Instead of swinging the bat, I'd listen to Whitney Houston on my Sony Walkman and I'd lip-synch my favorite of her hits. "The Greatest Love of All" had been released and skyrocketed to the top of the charts. I'd seen the video at one of my friends' houses and was mesmerized by Whitney's powerful voice. She was so gorgeous and glamorous in the two or three different gowns she wore in the video.

When I lip-synched in the basement, I dreamed about being on stage with her. I got a lot more practice singing than I did swinging that stupid bat. That's how I mastered every note of "The Greatest Love of All," moving my mouth and facial expressions exactly like Whitney's, even the jaw trembling from her raging vibrato.

■ ■ ■

I lost time from doing the things I really wanted as a child and a teenager to baseball and other sports. We lost time as a family, too, because of my father's obsession. We stopped taking any vacations because schedules of practices and games were more important. Dad even missed my sister's wedding rehearsal dinner to coach a high school football game under the lights. If nothing else, it could be said that he was dedicated to the community.

There were so many other things I wanted to do instead of sports. I wanted to try out for Merrimack Junior Theatre, or Confetti Kids show choir. I wanted to go to New York to see Broadway shows, and to see *The Nutcracker* at the Wang Center in Boston. But none of that was allowed; in fact, it was seriously discouraged. Eventually, I was afraid to even mention any of my interests. After all, if my father lost it because I liked dress-up time as a preschooler, he wasn't going to be too keen on me wanting to be a singer or a dancer as a teenager.

Chapter 3

The Greatest Love of All

took a deep breath so I could belt the high note. Not just any high note, the one that Whitney hits: "The greatest love of aaaaaalllllllll . . ." *Nailed it!* "Is easy to achieve . . . Learning to love yourself, it is the greatest love of all . . ."

I looked at my image in my bedroom mirror, one of the only places I ever sang. I was so impressed with myself that I'd made that note. *If I can hit that one,* I thought, *then I guess I can sing!*

I was practicing my audition song for our sixth grade musical, *Freedom Bound.* Because everyone in the sixth grade at Sanborn had to be in the play, this time my dad couldn't veto my involvement like he'd normally do for this kind of thing. It was part of the curriculum, and also a rite of passage in our school. I didn't care what the reason was. I was actually able to do something I'd wanted, something my father had vehemently discouraged from the time I was four or five, singing "You Light Up My Life" for my mother and our dinner company. Since then, most of my singing was relegated to the confines of my bedroom or the basement, except when my dad was on a business trip. I was afraid to sing when my dad was around.

My music teacher, Mrs. Grimes, saw that I enjoyed singing and always encouraged me in music class. And Mom paid for a few piano lessons here and there. But thanks to Dad's attitude toward my involvement with anything creative, plus the overbearing schedule of all things sports, singing was something I grew to love only in secret.

Much to my father's dismay, I got the male lead in the musical. I played John Anton, an immigrant from Europe moving his family to the United States for a better life. Clearly there was a history lesson embedded in the choice of musical. I had three solos throughout the play, and I took rehearsals and line memorization very seriously. I practiced constantly with my friend, Abbey, who played my wife, Sophie, and loved every moment of it. Even though I had a bit of stage fright in the beginning, by the end the joy of singing and performing bolstered my confidence and made me happy.

I think I might have been a little *too* excited for my father. He was intent on informing me that most men who were in musicals or theater were not real men. "Guys who do theater are girlie," he said. He was also adamant that the budding love I seemed to have for theater was to come to an end. After *Freedom Bound,* he insisted I was not to get used to doing "these sorts of things." I begged my dad to allow me to audition for the musicals produced by Merrimack Junior Theatre, a community theater for kids and teens in town. "Dad, can't I try out for the MJT musical?" I pleaded. "There are other guys who play sports who are trying out! It doesn't mean that I'll want to do theater all the time, just this once. Please?" I enlisted my mother to campaign on my behalf, too. Still, my father said, "No. And there will be no further discussion."

Instead, I'd have to settle for attending the musicals year after year as an audience member. I was overcome with envy watching other kids perform in shows like *Bye Bye Birdie* and *West Side Story.* I'd go backstage to congratulate the performers, some of whom were girlfriends of mine from school, wishing I could join them. I couldn't help but notice that there were always fewer guys in the musicals than girls, and that some of the guys who did participate matched my father's description—they were effeminate—but others did not. The choreographer and assistant director seemed to fit perfectly my father's descriptions of male thespians. They were loud, animated, and flamboyant, and sometimes outrageous.

Because I couldn't ever be in the shows, I would often go to more than one performance to study the productions. I'd go with a different set of friends to each performance and fib to my father about what I was really doing. Eventually, I think some of the adults involved with the theater group started to notice me backstage.

The choreographer, Denny, who'd been involved with MJT and Andover Community Theatre for a long time, approached me one night and said, with the lisp my father had always tried to prevent from coming from my own lips, "I see you here all the time, why don't you audition for one of the shows? We can always use guys."

"Okay," I said, nervously and quickly walked away.

It was a lie. I knew my dad wouldn't let me. But I didn't want to get into it with a stranger. Besides, even though I'm sure he had no ill intent, Denny made me uncomfortable. I think it was one of the first times the homophobia I'd internalized from my father surfaced in my own unconscious thinking. Although I didn't realize it at the time, I was afraid of Denny from the moment he spoke to me because of all the harsh things my father said about effeminate men. I was certain to avoid him at all costs at future shows.

Still, despite the seeds of my learned fears and biases sprouting roots, I wanted so much to be a part of the theater. In the seventh grade, I entered a singing competition behind my dad's back after being coerced by my friend Bianca and her parents, performing "Hold Me in Your Arms" (another Whitney Houston hit duet) and winning first place.

Mostly, I attended performances as an observer, watching, sometimes breathlessly at the talent that existed in my town. Many of those talented young actors were encouraged by their parents to pursue their dreams. Some went on to perform in regional theater, national tours, and even on Broadway and television. Auditioning and performing just weren't options for me. My dad never budged.

■ ■ ■

Freedom Bound was performed at the end of the school year, right around what was part of our sixth grade graduation week. I'd attended Sanborn School since we moved to Andover when I was in the second grade, and graduating from sixth grade—its highest grade—was a milestone.

I'd always loved school and thrived at it. There, I escaped the difficult realities of my home life. At an early age, I did my best to excel and immersed myself in as many activities as I could. That year, I completed the Andover's Integrated Reading System (AIRS) program early, and four other classmates and I started a school newspaper as a special post-AIRS project. We wrote our own articles and laid it out on an ancient Apple computer. We even had graphics and pictures in black and white.

I liked most of my teachers at Sanborn, but especially my sixth grade teacher, Mr. Ripstead. "Mr. Rip," as we called him for short, had been particularly fond of my brother, whom he'd had as a student a few years before. Jared wasn't the best student. He was a bit of a class clown, always seeking attention. Mr. Rip found a way into Jared's heart and mind, just like he had into mine. I was much easier to handle than my brother, but Mr. Rip looked at each kid as an individual. Actually, he was one of the first of what would become a series of important teachers in my life, particularly male teachers.

Socially, I was, for the most part, always surrounded by good friends. Although I slipped in and out of fitting into the really popular groups, I was not a victim of constant bullying by my peers; that was my dad's job. But there was one major exception.

I was in fourth grade when my best friend, Brandon, abruptly turned on me for unknown reasons. Instead of simply not being my friend anymore, he was determined to make sure I wasn't friends with anyone. By fourth grade, I'd become adept at playing mostly with the boys on the playground. Ever since Hudson Country Day and the severity of my father's threats, I did all I could to play with the *real boys* on the playground, despite never feeling completely comfortable with them.

Brandon rallied all the boys with whom we played kickball and gathered them in a circle. He "dumped" me from the group publicly.

Brandon literally decreed out loud, "Jon, you're dumped!" I'll never forget it. The words stung me in a way only my father's had been able to before then. They exiled me from any future games on the playground, and even worse, I wasn't welcomed at their birthday parties and sleepovers for quite some time.

The worst part was that after I recoiled and retreated and sought comfort from my loyal girlfriends—playing hopscotch, jacks, and four-square as familiar refuge—the boys gathered in a group and chanted under Brandon's leadership, "Air brain, air brain, air brain . . . YOU SUCK!"

I cried sometimes in Samantha's arms, and other times I just ignored them. I didn't tell my parents. I worried that because I was playing with the girls again, my father would lose it. And I had learned the hard way that when I told my mom things that I didn't tell my dad, I'd just get her into trouble. Suffering in silence was the only option.

Later in the school year, I was welcomed back into the group. They had ulterior motives: because I was close with so many of the cool girls, the boys saw me as an ally in getting their attention. Brandon and I were never friends again. I understood the magnitude of how mean he had been to me. It was the first time a boy other than my father would break my heart. I grew more intimidated, even scared of Brandon and what he was capable of, so I mostly stayed out of his way. I tried not to piss him off and I didn't attempt to get him back.

Brandon ended up going to private school in a neighboring town, and we rarely saw one another again. Over the years, I often wondered why Brandon turned on me. Only years later would it dawn on me that he may have seen in me so many of the characteristics that my dad dreaded, and they bothered him, too.

There's no question I gravitated toward boys, and often formed intense relationships bordering on infatuation. From a young age, I had a tendency to zero in on one guy at a time as a best friend, and Brandon filled that space for me for a couple of years in elementary school. I spent day after day at his family's house, escaping my own at Crescent Circle, and loved being around his mom in particular. She drove a silver sports car with a manual shift and I'd always beg to sit in the passenger seat pleading to help her shift the gears. Brandon would sometimes tell me that I was annoying because I begged to come over to his house so much. When I was at his house, I also begged for the processed cheese, cookies, and chips his mom stocked in their fridge and pantry. It was thrilling getting to eat the things that my dad didn't allow in our house.

Maybe Brandon sensed I was different. Did he pick up on the feeling that I had strong, singular sentiments for him? Even though neither one of us really knew what romantic feelings were at that time, was Brandon my first boy crush? Regardless, I got too close and Brandon pushed me away.

■ ■ ■

Following the successful run of *Freedom Bound,* one of the trips for sixth grade graduation week was an outing to Canobie Lake Park, an amusement park just across the Massachusetts border into New Hampshire. We boarded the buses and arrived at the park eager to jump on the flying pirate ship, or the flume, or to play Skee-ball so we could win cheap stuffed animals.

About halfway through the day, I stumbled upon a small building with music coming from it. As my friends and I walked closer, I realized it was sort of like an old-school karaoke station where amateurs could sing songs to a recorded accompaniment. The building replicated a small shed, and inside it were two recording booths behind glass doors. The booths were carpeted inside, and a large microphone hung from the ceiling. On the microphone stood a set of earphones, the ones with the large earmuff-looking headset.

One of the booths was occupied by a girl, singing Tiffany's "Could've Been," who wasn't very good. I thought she was brave for trying—and she was clearly having fun. My friends started pressuring me. "You should do it, Jon! You have the best voice, come on!" I was hesitant at first and embarrassed. Even though I had sung the three solos in

Freedom Bound, I was still insecure. "What do you have to lose? It is just for fun," Abbey said. I continued studying the surroundings, and finally after asking the attendant some questions about the process and the price, I gathered all the single dollar bills in my pockets and flung them onto his desk. He handed me a thick three-ring-binder filled with sheet music for hundreds of songs. There were so many to choose from! Without a moment's passing, I immediately looked in the index to see if they had the "The Greatest Love of All." *Jackpot!* It was settled. I was going to take a leap of faith and do it.

Inside the booth, I put the enormous headphones onto my head and adjusted them to fit tightly against my ears, blocking out the faint chatter outside the booth. "Hello, Jon, can you hear me?" a loud voice in my ears asked.

"Yes," I answered timidly.

"Okay, you get one practice run and then we're going to record. Are you ready?" I felt like I had been preparing for this moment for quite some time, singing this song in my room or lip-synching it in the basement instead of doing my baseball swings. I was as ready as I'd ever be. The only thing making me nervous was the realization that the people inside and around the building could hear the person singing inside the booth. I didn't want people to think I was terrible. "Here we go," the engineer said from inside his booth, and the synthesized, amateur piano introduction started.

There was no turning back. Other classmates who were passing by got wind that I was in the booth, and many stopped to watch and listen. I took a deep breath and started to sing the words just like I'd done so many times before. I imagined myself in my room, while my father was away on a business trip. I closed my eyes, shutting out the people gawking at me from outside the booth. I let loose and sang freely, without abandon.

What came out on the tape was one of my proudest moments. When we got back to school, Mr. Rip, who'd heard all the rumblings from my friends on the school bus about what I'd done, decided to play the cassette for the class. I was so nervous. What would everyone think? Was it really as good as I'd remembered? I braced myself as he put the tape in and hit play. *Not bad,* I thought. The other kids more than agreed, cheering and applauding. Mr. Rip said I should send it to *Star Search,* a popular TV show at that time hosted by Ed McMahon, on which amateur performers vied for a cash prize and stardom.

For a moment, I imagined walking on stage and singing the Whitney Houston song perfectly. I dreamed about not only winning, but getting a call from Whitney herself asking if I would sing the song with her on stage sometime. The daydreaming took me all the way home that afternoon, and I was so excited about what I had done that I couldn't wait to play the tape for Mom.

When I got home, I ran into the smoke-filled room where my mom, who must have just snuck a cigarette, was watching one of her favorite soaps and scurried her down to the den in the basement, where we had a stereo with a cassette player.

"What are we doing?" she asked.

"Just listen," I said. The music started and Mom, still, holding my hand, slowly let go and moved to the couch where she sat down. She immediately knew it was my voice. She grinned, then, wiping away some tears that had begun to fill her eyes, she listened with a smile until the last note was sung. She patted the cushion on the couch next her, inviting me to sit.

"Do you know how beautiful that was?" she asked, looking at me lovingly. "You have a wonderful voice, Jon." She said it in a way that was both encouraging, yet defeated. I could tell she knew I'd never be able to pursue singing as long as my dad was in charge. "I am always so proud of you, do you know that?"

In that instant, the sound of my father's garage door startled me. We'd all trained our ears to the different sounds of my mom's and dad's respective garage doors. I instinctually ran to the stereo and hit eject. My mom looked nervous, too. She stood up straighter in her seat, and her body stiffened. There wasn't enough time for both of us to get upstairs, so we stayed put.

"What are you guys doing down here?" Dad asked when he got inside. "Jon, have you done your swings?" I gave my mom a look meant to let her know she should go along with me.

"Yeah, Dad," I answered. "I just finished."

"What's that in your hand?" he wanted to know.

"Oh, nothing much," I resisted.

"Jon made a beautiful tape at Canobie Lake today and he was just playing it for me," my mom jumped in.

"What kind of tape?" he demanded, his voice getting the accusatory tone that so often came with his questions.

"I sang the 'Greatest Love of All' in the recording booth there," I said, reluctantly. "Do you want to hear it?"

"No!" he barked.

"Mr. Rip said I should send it to Ed McMahon at *Star Search*; he thought it was that good."

"*Star Search*?" The idea of this really freaked Dad out. "I don't think so, Mister! No son of mine is going on *Star Search* to sing some silly song. We've already talked about this. Just because you were in the sixth grade play, don't get any ideas!" I started to talk, but he cut me off. "We are done having this conversation!" he bellowed. Now get back to your push-ups or sit-ups or something. You're getting a belly!" My mom looked at me knowingly, but could say nothing.

I listened to the recording on my cassette player for weeks afterward. I always kept the volume low so my dad wouldn't hear it. I'd sneak watching *Star Search* from time to time and always wondered if I would have been invited to sing on that stage.

My prayers to God now went beyond the regular mantra of wishing that my parents would get along and that my dad would be nice. The prayers now included a hope to be discovered by someone hearing me singing at the top of my lungs in my bedroom when my dad was on business trips.

Of course, that never happened. I was left at Crescent Circle, ex-pelled each and every night to the basement to become the better baseball player, the real boy my father always dreamed he'd have, and that I never thought I could be.

*

Chapter 4

Life with Father

"Get out of here!" my brother yelled out to my father, who was on the other side of our dead-bolted door. It was dark outside, close to midnight. The front porch lights had been off for at least an hour, but the moon was half full so I could see the clouds of my father's breath. He was puffing like an old muffler. I kept running from the top of the staircase to my bedroom's windows to see which had the better view. I noticed that there was only one other set of porch lights still on at the beginning of Crescent Circle; all of our neighbors must have been asleep.

Jared screamed through the crack between the door and the bank of windows, "Go get a hotel room, we don't want you here!"

"This is MY house!" my dad screamed back. "Let me in my fucking house!" I could only hear his strained, angry voice from where I stood at the top of the stairs, but I knew what he looked like when he was mad—beet red face, veins swollen in his broad neck, spittle flying.

Jared tried to be stern, but I could hear the fear in his voice; he was only sixteen. "Your keys are in your car, Dad," he pleaded with him. "Just go stay at the Rolling Green Inn."

Jared turned around and looked up toward me at the top of the staircase with an expression meant to convey older brother assurance. But just as he did, my father burst through the dead-bolted door. It made a deafening crack, which echoed up through the house and sent a charge reverberating through my preadolescent body. I froze in terror, feeling as if I were in one of those dreams where you can't move your feet. At first, my brother yelped like an injured dog and sprinted up the stairs toward me.

"Oh my God!" he yelled. I screamed for Mom, like I always did, and Julie darted into her room.

"I'm calling the police!" she exclaimed. I ran into my sister's room behind her. She was panic-stricken. "I'm calling the police, you psycho, you crazy asshole!" My stomach turned; my throat closed. Even though this kind of behavior was familiar, I never got used to it.

I heard a smash and then silence. We wouldn't find out until later that adrenaline had gotten the best of Jared and he mustered the guts to turn around on the stairs and lunge at my father, knocking him off his feet, and slamming him into the foyer folding closet doors. Dad fell clear through them as if they were cardboard.

The subsequent silence made it seem the fracas was over. *Is he gone?* I wondered. I emerged from Julie's room cautiously grasping the doorframe for support. Suddenly, I heard my father's heavy feet pounding up the stairs, as he desperately beseeched my sister to hang up the phone.

"What will everyone think?" he pleaded.

She didn't hang up. "Please, get here right away," she begged the police.

When he realized she was crying to the police, immediately he turned around, stumbled down the steps, falling on his ass, and ran out the gaping hole that used to be our front door.

My mother was as upset as I'd ever seen her, hyperventilating between sobs, her legs wobbling in the frame of her bedroom door. She had her head pressed up against the white molding of the doorway and kept moving it forward and back, banging her forehead each time. As I crept toward her, I reached out my hand, "Mom, are you okay?" I asked. She didn't speak. She could barely breathe.

I looked down to the foyer, and there, on the floor, lay our front door. Shards of the slate welcome sign that once hung so perfectly from it spread across the marble tile. There was cracked molding scattered everywhere, along with chunks of jagged glass from the broken sidelights.

By the time the police arrived, we'd all gathered in the kitchen. I looked out of the massive hole from our house to the outside and could see that a few more front porch lights were on, after all the commotion. The officers slowly walked through the open door, and as their boots crunched the shattered glass, they greeted us all with expressions of concern.

My brother lifted me onto the countertop just next to the sink in our kitchen, as if I were just a little boy, and my sister consoled my mother, who was telling the two officers what had happened. I remember thinking how big the policemen were with knee-high, black leather boots and heavy utility belts. The fluorescent light above us made everyone's faces look whiter than they normally were. We were all still recovering from what had happened but did our best to explain everything to the police. They must have been surprised to get a call to come to a house in such a serene neighborhood.

■ ■ ■

Our house stood at the top of the hill, immaculate and regal. It was painted gray, trimmed with pure white. It had barn-red shutters that matched the front door and elegant drapes visible from every window. Flower beds were exquisitely edged, and the plush, green lawn was groomed each week in the spring and summer. In the fall, the tall trees in front of the house shook their rusted, paper-thin leaves to the ground, covering the hill, sometimes completely, for days at a time. Outsiders admired our spot high on the hill of Crescent Circle with its impressive view.

The house was a three-story New England colonial: a square box with a box attached on the side. To many visitors, it seemed the perfect house enveloping a perfect family and their little white and beige bichon frise–poodle mix, Buffy. Most people in our small town thought we were the ideal all-American family, and that's how my father liked it. He worked for many years to reach this pinnacle in societal admiration. It was his outward symbol of success, and he was determined to keep that image intact, no matter what the cost. The way we looked and dressed was all part of a façade that I imagine made him feel he'd achieved something.

Considering his very humble beginnings in a two-room apartment with his two brothers and his parents, he indeed had achieved a great deal of success. After all, he'd become a named partner in his manufacturer's rep company.

But despite Dad doing very well, I never felt well-off. I had the sense that he always thought his luck was about to run out. From a young age, I worried about money because Dad would often come home after a meeting that hadn't gone well and report that it was only a matter of time until we'd lose everything. I can't imagine what that pressure must have felt like for him.

When Julie was a baby, he'd gotten a lucky break with a new job that got them out of Lynn, Massachusetts, a town he described as "the rough and tough" North Shore "city of sin," where his identity was tied to being a star athlete, a devout Catholic, and, most of all, Italian.

Outsiders were either naïve about life inside our house or just wanted to believe the charade. Dad dedicated hours of his time to athletics in town and helped a lot of kids reach their dreams of playing a sport in college and some even in the pros. I'd often think, *If only he'd look after us the way he did the other kids.* Mom rarely, if ever, talked to anyone about Dad's rages, perhaps out of fear of what he'd do in retaliation. Or maybe it was her longing for her own "American dream." She'd grown up in the same city as Dad. She, too, came from modest means; her father was a welder and her mother a homemaker. Perhaps, by the time they'd made it to Crescent Circle, Mom didn't want to let go of what my father provided for us, even though it came at a great emotional cost.

Only a few insiders—a couple of close friends of mine, Jared's, and Julie's—knew what it was really like living inside our home.

■ ■ ■

The night before Dad broke down the front door, he had smacked Jared all over with his open hands for getting a C+ in Spanish. That was when the four of us mustered the collective nerve to tell him that we could no longer live with him. I suppose my mom had weathered enough under his rule to feel she no longer had much to lose. My brother, sister, and I had anxiously longed for the day when she'd tell us we were leaving, but that's not how it happened. We finally went to her. We'd seen too many Cheez-Its boxes or bottles of vinegar hurled at her from the kitchen as she sat in her chair in the family room quietly doing needlepoint. Her creations of perfect houses, or town greens and gazebos, ironically hung throughout our house.

All three of us kids had heard too many times that the rolls of fat on our stomachs were embarrassing. We grew tired of the sit-ups, push-ups, and jumping-over-the-turtle-stool drills he'd made us do in front of him. Julie was tired of hearing that hockey cheerleading was for "sluts." Jared had had enough of his daddy loving him only when he hit home runs. And I'd been chased throughout the house too many times by him with the belt that he'd pull from his waist, threatening to use the buckle because I forgotten to shake someone's hand like a man.

"Enough is enough," we told our mother, huddling close together, as if we were combining our courage to face him together. After years of us begging her to leave him, to no avail, we all timidly tiptoed into his room that night. Jared spoke on behalf of us all; Dad seemed to listen more to my brother. We stood behind Jared pretending to be brave.

My father's initial reaction was alarmingly calm. I expected him to get enraged as he always did, but instead, he was eerily mellow. It was almost as if he'd been possessed by another personality, one we'd never met before.

His eyes glazed over, he looked in our direction with an expression that said, "So this is how you ALL feel, huh?" Then his eyes darted at Mom. "Well, you have finally done it, Judy," he barked. "You finally brainwashed them to make them really hate me. This is your fault. You know that." He slowly walked toward us, never taking his eyes off my mother's. "You'll never be able to survive without me and you'll regret this. This is all mine," he said, holding his hands out wide in the air. "This whole place. I've done this all by myself, with no help. I earned this, not you. You'll be out on the streets and in the slums."

I think Mom believed him, but even though he wore a vindictive, menacing look, Jared, Julie, and I knew he was bluffing. And we didn't care. We'd already thought about being poor. That was better than this. We'd survive without him just fine.

"Get out of my room, you cowards," he growled, his voice rolling with phlegm, trying to hold back tears. "You're all nothing without me." We backed up out of the room slowly, not turning, so as to keep him in our sights. We didn't trust him; we never knew what he was capable of. The three of us kids dispersed into our bedrooms and shut our doors. I climbed into the bottom of my closet with my blanket and pillow and left my bedside table lamp on. I shut the louvered closet door and kept a lookout in between the slats as long as my eyelids wouldn't fall.

■ ■ ■

I had been too young and too protected by my siblings to recall for the policemen the exact details of the following day, but I listened to Jared and Julie as they recited their accounts. They said the day after telling my father we wanted him to leave, he drove to my school, Jared's school, and Julie's school to tell us that he loved us, no matter what was to come. I do remember thinking that it was strange when my father showed up at West Middle School's horseshoe drive during recess and summoned me over. He rolled down the window and told me that he loved me. I was bewildered. He didn't say that too often.

Jared and Julie continued. They found him hiding in the boiler closet of our basement when they got home that evening and he jumped out at them and yelled, "RAH!" They said he looked like he was in a fog and clenched his brown leather briefcase to his chest. At that point, I guess Mom threatened to call my father's brother, Uncle Tony, who lived about forty minutes away, but my dad panicked and begged to go get something to eat. He said he just needed air.

So, Jared and Julie took him to Harrison's Roast Beef in North Andover. When they got in the car to return, as soon as Jared started the engine, my father reached over and tried to take control of the car. He punched my brother to free him from his grip of keys. Jared didn't want to lose control of the car and screamed and yelled as my sister started to hit my father from the back seat. Afraid that people in the parking lot would intervene, Dad jumped out of the car and ran down the busy Route 125.

I'd later heard that Dad was fetched by the head varsity basketball coach in town, Donnie Fabrizio. My sister and brother returned home and told my mother what had happened. Dad was gone for hours and the house was silent. They locked all of the doors and unplugged the garage doors so he couldn't use his remote or the keypad to let himself in. That's when coach Fabrizio dropped him off and Dad landed at the front door step demanding to get into his house.

The police took copious notes and were attentive to every detail. They tried their best to make sense of a story that must have been as surreal to them us as it was to us. One of the policemen, Officer Miller, was particularly surprised, as he had played for my father on the high school football team years before. My father had spent a lot more time on the football field than at his office or at home.

For the first several years after we arrived in Andover, people thought my father was a hero. In time, there would be some who complained about his coaching methods, but still, most people revered him. Even to this day, some attribute to my father their success in college sports, or even professional sports.

Officer Miller explained to my mother that she had a couple of options. The long-term option was more complicated than I understood at the time. The short-term one, which he recommended, was to get a restraining order on my father. I understood that. I knew it was the best way to keep my father away as we figured things out as a group.

The officers told her that she'd have to head down to the station to complete the order.

After the cops left the house, my mom ordered me to bed, as it was a school night. I had no idea how I was supposed to go to school the next day and face all of the kids and teachers.

I went upstairs and closed my door and put my desk chair behind it; I was not convinced that my dad wouldn't be back that night. I climbed up into my bed, which was a loft over my desk and bureau. Once I got under my covers, I made the sign of the cross and began my nightly mantra to God. I prayed for forgiveness for all of my sins, I promised to be a better kid, student, and athlete, just as long as He would stop my dad from being the way he was. I even said the Act of Contrition, something I was forced to memorize very early on in my Catholic rearing.

I begged God to tell me why I had to have a dad like I had and why Mom and Julie and Jared had to go through what they did. I prayed for all of this to stop and for my dad to just go away. I even started to pray that God would make my dad go away and leave us alone. I wondered if it would just be easier, would we all be better off if he'd just die? And then I promised God I'd make bad thoughts like that go away. I kept praying, my hands folded over my chest, my head looking straight up at the ceiling, as if I could see up through the roof of our house and up as high into space as God could possibly be.

I woke to the buzzing of my alarm at six o'clock in the morning. It was still dark outside when I pulled the shade away from the window and peeked around it. I was looking to see if the police were still outside. There was no sign of their patrol cars.

The chill in the hallway was more than usual, which reminded me that we no longer had a front door protecting us. My mom must have been the one that hung some towels with duct tape to cover the opening, but it didn't stop the cold from leaking in.

The beating of the shower water awakened me. As I had done day in and day out, I brushed my teeth, blow-dried my hair, and put on my bathrobe. As I walked downstairs for my ritual of breakfast in front of the *Today Show* with Bryant Gumbel and Jane Pauley, I noticed that the television was already on in our family room.

Dad was sitting in his spot on the couch. He was glaring at the TV in a trance. The heaviness that overcame my body whenever he was around hit me like buckets of rain. I immediately felt soggy and weighted down.

I continued with my morning routine. I poured Cheerios into a bowl and drizzled some milk over the small circles. I walked slowly toward the family room and past Dad on the couch to my left. He didn't say anything. I didn't either. I looked out the large bay window and saw his car was parked under the basketball hoop in the driveway.

I sat on the floor directly in front of the TV, as if to block him out completely. My back got stiffer and stiffer and I got more and more upset. I was unable to pretend that life was anywhere near as sunny as weatherman Willard Scott's forecast for the day. I couldn't understand why my father was here. *When did he come back? Why did Mom let him in?* I thought. As I left the room, not even glancing in his direction, Dad said in an angry and quivering voice, "We will never talk about this ever again. Ever." And we did just that—never talked about it again, never knowing when he came back that night and why Mom let him back in.

■ ■ ■

Things got worse. Holidays were nightmares. One Thanksgiving, when I was around thirteen years old, my father hadn't yet arrived home from Andover High's Lovely Field after the football team's loss to Central Catholic in the annual Thanksgiving morning rivalry. This loss was our first problem.

When Jared and I got home from the game, the energy in the house was jovial. I was laughing and joking in the kitchen with my mother and her parents, Nana and Grampy Youngdahl, as well as my dad's parents. You could smell the turkey cooking in the oven and the sweet cinnamon buns that my nana brought from an old bakery in Lynn. My mom looked festive in her red holiday sweater and white cook's apron as she moved comfortably around the kitchen.

I set the table with Mom's china that would sit in the large dining room hutch the other 364 days of the year. I removed the silver from the mahogany buffet and grabbed the crystal wine goblets. Everything looked perfect: flowers, candles, and linen napkins, white with hand-embroidered blue flowers. I loved setting the table and making believe it was a royal table somewhere else.

As the food continued to simmer in the kitchen, we all gathered in the family room and snacked on tangy orange-and-red cheese rolled in nuts, mixed nuts, and crudités while watching the Macy's Thanksgiving Day Parade. We were all talking about the happenings in town, Jared's upcoming fall dance at school, and a recent language arts test I got an A on that my mom was showing my grandparents. The chatter in the house seemed like it was at my friends' homes— relaxed and easygoing.

Suddenly, below us, the loud groaning and creaking of my dad's garage door was activated. On weeknights, when his garage went up, we would all scatter. As his door was rolling up its tracks, I had my usual reaction: my chest tightened, my heart fluttered faster, my hands got sweaty, and my shoulders curled downward.

I jumped up and stuffed down the piece of cheese I had in my hand; I didn't want to get yelled at for eating it—"That's what makes you fat," he'd always remind me. I tried to look as busy as possible helping in the kitchen. Jared disappeared upstairs to his bedroom and closed the door behind him, pretending to do his homework. My mom immediately went to the stove and turned inward. Julie, who was home from her sophomore year in college, hadn't yet returned from her outing with her friends at Justin's, a tavern downtown where all of the home-comers would go for postgame libations. My grandparents just sat in front of the television staring blankly as the mood plummeted like a deflated Macy's balloon.

As I heard Dad's lumbering footsteps coming up the stairs toward the kitchen, I quickly snuck another piece of cheese and a cracker and tiptoed into the foyer and up the stairs to my bedroom. I closed the door quietly, so he would not know that I was up there. Just seconds after closing my door, I could hear his rising voice, complaining about the squash. "This is too runny, Judy. Why is it you always mess something up?"

Twenty minutes later, my mom called me and Jared downstairs to eat. Julie still hadn't arrived home.

"Where is your sister, Jared?" my father questioned.

My brother looked down and said, "I don't know. She said she was going to Justin's with a bunch of her friends after the game."

"She better get home soon because we are having a family dinner and she is not going to ruin it," he continued with red flowing into his face.

My mom took out the electric beaters and added whole milk to the smashed, already boiled potatoes. As the beaters started running, I asked everyone for their drink order and poured their requests into the crystal goblets. I knew my mom was trying to delay the meal somehow to give Julie enough time to get home, but after a while there still was no sign of her. Mom could only buy so much time until my father would freak out over not eating exactly at two o'clock.

"Well, dinner is ready, let's sit down," my mother said with hesitation. My dad took his seat at the head of the table and the rest of us took our assigned seats. There was one seat left open, to the left side of my father. That was Julie's place. Somehow I managed to put my grandmother, his mother, next to him on his right. Nana Rose was in her early eighties at the time. Her white hair was sparse and frizzy from bimonthly permanents, and her hands were crinkled and crumpled from arthritis. She could barely walk now, even after having knee and hip replacements. She didn't say much anymore; she was disgusted with her life, and when she did talk, she complained about the agony she was in. I imagined that my father would be just like her when he got older, although I always believed that he would live forever.

I sat with my hands folded on my lap. I didn't say much or look at my father; my survival strategy was keeping a low profile and not doing anything to break order. I focused on my mother, at the other head of the table, beginning to serve the plates, trying to make this Thanksgiving an uneventful one.

My dad sat at his seat, waiting for his meal as my mom did everything, with a little bit of help from her mother. My stomach ached, as it always did when my father was around. I did not want to cross my legs the wrong way, or hold my fork the wrong way, or perhaps have my pinky stick out too far when I took a sip of my apple cider. I didn't want to take too much on my plate and then not eat it, or perhaps even worse, get scolded for eating too much. And even though I was not the only one who couldn't seem to get anything right, I still kept trying; all I wanted was for him to say that I was a good boy.

There was little conversation at the dinner table. Nana and Grampy were eating the dark meat off the turkey legs, the highlight of their culinary year. My brother and I kept looking at one another but didn't dare say a thing. Mother kept quiet, too. I knew she was praying that my father wouldn't complain about what she had prepared this time.

My seat had a view of the neighborhood out on the cul-de-sac, and I could see the Steins and the Cohens playing out in the circle, riding their bikes and enjoying the last days of autumn in northern Massachusetts, despite the cold. Then, I saw a blue Honda Accord coming up the hill. The neighbors playing in the circle moved out of the street and waited on the grass as the car stopped in front of our mailbox. It was Julie.

I feared for my sister, as I could see my dad's temper rising. When he saw her close the car door, he slammed his fork and knife down on his plate and walked out to the foyer. "No respect," he muttered under his breath, "no respect whatsoever." I saw Julie was heading toward the driveway and so she'd be coming in through the first floor. I wanted to sneak out of the dining room and run out the kitchen's sliding glass door to meet her in the driveway to warn her. But I couldn't. Getting up from the table without being excused was a punishable offense. I heard my mom's garage door going up as Julie punched in the code. When my father heard the door going up, he started to head downstairs. Mom jumped up out of her seat and tried to put herself in his path. "Sit down, Judy," he said. "I'm going to have to teach our daughter a lesson."

As I continued to sit at the table, I could barely eat because of the screaming and crying from downstairs. After a few minutes, there was silence and my father came back into the dining room. He was red and sweaty from yelling so much. He grabbed the dining room's bronze doorknobs and slammed them shut, leaving us in the room.

I could hear his nasty voice. "Get up those stairs, Sister! How dare you embarrass me in front of your grandparents. You disgust me!" I heard my sister's feet running up the stairs and into her room. From upstairs I heard more screaming and slamming. I could picture my sister trying to get into the dead center of her queen-sized bed because it was harder for my dad's belt to reach her there.

What made matters worse was that Julie had come home with booze on her breath and, even though she was in college, in my father's eyes, by drinking in public she had failed at upholding The Image.

We all just sat there at the table, feeling helpless, as my mom slowly chewed her turkey and my grandparents looked down at their plates. I was sick to my stomach.

When Dad returned to the table, his comb-over off-kilter from the outburst, he made a declaration to Jared and me: "If either of you ever come home with booze on your breath and are late for a meal that your mother puts together and that I pay for and put on this table, you will not see daylight for days. Your sister is now in her room, with no dinner, and she will be there for as long as I say. Do you hear me?" Jared and I just looked down and didn't say anything. "Do you hear me, Misters?"

"Yes," we said in soft, cowardly voices.

The turkey that earlier had looked plump and juicy to me now looked limp and pale. The stuffing, once succulent and savory, now tasted sour. The cinnamon buns oozing with sugar and caramel coveted just a few minutes earlier now looked like poison. I refused to eat, which I knew would get me in trouble and sentenced to my room. Maybe that's what I wanted—and that's what I got.

Dad warned me not to go see Julie as he sent me upstairs, but I disobeyed him. I tiptoed up to Julie's room and slowly slithered through the small crack in her door. I saw her curled in the fetal position on her bed, crying into her pillow. I snuggled up behind her and gave her as warm a hug as I could. Julie smiled back at me, her eyes glassy with tears.

Later that night, my mom knocked on my door, then came and sat next to me on my bed. I was lying flat on my back, like I always did, looking up at the ceiling wondering about my friends Samantha and Chad. *I bet their Thanksgivings weren't like this,* I thought.

Mom stroked my hair with her long, ruby red nails. "I know why you didn't eat, Jon," she said. "You're a good brother, but you don't need to do that. I'm so sorry that this day was ruined. I'm sorry that I can't make it better. Please just know how much I love you." She kissed my forehead.

I looked up at her eyes, filling up with her nightly tears. I wanted to grab her and my brother and my sister and run away and never look back. But I knew that wasn't possible, so throwing myself in between my siblings and my father's belt, or boycotting food, or yelling back were things I'd just have to keep doing. Somehow I decided I would do what I could to protect my family. I was learning that keeping a low profile wasn't working. It became clear to me that life inside our house on Crescent Circle was never going to match its perfect exterior, no matter how badly we all wanted it, not even on a day like Thanksgiving.

✳

Chapter 5

And Then There Was Chad

I t had to be the best gift ever—that's all there was to it. Since he'd started dating Maria, she was the only thing he could talk about. And even though I'd been the one who'd set them up, I was determined to make sure my gift surpassed hers. It was Christmas after all, and it had been nearly four years since we'd become best friends. I wanted to commemorate that with something meaningful. We'd been through a lot together since meeting during our first season on St. Robert's traveling basketball team when we were in seventh grade.

■ ■ ■

The gymnasium lights were glaringly bright, and like so many other sports venues, it smelled. So did my hands after I passed the basketball back and forth with my teammates for our warm ups. I think the smell on the ball came from all the guys licking their fingers before touching it to get a better grip. *Gross!*

"Layup formation!" my father yelled out to all of us. As I got in line, I could feel how tight my too-small basketball shorts were around my prepubescent, expanding midsection and meaty thighs. The white undershirt beneath my mesh tank top was skintight, too, but I was feeling too uneasy about my body to go shirtless under the tank. I would actually pray to God the nights before our practices that I would get picked for "shirts" when we had to play "shirts-n-skins." *Me and skins just isn't going to be pretty, God, so please spare me!*

In front of me in the layup line was a thin, handsome guy from the other side of town whom I'd heard about from Dad after tryouts. He had thick, brown, wavy hair and wore a Celtics tank top without a shirt underneath it. His arms were biceps on top of bone. Some kids would call him "toothpick," but that didn't seem to matter to him. He was definitely sure of himself. He was full of bounce and couldn't stand still, almost as if he were on a pogo stick. He was lighthearted and seemed to want to find that in me, too. He kept trying to engage me in conversation, cracking jokes as we waited for our turn to dribble to the basket and make our layup.

"Shhh," I said, trying not to be as drawn in by him as I was, and to fight the impetus to smile. It was a challenge. There was at least a quarter smile I couldn't contain, even though I was terrified for both of us. "You don't know my dad; he's gonna kill you if you keep cracking jokes."

"Oh, so you're Jon, the coach's son," he said. "You think I care what he thinks? I've heard about your dad, but I'm not scared of him. I bet I can lighten him up. I can get him to smile!"

The ball bounced into his hands and he took off dribbling toward the basket, did a spin before he got to the hoop, and tossed the ball with finesse directly into the basket. "Woo-hoo!" he yelled. "Yeah, that's right, baby!" I watched him make his way under the hoop and sprint with excitement to the other line on the opposite side of the court. The rest of the team chuckled quietly, a few giving him high fives, a bit unsure of how my dad would react.

"Chad! Who do you think you are? Some kind of rock star?" my father scolded. "Not on my team. I'll have none of that crap on my court!"

Then it was my turn to get yelled at. The ball came at me and bounced near my feet. As I tried to grab it, it ricocheted up and hit me in the nose. *Shit*, I thought. *Here we go: Three. Two. One.* "Wake up, Jon!" my father screamed. I was mortified, and I wasn't done.

I slowly jogged and dribbled toward the hoop—doing both at once was a serious challenge for me—positioning myself underneath the basket. I shot the ball up and it hit the bottom of the backboard, rebounding back at my head. *What a nightmare.* I blocked my ears mentally, anticipating what would surely spew from my father's mouth. But it never came. Maybe he'd missed it.

When I was back on the other side of the court, I was once again behind Chad in line and he turned and introduced himself. "Hi, I'm Chad," he said, offering his hand for me to shake it. "It must blow being the coach's son!"

"Well, sort of," I admitted, "especially since I really don't feel like being here. The only reason I made the team was because he's the coach."

"Don't say that, dude," he said. "Come on, you'll get it, just keep practicing!" He patted me on the back like I was a puppy dog. *That was nice,* I thought.

Chad could tell how uneasy I was not only on the court, but also in the form-fitted, tight clothes I kept pulling away from my body. In an odd attempt to comfort me, he started making this clicking noise with his tongue and the roof of his mouth. Pop! "Aw, the earsies," he baby-talked, grabbing my left ear. "I just love the earsies." Then, using one of this thumbs, he pretended he was holding a piece of my ear in his hands. "Look at the earsies; I grabbed your earsies!" Then he laughed out loud. *That was odd,* I thought. *But cute,* I countered. I couldn't help but be taken with his juvenile, jovial spirit. I caved: I let go a full smile.

One of the things that struck me most about Chad when I first met him was how unintimidated he was by my dad. While I was busy obsessing over whether I had the courage to take my dad aside and tell him *I just had to be shirts* if we were to play shirts-n-skins at the end of practice, Chad was off impressing him with his athletic skills. Chad was good. Really good. My dad picked up on that quickly and put him in the group of five starters. Of course, I wasn't one of them.

As Dad taught the starting five a zone defense, I sat off on the sideline with my eye on Chad. He was narrow but still strong somehow. He was goofy, but in an attractive way. He was lanky, but fast and clever. He had braces, but big red lips that drew my attention much more than the metal inside of them. His hair was floppy and free, but in a boyish, endearing way. His shorts were mesh and the bulge in his crotch was generous for our age, I thought. *Whoa*, I asked myself, horrified, *why am I looking there?*

Chad goofed off while Dad tried to coach the starting players. It seemed as if he had a hard time keeping focused on the task, and as if he needed to be the center of attention. At one point, he said something that made the entire team laugh out loud. But my father wasn't having it.

"Enough!" he shouted. "Chad, I've warned you three times during this practice. Three strikes and you're out! Now give me a hundred laps around this gym or run around it until the end of practice."

Chad turned red, seemingly surprised that his charm hadn't worked on my father, and he started running around the gym. Every time he'd run by me, he'd give me a little punch toward my belly. Sometimes he hit me softly, sometimes he'd miss. Either way, I liked it.

■ ■ ■

Four years later, the question of the perfect Christmas present for Chad loomed. Since I'd already redecorated his room with sports posters and memorabilia for his most recent birthday that June, I had to come up with something different, *something even better.* *He doesn't need clothes,* I brainstormed, *but still, I could get him a great outfit from the Gap. A watch?* I ruminated about his gift for days before deciding. And then it hit me. *A trip to Loon Mountain for February vacation?* Yes! It was the best idea ever and Mom had agreed to take me and a couple of friends skiing to one of the homes of a business associate of Dad's right on the slopes of Loon. *Perfect,* I thought. *He'll love it, and it'll be a blast for both of us.*

Chad and I had developed a great friendship. Although it was a relationship of mostly laughter and silliness, he also had a soft, deeper side that others didn't get to see. He was thoughtful and emotional at times. At night, with him on the floor covered in blankets and pillows in my bedroom at Crescent Circle, or us in the two twin beds in his room on Chestnut Street, he'd talk to me about his deepest worries.

He often wondered aloud in the middle of the night why his father had left him at an early age, and wondered if he'd ever see him again. It struck me as funny: Chad would have done anything to see his father just once, and I'd do anything to never see mine again. We had very different upbringings and were very different guys, but there was an empathetic rope that kept us tied to one another.

Even though he was a goofball, he was a solid friend who came to understand what I was up against with my dad, and stood up for me at practices and at games. He'd volunteer to come over to my house and keep me company on the many nights when I feared my dad the most. One of the best ways to keep my dad on his best behavior was by filling the house with as many friends as possible. More often than not, however, I was at Chad's.

Starting in middle school and all through high school, I always begged to go to Chad's the way I'd begged to go to Brandon's in elementary school. I loved being there. I loved his mother, who, like mine, was beautiful, funny, and kind. She was fun to be around. Chad's stepdad was nice enough, too. He was a guy's guy, but not overly macho, like my father was. I felt comfortable in their home, and they never ever closed their door on me. There were many late nights sitting at their kitchen table after parties or during sleepovers when Chad's mom and I would chat for hours. Chad would be in the other room watching a movie or talking to some girl on the phone. They were like my extended family and we were like brothers. At least in the beginning.

As time progressed, I felt myself getting more and more protective of my time with Chad, and I'd ache with jealousy when he'd decide to go out with a girl instead of me. "But that's what we're supposed to do, Jon," he'd say. "Don't you want to get some action?"

He was a sex-crazed, red-blooded teenager with raging hormones, who was magnetic and gorgeous in so many girls' eyes so it was hard for him to turn away the attention. I never blamed him. It must have felt good to have all that glory. I was just jealous.

It was so easy for Chad. Just about any girl could be the right one to get his rocks off when he needed it.

I, on the other hand, struggled to find the perfect girl. I never felt as if I wanted to kiss one or touch one the way Chad or my other guy friends were so desperate to do. Sure, I thought a lot of girls were pretty. I just didn't find them "sexy or hot," the way Chad described them.

I'd had some crushes, like my seventh and eighth grade obsession, Meredith, to whom I'd send endless love letters on white lined paper, and from whom I'd receive endless rejections. Maybe it felt safer to pursue with full force a girl I knew didn't like me back. Luckily for me, Meredith had the patience and grace to see past my almost stalker-like persistence, and we came to enjoy a wonderful friendship that still thrives today.

The next object of my affection, Carla, appeared during my freshman year, but we dated for only a week or two. I'd go to her soccer games under the lights and cheer her on, or we'd go to parties together, but I always found a way to avoid being alone with her. At first she cried, confused by my lack of interest in her breasts. Then she dumped me.

In my sophomore year, there was Kim, whose beautiful blue eyes gave Chad's a run for his money. We'd talk on the phone late into the evenings on my private line. I liked telling everyone that I had a girlfriend. For at least a while, it kept my dad off my back. For years, he'd been interrogating me on the mornings after parties and movie dates. "You get any action, Jon?" he'd ask. There was no question: he wanted me to get with a girl, and he wanted me to like it. But I never did either. Kim only lasted a few months until I broke it off because I began to feel like she wanted to make out.

Then, through my friend Samantha, I met Sophia later that year. She was a freshman and they were on the gymnastics team together. Sophia was beautiful with soft, flawless, tea-with-milk-colored-skin, dark hair, and three-quarter-moon, half-Asian eyes. She was different than the other girls who were interested in me. She wasn't as aggressive or demanding. She liked English class and did creative writing like I did. Sophia was a student leader, too, and very active in sports. We had a very special connection, and while Chad couldn't keep a steady girlfriend, I zeroed in on the blossoming, increasingly ambiguous, and confusing-to-me relationship with Sophia.

For the most part, the girls in high school seemed to be drawn to me for different reasons than they were to Chad or my other best guy friends, Charlie, Vinny, or James. They'd come to me for advice about the other boys and how they could get their attention. They'd confide in me about their dates and the details of their make-out sessions.

During their breakups or fights with boyfriends, mine was the shoulder they'd cry on. And I wasn't averse to giving sex advice. I even showed Samantha how a guy "might prefer" a blow job, using a soy sauce bottle. After showing her, I wondered, *um, how do I know how to do this?* Then I remembered how my guy friends had told me who gave the best "head" and why, and I had listened intently.

I also served as a confidant to my guy friends. Many of them told me things they dared not tell the others. I was there for Charlie when he decided to move into his dad's house and leave his mom's because they were fighting so much. I'd sit and listen to James try out a new song he'd just written. I was there for Vinny when Samantha inadvertently broke his heart. My role was something like that of rabbi or ombudsperson, counselor or advocate. I was good at giving out advice, but not so good at seeking it.

I was able to help the guys through their girl dramas because I understood the girls better than they did, at least the girls' feelings. I helped the guys act a bit more emotional and available for the girls. I'd encourage them to be sensitive to their feelings and to listen to them, and discouraged them from only wanting to get to third base.

Out of all my guy friends, Chad was the most overtly sexual. He knew he was hot and used that to lure in girls from all over. Freshman, sophomores, juniors, and even senior girls—they all wanted to get into Chad's pants. I was always surprised to learn that some of the girls were just as horny as Chad. I spent a lot of time coaching him about girls, too. I'd take him to downtown Andover and help him pick out cards to send them, or remind him to get his girlfriend flowers. It always panned out for Chad; the girls were always profuse with their thanks. "How do you know this stuff, buddy?" he'd ask me. "She loved it!"

Sometimes I even introduced Chad to girls. There was a long line of girls I'd set him up with. Like Kendra, who shared her first kiss with Chad on a chairlift heading to the top of the mountain at Nashoba Valley, with me next to them twiddling my mittened thumbs. And briefly, Samantha. She was charmed by him a year prior when he accidentally locked them in her bathroom. He got them out by escaping through the skylight in the ceiling, but only after stepping up on the towel rack and breaking it off the wall. He's lucky he didn't slip off the roof and break his neck. At first, she banned him from her house because she took the blame for the damage. But later she caved.

There were so many other relationships that just never lasted, for one reason or another. Except for the one that seemed to last forever, or at least through junior year: Maria. Maria was a stunning, Italian-looking girl with midnight-dark, curly hair, and brown eyes with long, almost fake-looking eyelashes. She was pretty and she was sweet. I thought she was perfect for Chad. I'd set them up around the time Chad started to develop panic attacks. One day at school he felt as if a two-hundred-pound person were sitting on his chest and he couldn't breathe. I thought he was having a heart attack, but it was later diagnosed as anxiety.

Maria seemed like an easygoing girl, and they had a great connection. She comforted him. Their relationship got serious, fast. I hung out with them a lot, usually with another girl as my "date." Abbey, Maria's best friend, and I would squeeze into the back of Maria's two-seater sports car, and together we'd all drive around. Maria would shift her manual transition through town for hours. Abbey and I would be dying of laughter in the hatchback trunk, singing along to the blaring stereo, flat on our backs looking out the bubble window at the stars zipping by us. Later, one night when I slept over at Chad's house, he told me Maria had been giving him handjobs up front while Abbey and I were in back, clueless.

I was naïve about the entire sex thing. Chad's relationship with Maria enlightened me quite a bit. Because he told me everything, I heard stories of them making out, of her giving him handjobs and blowjobs, how he'd "go down on her" and love it. "Um, please stop!" I'd insist. "That is really disgusting."

"Come on, Jon, you'll love it too one day," he promised. "You'll see, buddy!"

I don't think so, I'd protest in my head.

Eventually he and Maria had sex, and Chad was ecstatic about it. In a short while, they were having sex multiple times a day. They'd leave school to have sex. They'd have it at her house, at his house, in her car, in his car. They'd have sex any time they could get him inside of her. He may have even been falling in love with her. He was certainly in lust with her. Whatever it was, I was losing him.

To keep a grip on him, I was willing to listen to the stories of his "sexcapades" with Maria night after night. I'd hear his groaning complaints about her possessiveness, and the elation in his voice when he'd describe his-and-hers euphoric orgasms. He talked about sex in a way that I wouldn't be able to relate to for years.

While it annoyed me on one hand, for reasons I couldn't quite grasp at the time, I did find myself, on the other hand, always getting aroused by his stories. In the twin bed next to his, I'd have to keep my erection from tenting the sheet as he'd describe their intercourse in vivid detail.

That's weird, I'd think. It seemed strange that I'd find pleasure in hearing his stories. Instead of imagining Maria naked, I'd always imagine Chad in his briefs with his shirt off, kissing her, caressing her, fantasizing, scene by scene, as he described it.

I liked seeing Chad in his briefs. It was kind of an everyday thing, nothing really at first. All guys changed in front of one another in the sports-centric life I was forced into. Guys in locker rooms in their underwear was normal. I never thought anything of it, until junior year, until Chad.

Of course, it was normal for Chad to do the kiss-and-tell thing. All the guys did. But I think he knew I was a captive audience. I would sit and listen and then wonder what his penis actually looked like. *Was it different than mine?* I wondered if it would hurt Maria when they did it because he said it was so big. Despite my wondering, I never really wanted to actually see it. I think that was a line my Catholic guilt made it hard for me to cross. In hindsight, I was jealous of the other guys in locker rooms in high school who had seen it when, as a joke for attention, Chad would whip it out. Or they innocently saw it in the group showers that were so much a part of our lives in the late '80s and early '90s. For me, Chad's penis would remain a sacred mystery. I liked wondering about it, hidden behind the white briefs when he'd walk around in his room, sometimes grabbing it with both hands.

After several months, I'd grown tired of the stories about Maria. I was frustrated, really, that Maria and Chad were spending more and more time together alone. Not only were they sneaking away from school during the weekdays, but their weekends were solely devoted to one another.

The twinge of jealousy that fluttered in me from time to time during our freshman and sophomore years when girls took too much of Chad's attention turned into full-blown sadness. I'd been prone to melancholia in middle school and the start of high school, especially about my upbringing, but I remember hurting over Chad in my junior and senior years like I'd hurt over Brandon, only much worse. Still, in my early teens, utterly confused and even ashamed, I couldn't make sense of the intensity of feelings for Chad, so I began what would be several years of swallowing those feelings down, hard.

Even though we saw each other less senior year, we remained best friends. We'd go skiing together and go to all the same parties. We'd travel to Florida with our moms to watch our brothers play college baseball during spring training. I'd escape my father's ire and go to Chad's house, sometimes only to be left alone while he was out with Maria. We had lockers next to one another's at the high school. And although I was convinced that, in the last two years I was invited, he'd rather have had one of his girlfriends along with him in Ocean City, Maryland, where we'd gone every summer with his family since the eighth grade, I still went along.

My constant nagging about being left out for Maria must have driven Chad crazy, but he didn't complain. He was committed to both Maria and me. This became our biggest issue and we bickered more than ever. I wanted him all to myself and he wanted us both—the girl-friend he loved to have sex with, and the devoted best friend whose love he conveniently took to be undying loyalty.

I at least got to be with a Maria-free Chad at Loon Mountain after I invited him as his Christmas present. Maria wasn't a skier, so she got left behind—which made my gift for Chad perfect for me, too. At Loon Mountain I only had to share him with my mom and my other best friends: Kendra, Charlie, and Samantha. (Dad wasn't a skier so he got left behind, too.) We skied, we ice-skated, and we stayed up late at night laughing and playing *Pictionary*. Chad let me know how grateful he was for his gift, and it made me feel beyond great. Few things pleased me more than knowing Chad was pleased with me. What's more, for once I'd outdone Maria, whose Christmas gift to him was so unmemorable that, well, today I don't even remember what it was.

✳

Chapter 6

Running over the Creek

I prayed for rain all summer. If I had known how to do a rain dance, I would've done one. By the time I was fifteen, I'd fought many tough battles against my father and maybe even won a couple, but there was one I had no chance of winning: getting out of baseball. And so I prayed that just about all our practices and games would get washed out.

While a broken growth plate in my hip was all the ammunition my mother needed to help me escape the horrors of football for good, a broken eye socket, a shattered bone in my left wrist, and sixteen weeks of casts, splints, and physical therapy hadn't been enough to get my father to let me off the hook with basketball. Instead, it took me shooting endless air balls and embarrassing him on the court so often that he just gave up. When it came to baseball, though, he dug his heels in, and he wasn't going to give up.

Despite many nights of tears and petitioning, I had no choice but to keep playing, to keep practicing, and to keep going to the baseball clinics. After winning the town championships with the Red Sox in my last year of Little League, my next step in the town's standard baseball progression was to try out for Pony League or Babe Ruth League. Of course, my father ran the program, so even though I had to go through the tryouts, it was assumed that I was automatically on the team. I felt guilty taking another kid's spot, one who wanted and deserved to be there.

Pony League was for thirteen- to sixteen-year-olds and my dad coached the Blue team; Danny Martin coached the Gold team. Making the team despite my wishes was a sentence to three more years of misery.

As an escape from the hideousness of baseball, and in an overt adolescent act of rebellion, in the hours I wasn't playing on the high school diamonds, I began to find my way onto the tennis courts at Indian Meadows, the country club we belonged to. Tennis was acceptable to my father, but only as part of my activities at the club. In fact, he played tennis himself, in leagues mostly in Hudson, Ohio, when we lived there, and at the beginning of our time in Andover. But, according to him, it was not to interfere with my workouts and baseball practices, and it was not a sport real men played in high school or college.

We belonged to Indian Meadows because it was good for our image. My dad didn't go much, so I actually liked going there. In the summers, when there wasn't a game, I'd meet Samantha and Deborah and our other friends, and we'd lay out by the pool and read magazines and chat while we ate grilled cheeses with bacon and french fries from the Grill Room. At an early age, my mom was quietly getting me tennis lessons from a private coach at the club. Lorna, who ironically would later become a therapist specializing in eating disorders, saw that I had real ability in tennis and told my mom that I should keep playing. This was good news, because I genuinely liked tennis.

Most summer mornings, just as the water from the early morning sprinklers was evaporating off the lawns on our block, I would get on my bike and ride over to the country club. On game days, Pony League players were forbidden to swim in the midday sun because my father said it drained us. He didn't mention playing tennis as part of that rule, so I did. I began playing several hours of tennis each day.

I started winning matches. I climbed the ladder at the club, and Lorna asked me to join the team that played other clubs. I did, and I got even better because of playing so often.

The summer I was fifteen, my dad knew I was playing tennis, but he didn't know how much I was playing. I was secretly playing five or six hours of tennis a day. It didn't much affect my baseball performance because I was still just the second string catcher. Winning was most important to my dad, and even though he insisted on having me in the game, he knew that with me on the field and at bat, he increased his chances of losing.

For me—and my dad—a lot hinged on the presence of Mark Stevens, a great athlete and much better catcher, the first string. As long as he was able to be at a game, I didn't have to play much—only when it was a landslide in our favor, and at the very end of the game. Usually, that meant I had to catch the last two or three innings, and spend most of my time in the game running to the backstop behind home plate, to retrieve all of the balls that got by me. *This is humiliating*, I thought. Some people assumed that because Mark was so much better than me there was a rivalry between us, but nothing could be further from the truth. I was grateful for him.

Baseball, to me, was no longer about playing, because I didn't play the majority of the time. Baseball became about time lost, the inordinate amount of it I had to spend at practices and at games. It began pissing me off. I thought about how much of my life I was wasting being forced to do something I didn't enjoy. And so I'd pray for rain.

More and more, I found myself diverting my energies to tennis. I would work for hours on my serve. I'd hit the ball up against the backboard. I would call kids or even adults to play with me, in the morning, midday, or under the lights at Indian Meadows on nights when I didn't have baseball games. Maybe deep down I thought that if I got good enough at a sport, any sport, and truly excelled at it, then my dad would like me. Maybe I'd be able to negotiate a deal with him to play full time. Maybe he'd even be proud of me.

■ ■ ■

That summer, as luck would have it, it never rained. It seemed as if the more I'd pray, the less often it would rain. I wondered to myself if it was God's way of punishing me for being defiant against my father, or for not following the Ten Commandments. *It has been a while since my last confession,* I realized. Maybe that was it.

Pony League interfered with my tennis schedule. I began missing tennis matches and missing out on tournaments because baseball was so demanding. And when you play for a father who's an oppressive coach, calling in sick isn't an option. It wasn't much of an option for the other players either, because he'd show up at their houses to make sure they weren't swimming in their pool after they'd called to say they were upchucking in the toilet.

Mom knew how much I hated baseball and how much I hated playing for my father. And even though all my teammates were nice, I really felt like I had nothing in common with them. I would tell her about it as I sat with her on our back deck overlooking the woods, while she smoked. (As I got older, she stopped smoking inside, so the deck was where you'd find her most of the summer. In the winters, she had a folding lawn chair that she placed in the garage with a quilt and a blanket, and she would sit out there by herself and smoke.)

"I want to quit baseball," I told her.

"Why, Jon?" she asked.

"For so many reasons," I said. "I'm so uncomfortable with the other guys on the baseball team," I told her. "I hate when they talk about girls' 'tits' and 'asses.' They're always grabbing their crotches and spitting."

As the midsummer sun cast shadows through trees, Mom reached over and gave me a hug.

"I know how much you hate it, Jon," she said. "But you're halfway through the season. If you quit, there might be something you'd miss learning from sticking it out."

I frowned. I had been looking for her to somehow let me off the hook.

"Instead of quitting, why don't you play more tennis?" she suggested. "You love that—it's challenging and invigorating for you. Just keep at it. Then, when the spring of your high school freshman year comes around, try out for the varsity team and make it. Then see what your father does! You show him!"

■ ■ ■

Freshman year hadn't been as bad as I thought it would be. Having my brother Jared there to show me the ropes helped a lot. He was a three-sport athlete, popular, good looking, a lady's man, and president of the senior class. That was a powerful combination in high school. Because of my bloodline, I was protected. I was a prime target for upper-class bullies, but he and his friends made sure the bullies stayed away from me. It also helped that my dad coached so many of the upperclassmen. It didn't matter that I mostly hung around girls' lockers and I dressed impeccably like a preppie, with popped-collared shirts and sweater vests; because I was Jared's brother and my father's son, I was off-limits.

On the other hand, I had to spend a lot of time impressing upon teachers, who'd had Jared before me, that I was a different kind of student than he was. Jared didn't apply himself in classes the way he did in sports. Slacking off in class seemed to be a way for him to uphold his jock image. But it came at a high price. He was often grounded or got the belt from my father for getting Cs or Ds on exams.

I did everything I could to create a "brand" of my own. I'd been popular with the teachers at Sanborn and at West. I'd won the Daughters of the American Revolution Award at our eighth grade graduation ceremony for being a good citizen. It would be work, but I was up for the challenge of proving I was different than Jared in the classroom.

The schoolwork was a lot harder than in eighth grade. I took the level one classes seriously and I studied constantly. I collected as many As as I could, but mathematics always brought me down. I felt lucky if I got B-minuses in algebra or geometry. It didn't matter to my father, though, that even my lowest grades were better than my brother's. At the end of freshman year the class rankings came out, and even though I was thirty-ninth, it wasn't good enough. My father told me that anything less than a top-ten ranking was failure.

My relationship with Chad proved to be even more beneficial to my social standing at the start of high school than my brother's. He exuded an upbeat, bouncy energy, and a lightness that brightened the school's dark, locker-lined corridors as he passed through them with his big laugh. Even though he liked to goof around, he was always positive and kind, never saying anything mean about anyone. He brought a lot of attention to himself and he had a lot of followers, especially the girls who continued to think he was "hot"—his aqua eyes set against wavy, Superman hair that often climbed like vines around a baseball cap. I didn't realize it at first, but coming into high school as Chad's best friend had advantages for me. I'd heard from time to time that a few girls said I was cute, too, but at Andover High School, being as hot and popular as Chad was took you a lot further. It meant access to the best parties and to upper-class events. I wasn't much of a partier, but my friendship with Chad was still a form of social currency. It prevented me from falling into obscurity freshman year—that crucial year that set the tone for the three that followed.

Because of Chad, even that first year I was invited to semiformals and dances, and some parties, and yes, I was even asked to prom—by a senior girl who scared the living shit out of me! So I didn't go. But, case in point: I was asked because I had access to Chad.

■ ■ ■

The winters in Massachusetts were toughest in March. It seemed unfathomable that there could be more snow so late in the season, after so much of it had already fallen and kept us cooped up inside since December.

But despite the frigid temperatures, spring fever took hold during that month in my freshman year. I'd spent many winter days playing tennis, and my mom was incredibly supportive, driving me to workouts and practices and covering the costs of the expensive sport. I don't know what she'd say to my father when I wasn't around, but somehow she had gotten his approval to keep financing it. My guess was that playing tennis helped me thin out quite a bit. He needed to pick his battles.

I had risen to the top of the Rolling Green ladder in my age group. I was winning singles matches, and having learned to be a good doubles player, I was winning those, too. Our team played other clubs like The Willows and Cedardale, and we became one of the best teams in the league.

As the banks of plowed snow on the side of the roads began to shrink, and the brown, soggy grass began to show itself, postings for spring sports tryouts began to cover my school's cement walls. Varsity, junior varsity, and freshman sign-up sheets for track, baseball, tennis, and softball were quickly populated with signatures. Each night that spring when my father wasn't traveling, he'd ask me when baseball tryouts were. He accepted that I had no shot at the varsity team, but he pushed me to make junior varsity. He'd already begun lobbying the coaches. What he didn't yet know was that my name was on the tryout list for varsity tennis.

Mr. Bartman, one of the guidance counselors, was the boys' varsity tennis coach. I went to see him on the Friday afternoon before tryouts the following Monday.

"How hard is it to make the varsity squad?" I asked.

"Pretty hard, Jon," he said. "Tennis is a big sport in this town, so there's going to be a lot of competition."

I'd heard of guys like Paul Benner and Stan King, who'd been playing tennis for most of their lives, and were really good. But I knew that I'd worked hard and was ready for the tryouts. In contrast to my insecurity about playing just about all other sports, I had confidence in my tennis playing. I was running out of time to have my name show up on the baseball tryout list. The good news was that because some of the tryouts for tennis could take place inside, they were always a week or two earlier than the ones for baseball.

After a grueling set of weeklong running drills, sprints, timed-mile runs, and match after match at the indoor club, I tried out. The tryouts were mostly individual singles matches. I guess the proof was in the pudding: the more you won, the more you kept playing. I had doubts because so many of the guys, like Paul and Stan, had been playing all their lives. They hit the ball so hard, and their serves were so good. But even though nerves kept me from playing my best at the tryouts, a few days later I learned, to my great surprise, that I ended up high enough on the tryout ladder to make the varsity team. Even more impressive, I was high enough on the ladder to be chosen as the second half of the second doubles team. It was a massive victory for me. It was the first athletics team I made without being forced by my father to play, and that I actually made on my own, without him pulling his weight as coach. I did this on my own terms and was victorious in my own way. Elated, I told all my friends and my mom. But it had a downside: My name wasn't going to be on that baseball list, and I was going to pay for it.

There was never a good time for us to try to free ourselves from our father. My father didn't allow anyone to make his or her own decisions. There was something about taking complete control of our lives that seemed to make him feel better about himself. None of my friends could quite comprehend why telling him that I made the varsity tennis team was a frightening thing—news that he would consider bad.

I waited until the second night after he returned home from a business trip to tell him I wasn't going to play baseball anymore. Usually he was in a better mood a day or two after he'd been on a business trip because he was less tired. I needed to have as many positive things as possible on my side.

I got one last pep talk from my mom, gathered my strength, and went forth, climbing the stairs to his bedroom, where I found him taking off his watch and placing it in the valet on top of his tall bureau. "Dad, do you have a minute?" I asked, trembling. "I have some good news to share with you." I said it as positively as I could.

"What is it, Jon?" he asked, impatiently. "I have a Little League meeting tonight and I can't be late. I'm up for becoming vice president of the league." My palms were sweating and my heart was doing that familiar racing it did when I was in his presence. My anxiety around him became an everyday part of life. The adrenaline elevating my heart rate, the blood rapidly pumping through my veins seemed to give me the strength to get through whatever horrors he threw at me. It felt almost like a workout.

"Dad, don't get mad," I said, "but I made varsity tennis. I got the news from Mr. Bartman after school yester—"

I'd barely finished getting the words out of my mouth when I had to duck for cover, as he started throwing various items from the top of his bureau at my head.

"How dare you come in here, Mister, and tell me what you're going to do!" he screamed. "You are not going to play *that* sport, and you are not quitting baseball! You don't have a choice!"

He went on and on. "You are not going to embarrass me and play some sissy sport in high school. I should have never listened to your mother. She babies you. She coddles you and look at what it does; it makes you choose some pussy sport like tennis. How dare you?!" He went into their ensuite bathroom and slammed the door, nearly splitting the wood in half. I ran out of the room as fast as I could, hoping to escape a beating or more yelling. I ran downstairs and screamed at my mom, "Look what you made me do! And now I can't play!" I ran down to the first floor and called my friend Kendra. I told her what my dad had said. "Can I please come to your house now?"

"Of course!" she said.

I hid in the basement for as long as I could, listening to my father scream at my mother. I was waiting for him to leave so I could make my escape.

"You are ruining him, Judy!" he hollered. "He is not to ever play tennis again! He's going to play baseball, as a catcher. End of conversation."

I went under the basement staircase, where we had a Nintendo set up, and I started playing Mario Bros. to mentally escape, but I couldn't stay distracted from the yelling upstairs. My mom had become a bit fiercer in her fighting back over time, and I remember her really advocating for me on this one.

"Jesus Christ, Jimmy, he made varsity tennis," she said. "Most fathers would be proud of their sons, but all you think of is yourself and your image! You're ruining these poor kids!"

She got more backbone as we got older, maybe because I was the third child and she was sick of his tyranny, but she at least yelled back now. I knew she would never win in any fight against him, but at least she stood up for me. Jared and Julie really never had her to help them fight their battles. She was still too weak at the time when they were in their prime teenage years.

When I heard him coming for the basement door, I quickly turned off the TV and the Nintendo and sat quietly in the corner hoping he wouldn't see or hear me. His garage door went up, his Lincoln started, and the garage door went back down. This was always a sound of relief. *He's gone.* I went back upstairs and cried to my mother, begging her to do something. She looked at me with defeated eyes and said, "I tried, Jon, there's nothing I can do."

"Then I'm running away and I'm not coming home until he lets me play tennis," I insisted.

After packing up my clothes for school and all of my books, I went downstairs and out the front door. *I need to get out of here, and fast,* I thought. I ran down our street, took a right onto Windchannel Road, and a left onto Robin's Way. Behind Jessica Cohn's house were a path and a creek that separated our neighborhood, Rocky Acres, from Tabatha's Lane.

When I got to the creek, I saw the neighbors' lawns across it and thought about the quiet, loving house that Kendra lived in with her parents and her little cat, Gabby. The sun, low in the sky, was casting rays of light ahead of me, between the trees. Many times in my childhood when my father made my mom cry because she embarrassed him at a dinner party, or put red marks on my sister's legs because the skirt she picked was too short, or locked my brother in his room for booting a ground ball, I would run to the creek and imagine what it was like to live across it.

I'd never crossed it on moments like this because I was always so afraid of the consequences. I was always afraid of what would happen to my mom or my brother or my sister in that house with my father there, without me, so I always turned around and went walking back, giving in to his rule. But this day was different; I couldn't give up what I had achieved on my own. I backed up far enough so that I could leap over the rushing creek, took a deep breath, ran to the bank, and jumped. I cleared the cavern and landed. Once I got my composure, I looked back. Seeing the darkness on the other side, I felt sad for my mom. I felt bad for my siblings, too, but I knew that I had to break free. I had to keep running. I knew it was an important moment in my life, but I hardly knew it would eventually become a habit that would end up taking it over.

There were only a few places that my mom knew I would go. It was either Kendra's, Samantha's, or Chad's. She knew I had good friends who took care of me when she could not. Those friends helped me survive. Once Mom knew I was safe, she somehow convinced my father that going to Kendra's house to come after me would be more embarrassing for him than just leaving me there. I remember Kendra's mom talking to my mom on the phone. I could hear her mom say how ridiculous this was. My mom probably didn't know what to say, and said nothing.

A few days later, my mom came to school and told me I'd won the battle. She'd called my Uncle Tony and somehow he'd been able to convince my father that my playing tennis was not the end of the world. It took some additional phone calls, but eventually, my uncle's pressure, coupled with the embarrassment of others knowing that I was living at Kendra's house because of him, gave me the edge.

"Before I come home, Mom," I said, "I need assurances that I'm not going to be in danger. And I don't want to have to deal with any of his nonsense."

"It will be fine, Jon," she promised. "You can trust me."

That following Monday, I went to my first varsity tennis practice and defended my place as number six on the ladder. I got home that night and my mom had prepared my favorite meal, macaroni and cheese and fish sticks. I ate at the kitchen table as my mom sat with me and drank a soda. My father sat in the family room, by himself, flipping through channels of sports scores and recaps, and never saying one word to me. I went upstairs after dinner and turned on my lamp and began studying for a Spanish quiz I had the next day. As I gazed out of my window and looked in the direction of where the creek was, I sat peacefully and wondered whether I should have run over the creek long before.

Chapter 7

Mr. Andover High School

Everything I did had to be perfect. Even my closet had to be impeccably arranged. My jeans hung on hangers, organized from light to dark. Shirts were grouped from left to right: solids, plaids, stripes. Roll-necks and cardigans were folded like they were at the department stores and arranged by color on the top shelf.

One time when I wasn't paying attention, my good friend Vinny moved a bunch of sweaters from the top shelf and put them on the floor of my closet. When I found them there, I freaked, and he laughed as I grabbed them, dusted them off (even though there was no dust in my room), neatly folded them, and put them back into their right place. Fastidiously keeping my closet, my bedroom, and just about everything else perfect was the only way I thought I could make up for the flaw within me that seemed to emerge more forcefully each day. Pictures of my friends stood in pretty frames on my bookshelves. If anyone moved them even an inch, I knew. My room was the epitome of order and cleanliness. It was my sanctuary in a house of chaos, in a world that seemed to be crumbling in around me.

As my hormones began to erupt, I fought harder to stifle them. I went to church. I prayed at night, longer and louder in my mind. I wrote secret poems about remaining chaste and pure. And when that didn't work, I distracted myself with a full slate of activities at school. The more I did, the less time I had to think about my attraction to Chad and the less time I had to think about why I wasn't attracted to Sophia in the same way. I was frantic to bring up my class ranking.

I needed to make National Honor Society, or else. I wanted the students, teachers, and parents to like me, even though I was hiding this demon inside. *Maybe if I am perfect, they will still like me when they find out.*

Yet I didn't even know if what they'd find out was even true. I still wasn't able to confirm it. I just knew that something deep in my soul was off. I was a misfit, a fraud. I was nothing like what my father wanted me to be, and if left to my own thoughts and devices, I knew I was doomed. So I did all I could to be outside of myself.

■ ■ ■

"Come on you guys, let's get this together; everyone back on stage, we only have two days left to make this perfect," I said encouragingly.

It was my junior year, and Meredith and I were the coproducers, writers, directors, and hosts of the second annual *Mr. Andover High School Contest.* We'd been challenged by the girl-best-friend-duo who created the contest the year before to increase the attendance and to make the contest even better. I thought about competing myself, but I feared my father's wrath if I performed, and I worried that if I sang or danced, I would draw unwanted attention. So I took the reins as producer, a role that was mostly behind the scenes.

A couple of months earlier, Meredith and I sat in the high school library behind a long folding table, listening to a wide variety of Andover High School guys—jocks, freaks, headbangers, geeks, theater buffs, "populars," and "unpopulars"—telling us why they would make great contestants to become the next Mr. AHS. Anyone could audition; it was one of the few moments in high school when the caste system really didn't matter.

Some of the auditions were compelling; some were not. After a night of deliberations, Meredith and I picked the dozen guys who were to compete in the show in three main categories: casual wear, formal wear, and sportswear. They also had to compete in a talent portion of the show.

As the curtain opened and the spotlight shined upon us, Meredith and I walked on stage to the music of "Wonderful Tonight" by Eric Clapton. It was invigorating but scary to be on stage with all those eyes on us. As the show continued on, Meredith and I read carefully from the script we'd written. I looked out and saw the sea of faces before us. We had done it; every seat in the Collins Center was filled. *Perfection!*

Of course, we had to pretend otherwise, but naturally we were rooting for our friends. James performed "Cat's in the Cradle" and nailed it. Vinny sang Weird Al's "One More Minute" in a white tuxedo with a purple bow tie and cummerbund, and it was hilarious. And, Charlie, the front-runner, lip-synched and danced fabulously to a Michael Jackson medley, choreographed by Broadway-bound classmate Melanie Masterson. The audience members rose to their feet in cheer. We were sure Charlie stole the show—as he'd stolen the ninth grade presidential election from me as a write-in candidate!—but in the end, the surprise winner of the 1994 Mr. AHS Contest was Kyle Montclair, who had done a funny *Romeo and Juliet* sketch complete with a set and costumes, in which he played both Romeo and Juliet.

The show was a huge success, and Meredith and I received accolades for our work on it—plus lots of flowers and cards. Many people were waiting in line to greet us at the stage door of the Collins Center when we left after the show.

To celebrate our success, a bunch of us went out to our favorite hangout for ice cream and fries. Sophia, who'd been my steady on and off again, was now on, and rode with me. We giggled about the show and then talked about how we'd watch the movie *Aladdin* on Saturday at her house. We both loved watching that movie, and we both loved listening to Whitney Houston. I think we watched her movie *The Bodyguard* twenty times together.

"You must be exhausted," Sophia said empathetically.

"No, I'm fine. Really," I assured her.

"I don't know how you do it—how you find the time to do so much and to still do it well."

I don't really know how, either, I thought. I spent hours at night studying after one activity or another at school. Most nights I didn't get home from school or activities until nine o'clock. I usually studied until midnight or one in the morning and then got up the next day around six. I was pretty tired, but I had no choice. It kept me out of my father's way, and it kept me from thinking too much about things I didn't want to think about.

After downing a hot fudge sundae and some curly fries with ketchup, Sophia said she had to meet her curfew, so I had to drive her home. Sophia lived in East Andover, and it was about a fifteen-minute drive from downtown to her house.

As we drove, Sophia reached her hand out and grabbed mine. We had so far never been physical. We still hadn't even kissed. When she held my hand, my whole being felt limp. Nothing happened. It didn't excite me the way my guy friends said touching a girl excited them, whether it was their hands or their thighs or their boobs.

For a long time, I wondered if I was not attracted to Sophia, and I know she wondered the same thing. But the few times we'd broken up in the two years since she arrived at AHS as a freshman, I did date a couple of other girls and felt exactly the same; it wasn't just her.

I was interested in talking with Sophia and learning about her feelings. I wanted to be there for her, and hear about her problems and her joys. I wanted to be her confidant. But I didn't want to make out with her or have sex with her. When I tried imagining us like that, it felt like I'd be molesting her. I mean, molesting in the true sense of the word: bothering her. I didn't understand why girls would want guys to feel their boobs or touch their privates. None of it made sense to me.

As we pulled into Sophia's driveway, I got a little nervous. Dropping dates off, I thought, *this is when the kissing happens.* I dreaded drop-offs, not only with Sophia but with all girls who thought I was about to kiss them. I could tell that Sophia really wanted to kiss me that night, and I wasn't too surprised; I felt more handsome than usual in my three-piece tuxedo, with my hair flopped down nearly perfect, with a golden bronze tan from Andover Tanning. Whitney Houston's "I Wanna Dance with Somebody" was on the cassette in the stereo and we were both singing it. As I pulled down the driveway, I threw the car into park and looked out my driver's side window, turning my head away from her, as if I were looking at something in the dark. "Bye!" I said abruptly. "Um, bye, see you tomorrow," she said, apparently confused. "Do you still want to go for a walk through Baker's Meadow before we watch *Aladdin* tomorrow?"

"Yeah, that sounds great. I'll pick you up at ten?" I answered, still looking out into her side yard. When I turned, I saw that she was looking down, dejected and a bit drawn, with only a half smile. "Yes," she answered. "See you in the morning."

On the way to my house clear on the other side of Andover, I had plenty of time to think. *What is wrong with me?* I wondered. Why didn't I have any desire to kiss one of the prettiest, most talented, sweetest, smartest girls in the school? Many guys would have killed for the chance to hook up with Sophia, but she was mine, and I just couldn't. I was afraid of what I would find if I did kiss her. I worried that I wouldn't like it or that it would gross me out. *Then I'd really know,* I thought. *That would really confirm it.* I didn't want to confirm it. I wanted to keep the mystery of what was going on with me just that—a mystery. Then, at least, I could keep denying it. If I kissed her, or anyone else for that matter, the truth would likely emerge. And with the truth certainly came doom, especially in my house, and in my town. In my mind, I just knew that kissing Sophia was wrong, so I never did it. I knew it had to be a huge disappointment for her. I'd never live up to the image of her own Mr. AHS. That made me slump into a darker place.

To find the light, determined to figure it all out, I continued to learn new ways to be not only Sophia's, but everyone's version of Mr. Andover High. I became frenzied about excelling at everything. I couldn't just be on student council; I had to be the president. I was a founder of Growing Up, Taking a Stand (GUTS), an organization that vowed its members against drinking and drugging while in high school, made National Honor Society, and became a Big Brother to a young, Hispanic kid in nearby Lawrence.

I always had good intentions, and it was innate in me to do good deeds, but I drove myself crazy making sure that A-minuses turned to As and As turned to A-pluses. I ensured that everything I did was flawless, and in doing so, made myself sick. I did all I could to overachieve. I had to make up for my hidden, real self somehow.

Maybe that's when I started to lose weight without even realizing it. Looking back at pictures, I got to be pretty skinny, but sadly, I remember looking in the mirror at the time and seeing the chubby face that my dad used to ridicule when I was in Little League. I wasn't in good enough shape, I decided. I didn't have a six-pack like Chad or Vinny, another sign I wasn't good enough and another area in which I'd soon begin to overdo my efforts to be perfect.

I picked Sophia up at ten the next morning just like we'd agreed. I rang the doorbell. I figured I couldn't kiss her in front of her parents, but I could give her a hug. Sophia's mom answered the door and yelled up to Sophia, "Sophia, Jon is here." I looked up and saw her run from the bathroom into her bedroom in a towel. She looked like my sister looked when she ran from her room to the bathroom, one towel in her hair and another around her torso, just grazing her thigh. As I waited, Sophia's mom made me some tea and asked how things were at school and at home. I didn't say much about my home life, but I told her that school was going very well. She asked me if I had started thinking about college, and I said, "Just a little, it feels like it's so far away."

Sophia came down a little while later all made up and her hair blown out. Sometimes she really looked like a model with her beautiful eyes and pretty smile. I knew that I was lucky to be able to call her my girlfriend. "Bye, Mom," Sophia yelled out to her mother, who was now in their family room watching television. "We're going to Baker's Meadow for a walk and a picnic."

Baker's Meadow was a pristine nature preserve in Andover, with a footpath that encircled a large pond with cattails and lily pads and tall pines, oaks, and elms that I often felt looked over us like God. I imagined each one of those trees was God in his most beautiful form. There were beaver dams and ducks—mallards mate-calling across the water. It was a place where I loved to think and dream, especially when things were rough at home.

Baker's Meadow also became a special spot for Sophia and me. On the far side of the walking path, there was a wooden bridge built over a small outlet for the pond. It was a small well of water. The water was so still and clear, we could see our reflections in it when we leaned over the bridge. We dubbed it "the wishing well."

There, at the wishing well, Sophia and I would have our picnics and long talks about life and our futures. Often, we talked about how it would work when I was at college and she was still at AHS, and other times we talked about our futures way beyond that. Many people seemed to think Sophia and I were the kind of high school sweethearts who would end up getting married. It felt as if everyone expected that of us. Why not? We seemed perfect together. *Perfection.*

When Sophia and I arrived at the wishing well after the good hike from the road, we sat side by side looking out onto the pond. The sun was shining brightly, and even though we couldn't see it behind the trees, it was there, warming up the blue sky above us. Sophia had brought a couple of ham and cheese sandwiches on white bread, chips, and two cans of soda. She spread a blanket on top of the wooden bridge and we sat down enjoying the view.

After eating our sandwiches and a moment of silence, Sophia asked me why I never wanted to kiss her. "Some of our other friends are even having sex, and you haven't kissed me," she said. "Do you think I'm ugly, do you think I'm fat?" I felt horrible. I didn't know what to say, other than the truth.

"Of course not, Sophia, I think that you're beautiful. I'm just scared."

"Scared of what?" she wondered.

"I'm scared of what will happen after I kiss you." She looked at me bewildered. "I'm just really confused. I don't have a huge sexual drive at this point in my life, and I'm just nervous that I'll either do it wrong or be a bad kisser or something." Sophia still didn't quite understand, but I couldn't say any more. I didn't know how to articulate what I was feeling to myself. How could I possibly let her in on a secret I wasn't even sure was real?

I looked over the side of the bridge at the reflection in the water and hated what I saw. There I was, one of the luckiest guys at AHS with one of the most beautiful girls from our school, in a wide open preserve with no one within a mile of us, and I possessed neither the nerve nor the desire to kiss her. I hated myself. *I'm the one that's ugly and fat, not her,* I found myself thinking.

We sat on top of the wishing well in quiet silence and listened to the ducks and Canada geese. Sophia took out two pennies from her pocket and gave me one. "Time to make our wishes; you go first."

I took the penny and concentrated on it, holding it up to the sky and wishing as hard as I could that somehow, some way, all of this confusion would go away and the truth would appear. I closed my eyes and silently made another wish: *"Please, let me place my lips on Sophia's, and then let the earth move beneath me the way my friends describe when they kiss girls. Let me get all excited and want to go further with her, lovingly, but like a man. Oh Wishing Well, I wish to kiss Sophia, right here and right now."* Then Sophia took her penny and also held it up to the sky and silently made her wish. We both tossed the pennies into the water at the same time.

I waited a few seconds, then a few minutes. After fifteen minutes, the urge still hadn't come. Instead, Sophia said she was getting cold and she wanted to head back to the car. One foot behind the other, we crushed leaves under our feet, and I covered my mouth with my scarf so as to create a barrier between my lips and hers.

As we drove home from Baker's Meadow, we didn't say much. We were both crushed. I was hurting as much as she was. I dropped her off in silence.

A few weeks later, Sophia broke up with me, "for good this time," she said. She didn't need to give me an explanation. I understood.

■ ■ ■

At school, the weeks after the Mr. AHS Contest were particularly good ones. The principal and assistant principal gave me an award for all of my citizenship and service to our class and to AHS. I was elected editor in chief of our yearbook, I was the incoming president of the student council, and, when our third quarter grades were released, I had made high honors for the third semester in a row. My class rank was surely to rise.

And yet despite all this glory, it still wasn't good enough. I was never good enough. The yelling and screaming at home continued. I was reminded every day when I looked in the mirror that in my father's eyes, I was a colossal failure, as I would likely also be to everyone who would eventually find out the "disease" I was harboring inside. My fears and doubts haunted me more and more as the days went on. And even though to everyone else I looked like the ideal Mr. Andover High School on the outside, I was nothing of the sort on the inside.

✳

Chapter 8

The Unearthing

I was deep into my history homework when I heard my father's lumbering footsteps coming toward my bedroom door. Any second, he'd burst in. He'd never think of knocking.

"Jon, I'd like to talk to you."

Even though he wasn't yelling, as he so often was, I experienced the awful, tight feeling in my gut that I always got when my father wanted to talk to me. What was he going to criticize me for now? What new, ridiculous edict was he going to throw down? What small pleasure would be forbidden next?

"Sure, Dad," I said after a deep breath.

He was still in his suit pants and oxford shirt from work, but he had on slippers, which somehow made him seem less threatening. He looked tired, too, at the end of the day. His comb-over was even slightly askew. Usually there wasn't a hair out of place.

"I'm going to take you with me on a business trip next month," he said, standing in the doorway. His face bore the oddest expression—as if he were trying to smile, something he only really knew how to do on a baseball field or in a men's locker room, but his facial muscles weren't cooperating. "We're going to San Francisco."

This was puzzling to say the least. I'd never been on a business trip with my father before, and I didn't recall Jared or Julie being invited on one, either. Dad and I could barely endure a short car ride alone together without him getting angry and me getting upset. Was he out of his mind? Why me? Why now? I figured my mother had put him up to it. She was always hoping to find some way for us to connect. For as long as I could remember, it seemed as if he hated me, and that caused her tremendous anguish.

"Okay," I said, trying for a believable level of enthusiasm, "that'll be great."

There was an awkward pause as my dad seemed to consider what to say next. The fake smile went away and he shifted to the other foot. "I'm telling you now," he began, "you're going to see homos kissing and making out with each other all over the place there. It's disgusting and wrong, and you should just look away."

This startled me. How had he managed to work a harsh, negative reference to gayness into yet another statement? "All right, Dad," I said. "I've got it. I'll look away."

"Okay. Goodnight, Boze." That was my dad's nickname for both me and my older brother—short for Bozo as in Bozo the Clown. He'd only call us that on the rare occasions when he was in a good mood and getting along with us, or trying to.

After he left my room, I began to panic, first about spending so much time alone with my father, then about what it would be like to see all those gay men being so flagrantly sexual. What effect would it have on me? Would it look appealing to me? God, what if it turned me on? Could just seeing it confirm me as gay? And if it did make me gay, would I suddenly become the kind of person who had to make out in public? Ugh. That sounded repulsive.

Until then, the only seemingly gay person I knew was Mr. Chardiet, the Spanish teacher who'd inappropriately pursued me and other boys, and he was clearly pathetic and gross. Mr. Chardiet took a special interest in me freshman and sophomore years and it made me incredibly uncomfortable. He'd fawn all over me, calling on me more than anyone else in class. He'd invite me to stay after school for extra credit, and while I was there, offer to take me with him to his vacation home in Quebec. "You like to ski, Jon, don't you?" I didn't know what to say.

When he started calling me on my private line at home, seemingly drunk, at 10:30 at night, I got completely creeped out. The second time he called, I lost it, and hung up on him.

The next morning I told my parents, and shortly after that my father marched into the principal's office and exploded. I was immediately switched into a different Spanish class, Mr. Chardiet was reprimanded, and the incident, I was told, was documented in his permanent record. I heard years later that he continued to hit on boys in his classes.

Just my luck, the first gay person I encountered in my life turned out to be the nightmare projection of homophobes everywhere: a depraved pedophile who can't control his urges. That was an up-close picture of what I thought was gay.

Were all those "homos" in San Francisco going to be as desperate as Mr. Chardiet?

I dreaded the trip with my father. I could imagine nothing positive about it. He frightened me with his temper and repulsed me with his cloying, overwhelming cologne, his bad breath, and the way he spit all over everything when he got worked up and screamed. And yet I was so eager to please him, so desperate for his approval. I'd been twisting myself into knots for years hoping he'd think I was fit enough, skinny enough, masculine enough in the way I stood and talked. I was always careful not to eat fatty foods like cheese or *his* personal favorite, Cheez-Its, around him, not to limply bend my wrist, not to sway as I walked, not to emphasize my s sounds when I spoke. There was so much for me to remember to keep in line for his benefit. The effort gave me a stomachache, but it reassured me and contained me, too.

The next morning after Dad left for work, I approached Mom as she made me breakfast. "Mom, did you ask Dad to take me to San Francisco with him?" I asked. "I know you're always trying to get us to be close, but—"

"No, Jon," she insisted, cutting me off. "It was your father's idea." I stood there stunned for a minute.

"Well, this is going to be torture," I said. I racked my brain for excuses I might try, but quickly realized that was futile. "I can't get out of this, can I?"

"You'll upset your father," she answered. "You don't want to upset your father."

My mother lived in terror of upsetting my father. Even more than I did, she lived her life like a caged animal, all in an effort to never upset him.

My father harped on my mother for so many things. If it wasn't her wrinkles and smoking, it was that she was too thin. He couldn't stand it when she made jokes or, for that matter, even spoke in public. "You always say the wrong things!" he would scream at her. How they ever got together is beyond me. I never witnessed any intimacy or affection between them, and by the time I left for college they were sleeping most nights in separate rooms.

Once a year, at Christmas, my father would make a big show of giving her some big, gaudy piece of jewelry. For many years, she seemed to savor those moments and the clunky baubles that came with them. In her later years, though, she would wait a few days, then trade them in for something she liked better. Dad never paid attention to her, so he never knew the difference.

■ ■ ■

I don't know what I expected the trip to San Francisco to be like. I was afraid it meant I'd have to interact with my father a lot, that he'd try to lecture me constantly. But that didn't happen. The two of us barely spoke to each other—in the car, on the plane, on the way to the hotel. We were silent at meals, except for a little small talk here and there about school and the Red Sox. Dad took me to Alcatraz, but otherwise he went on his business appointments during the day and left me on my own, which was fine. I walked around by myself, checking out the tourist spots, like Fisherman's Wharf and the San Francisco Museum of Modern Art. I wandered through different neighborhoods.

Even though I kept an eye out, I never once saw any "homos" kissing like my dad had warned me about, which was fine by me.

■ ■ ■

Back home, I was able to keep things suppressed. Even though she'd said it was for good when we'd broken up the last time, I actually managed to win back Sophia, although it was tenuous. One afternoon after school, on a walk with Sophia in Baker's Meadow, she sat me down near the place we called the wishing well. Just when I thought she was going to speak, she put her head down. I could tell she was holding back tears. My fear that this was going to be a repeat of the picnic when I was confronted with the lack of sexual intimacy in our relationship was soon realized.

"Jon, I want to ask you again, don't you think it's weird that we never, like . . . do anything . . . like . . . physical?" She was trembling. I'd had a feeling this question was coming. "I mean, we never even hold hands," she said. "We're in high school. Everyone else is at least kissing and stuff. Is something wrong with me?"

"Oh my God, Sophia," I said. "It's not that at all!"

"Then what?" she pressed.

My heart was racing. I again didn't know how truthful I could be. I still wasn't ready to know the truth myself. Should I make it all about respecting her this time? About being raised Catholic? About my father forbidding all three of his kids from having premarital sex? Hey, if you started getting physical with someone, what was to keep you from going all the way?

Yes, that was good; I began there. But then a little bit of the truth leaked in. "I think I'm confused, Sophia," I said. "It has nothing to do with you. You are so, so beautiful! And I like you so much. I'm just . . . yes, I'm confused."

"Confused about me? About us?" she begged.

"No, no," I said. "Confused about me. Like, maybe I'm asexual? Or maybe I'm a late bloomer. That's what my mom thinks, anyway."

That conversation alleviated the tension for a little while. She still wanted to hang out and see where things would go, and so did I.

When I wasn't spending time with Sophia, I continued to keep extra busy with schoolwork and extracurricular activities. Priority number one remained to distract myself from the impure thoughts triggered by hormones that were trying to surface.

Complicating matters was my frequent proximity to Chad. Although our differences continued to become evident during high school—he shot three-pointers and I shot air balls—our yin and yang worked.

We played very different roles at AHS, but we were known as a pair. He commanded way more attention than I did. Sure, I eventually became the captain of the tennis team, but Chad was a star pitcher on the baseball team. I was student body president, but Chad stole the show at student government meetings, making a mockery of them by demanding things like better quality salami on the lunch line. I could do little but hammer the gavel, calling for order, while everyone in attendance laughed hysterically at Chad's antics. I was the straight man to his funnyman. I never laughed more than when I was with Chad.

Still, he and I had *one of those connections*. The kind where you complete each other's sentences. We'd had it ever since that night we met on the basketball court.

By our second year of high school year, we'd become inseparable. We even bought matching friendship necklaces in Ocean City one summer—blue and green football-shaped ceramic beads on leather chokers.

"There's a reason we have the same color beads, bro," he'd remind me from time to time. "We're gonna always be together. We're gonna always be best friends, Beans." I can't even remember where his nickname for me came from, but I liked it, and it stuck.

Spending the night at Chad's house had become an every weekend kind of thing by the time we were juniors. He would tell me everything, even the most personal stuff, like about how scared he was of his panic attacks. I would tell him about how worried I was about my funny but fragile mother, and about how much I liked Sophia. I'd try to leave out the part about how we weren't so much as kissing yet, but he always asked, "How far'd ya get, huh?"

That year my feelings for Chad, alarmingly, took on a different hue, something that made me uncomfortable to recognize. He'd always been something of a flirt; he flirted indiscriminately with everyone—male, female, young, old. Everyone loved him and he loved the attention.

In my case, I doubt he'd label what he did with me *flirting*, and I don't know if he had any inkling I might be gay. I scarcely knew it myself. But that year more than ever before, it felt as if Chad was not just teasing me but trying to seduce me.

"You're so cute, I could kiss you, Beans," he'd joke now and then. "Look at that face, look at those earsies." He liked to grab his "package" in front of me, too, and say things like, "Check this out! Can you believe how big this thing has gotten?" Did he ever catch me looking for a beat too long, before I rolled my eyes at him and started laughing?

Maybe it's just what guys do at that age, some kind of adolescent homoerotic play. As a middle-schooler, I often saw my brother's straight jock friends from high school fake hump one another. But for me Chad's antics were a tremendous source of confusion. Much to my own dismay, and despite my great efforts toward resistance, I was developing real feelings for Chad—both romantic and sexual. I started to make sense of the jealousy I felt when he spent more time with his girlfriends than with me, and why I found myself vying with them for his attention in every possible way. That year for his birthday I even redecorated his room for him with money from my own pocket. His mom let me in one day when Chad was occupied with some girl or something, and when he came home his newly decorated room awaited him. Because he was into sports, I bought him Michael Jordan "Air Jordan" posters and hung them so they looked perfect. In hindsight, I'm surprised Chad and his parents didn't think that was a little weird. We were sixteen and I essentially "Queer-Eyed" his personal space. If they did find it strange, they never said anything about it. And it didn't keep Chad from spending time with me, inviting me over, and inviting me to spend time with his family in Ocean City, Maryland, as I'd been doing every summer for several years running.

■ ■ ■

For two weeks at the beginning of every August, Chad's extended family would gather at Salty Sands, a condominium complex right on the beach in the heart of Ocean City. I was always there alongside them. It felt special to be included like that, every year, no questions asked.

Over the years, we'd fallen into a comfortable rhythm. We'd spend our days swimming and hanging out at the beach and our evenings cruising the boardwalk for girls—although Chad was the only one who picked them up. I was, conveniently, his "wingman."

The summer between junior and senior years, we made what would be our last trip there together. I had no clue it would be any different this time.

That summer should have been our best time ever. We were finally going to be seniors at Andover High! We were well positioned in the social pecking order. We were both popular, but for different reasons. Chad was more popular with the jocks and hot girls and was interested in hooking up and making out. He spent a lot of time looking in the mirror, asking me to assure him that he was good-looking. I had no trouble indulging him.

As for me, I never thought of myself as good-looking or attractive. I always thought that I was just kind of average and a little pudgy. My father would remind me all the time that I wasn't in good shape. (Years later, I would see that his assessment of my body was absurd. I was a little soft in the middle, but generally fit and trim. At times, around the one or two growth spurts I had, I was even skinny.)

Around the same time I had begun recognizing my own anxiety about my body, Chad's mom would get these melt-in-your-mouth butter donuts at the boardwalk in Ocean City. I'd scarf down one or two and hate myself afterward. I'd try to skip the cooler lunch on the beach that day to make up for it. "Nah, I'm just not hungry right now," I'd tell Chad's doting mom.

In photos from that summer, I'm pretty slim. Chad's cousin, Shaun, took out his camera and took a bunch of shots one night. It was when the sun was just beginning to go down, that great time at the beach when the sky is blue and the sand turns cool. Chad suggested we shower and change and try to get some nice pictures of the two of us, since it was such a beautiful night. Chad was as sentimental about our friendship as I was. In fact, Chad had never had a friend like me before: a sensitive guy. I listened to him. I was there for him. Chad valued our friendship and he often told me so. I valued being valued. I wanted to be the most important person to him in the world. I wanted to know him better than anyone else. I wanted to take care of him the way he took care of me—like on the nights when my father's ranting and raving was too much for me to bear and I'd run to his house to get away, or when he cheered me on while on the playing field where my father would berate me in front of everyone.

"Let's go, Beans. Let's get down to the beach before the sun goes down!"

Shaun took out the camera and Chad started striking poses—shirt off and standing in front of the water, sitting down near the dune grasses, crouching down in a catcher's stance. Insecure, I kept my shirt on.

"You're not gonna hook up with any cute girls if you don't flaunt what you've got a little, Beans," Chad teased.

■ ■ ■

Of course, I wasn't interested in hooking up with any cute girls. Chad, on the other hand, was interested in any girl with a pulse. In the evenings, as we cruised around town checking out the Ferris wheel and the waterslides at the end of the busy boardwalk, Chad looked for girls to conquer. I looked for girls who would talk with me about Walt Whitman, to no avail. I wound up talking to the surplus babes who were infatuated with Chad. They could tell I wasn't interested in getting in their pants, so they made me their confidante, telling me how much they wanted Chad, and trying to use my closeness with him to their advantage. How could I help them get Chad alone? Get him to kiss them? Spend the night with them?

It would have been almost comical, if I weren't fighting those same feelings. Chad had such a powerful allure. The women would just melt. "Oh my God, those aqua blue eyes!" one girl swooned. "They peek out from under that Philly's hat he wears and they slay me!" Of course Chad knew just what he was doing. He wore that hat strategically low and tight on his head, the rim curved downward, the angle like a vortex the girls magically got caught in. Another girl went on and on about his cute butt. "Just look at it," she squealed as Chad paid attention to a blonder, taller, skinnier girl. I couldn't have agreed more; it was a really cute butt, sticking out as it did from his tight, size-30 Gap jeans. His lips—full, red, glossed over with ChapStick— were another favorite feature among his fans, myself included.

Playing the role of horny American straight dude was always a big challenge for me, but it had never been harder than it was that summer. Never mind that I'd already had several summers of practice, bullshitting with Chad's many testosterone-filled uncles who did nothing but talk about women, sex, and football. It was torture for me. I hated the way they talked about women's boobs—frequently a topic of discussion on the heavily bikini-laden beach.

"Look at those knockers, Jon," one of the uncles would say. "I bet you want a piece of those!"

Um, no! Not really! Not only was I turned off by the discussion, but it made me worry. *Why didn't I want a piece of those?* When was I going to start wanting a piece? Could my mother be right? Was I just a late bloomer? But I'd nod right along and reply, "Oh yeah, a big piece!"

The late bloomer theory was becoming increasingly difficult for me to buy. Who were we kidding? I was having feelings for guys. Well, one guy in particular. In fact, I think I was maybe even—*oh, shit*—falling in love with him.

That unfortunate bit of information, which I'd been laboring to deny, came in loud and clear on the Tuesday night of Chad's and my second week at the beach. My eyes opened at 3:22 a.m., according to the blinking microwave clock. Chad and I had fallen asleep together on the pullout couch in the living room with the television on, its blue glow still coloring the room. The rest of Chad's family—his parents and two brothers—were asleep in the bedrooms down the hall.

We'd been particularly wiped out that night. We'd gone to the go-kart track, racing around a hundred times. It was just the two of us, having a great time together like usual, laughing nonstop. When we got home, everyone was already asleep. We turned on the end of the *Tonight Show*, and before long we were both out like lights.

When I woke, I used the remote to turn off the TV and saw that we were in the middle of a storm. Lightning flashed, making the room glow, and then, seconds later, loud thunder answered it. I found myself feeling uneasy. Ever since my family's early days in Ohio, where storms often led to tornado warnings, lightning had always tied my stomach in knots. I tried to put my fear in check and go back to sleep, but it was no use; I continued tossing and turning.

Chad, on the other hand, was dead to the world. He could sleep through anything, and predictably he didn't move. He was cuddled close to me, with his arm accidentally draped across my torso. Sleeping this way had become a nightly habit. He would have done the same thing to a pillow. I didn't think anything of it, except, the truth is, it felt good. *So* good. *Too* good. Chad was straight, I had to remind myself. This couldn't possibly mean anything. *We're like brothers,* or *he thinks I'm a stuffed animal,* I rationalized in my head.

But on that stormy night as I lay there, as still as could be, so as not to disturb Chad's dreaming, I couldn't help but realize that I wished it *did* mean something, and that it would lead to more. I hated myself for those wishes and began to wonder whether the thunder was God expressing his disgust over my not wanting Chad to let go of me, not gawking at the girls in bikinis on the beach, not being more like Chad. I heard my father's voice. "You really are a faggot," over and over, in my head.

I had to roll away from Chad without waking him. I couldn't take the closeness. The gentle touch of his leg hairs was giving me butter-flies. It felt so good, it startled me. I kept my eyes wide open, watching the storm's electricity create shadows on the walls. If I stayed awake, maybe I could will my urges to pass. I rolled back toward him just so I could watch him sleep.

With each flash of lightning, I could see the silhouette of Chad's nose on the wall, and his short brown curls flopping down onto his forehead. With his eyes closed, he looked peaceful and calm—not the hyperkinetic, all-American teen he was during waking hours. I always knew Chad was good-looking, that was obvious. But that night, for the first time, I found my friend to be utterly beautiful and, I had to admit, incredibly sexy. I felt something drawing me toward him. Something inside me was making me long to be even closer to him than I already was. The feeling of him next to me al-ways made me feel warm, but that night his skin touching mine made me shiver.

I started to feel a strong push-pull mechanism inside me, bring-ing me closer to Chad and then pulling me away in fear. One minute I was noticing how much I loved the feeling of his muscular legs next to mine, and how Chad seemed to use them to keep me from getting away from him. The next I was withdrawing my legs for fear that I wouldn't be able to lie there much longer without making the kind of move on him that he wanted to make on the boardwalk girls.

What are you doing? an alarmed voice said inside me.

Shut up—I like this, and he keeps moving closer, so who cares? said another voice.

Stop this! It's evil! said the first voice. (That's the one that talked the most, the one that always won the argument.) *You are going to hell for these thoughts,* it said. *Guys don't feel this way about other guys. Remember what Dad has always said. Stop it!*

Despite the internal ramblings, I kept looking over at Chad. I couldn't keep my eyes off him. I wanted him to wake up, but I also loved watching him sleep. I focused on his mouth and his plush lips, and I imagined kissing them. I thought about his hands, and about lacing his smooth, thin fingers in between mine underneath the covers. I wanted to grab Chad and pull him on top of me. I was almost certain he would kiss me back. He'd joked so many times about us kissing. *There had to be something behind that.* And what about all the times when he would grab himself proudly in front of me, outlining the bulk of his genitals, and say, "What do you think of this, huh?" I knew he was being provocative, and I would always look away and yell, "Stop, you're gross." But, it seemed he sensed I liked it, and so he kept doing it.

How many nights just like that one had he wrapped his arm around me in bed, unknowingly? If I didn't move, he'd leave his arm there all night. Only when Chad's baby brother woke up and started to cry early in the morning would I remove myself from his embrace, for fear that we'd be caught like that, entwined under the sheets.

Yeah, maybe Chad knew what he was doing. But maybe he didn't. Maybe I was reading too much into it.

I started to panic. I went from shivering to trembling, my breath quickening, my heart racing. I was caught between two diametrically opposed versions of myself. One was critical and self-punishing. The other was filled with lust and was, most alarmingly, ready to act. It was desperate to lean over and touch the ample penis Chad had so frequently flaunted. Would he wake up if I simply cupped my hand around his large mound, the way he would do in front of me, over his tattered, white briefs? Oh, how I wanted to see what it felt like! I wanted to kiss him and touch him the way he wanted all those boardwalk girls to touch him. But I'd do it better. I could just start and see what happened. Maybe he wouldn't even wake up.

But what if he did wake up? Would he freak out? Would he want me to grab him harder? Would he reach out and touch me in the same way? Would he lie on top of me and press himself up against me the way I desperately wanted him to? Or would he run away and cast me out of his life, forever? Would my father find out and humiliate me and kick me out of the house? Would my mother stop loving me, too?

I was alternately so horny and so disgusted with myself. I felt like I was being tossed wildly back and forth between the two feelings, thrown around by rough waves in the ocean just outside our condo. But as the minutes on the microwave clock ticked by, I moved more in the direction of disgusted. After each impure, dirty thought occurred to me, my body would shake with shame. I began to hyperventilate, to convulse, then cry, then sob. I took my hand and pushed my dick down in between my legs. I then locked my hands in between my thighs just above my knees and squeezed them. I rocked myself back and forth, my tears staining the light blue cotton pillowcase that I knew so well from Chad's room back home.

Chad took in a deep sigh through his nose and scooted over to me like he always did. "What's wrong?" he mumbled into my ear.

"I'm fine," I said, barely breathing, "go back to sleep." I watched his eyelids melt downward again. I told myself to concentrate on my breathing, to think of the waves crashing on the sand outside. Morning was near. This would all be gone when we woke up.

I lay flat on my back, folded my hands on my chest in prayer, and looked up at the ceiling. I repeated my mantra, this time with particular fervor: *Please, God, forgive me for my thoughts, these sickening thoughts. Forgive me, God. Forgive me for all of my sins. Please don't hate me for having these thoughts. I am so sorry for my sins. Please don't let me be gay. Please don't let me be gay. Please don't let me be gay.*

■ ■ ■

The following year at school—our senior year—should have been Chad's and my best. But that last summer in Ocean City had left me ashamed and scarred. It brought my sexuality to the surface in a way I wasn't ready to handle. So I did to Chad what I'd go on to do to so many other men in my life: I distanced myself from him, retreating into the shadows without so much as a word.

※

Chapter 9

Suicide Is Painless

I t seemed like we'd been in the car forever. Mr. MacMahon was driving about fifty-three miles per hour in a sixty-mile-per-hour zone in the right lane on Route 93 North. Cars were passing us on our left, their drivers beeping and giving us the finger. I wanted to duck down into the place where the floor mat meets the glove compartment so no one could see me.

The interior of his black, two-door Cadillac was sticky red leather, and the passenger seat engulfed me like an oversized arm chair. I put the armrest down as soon as I got in the car. I wanted a clear line between Mr. MacMahon and me. I was pissed.

We pulled off of the highway at the exit you take for Canobie Lake Park, but swerved around wooded, windy roads in the opposite direction of the amusement park. The streets were quiet. Cars didn't rush by us. The houses were set much farther apart than in Andover, with many gray, ash-like trees between them extending high, reaching for rays of sun behind the winter sky. Houses here seemed decrepit and landscapes ungroomed. Dead grasses had grown wilder and taller, and lawns were spotted with burnt, dog-stained patches and clumps of weeds. Everything seemed to be gloomy and foggy. Or maybe it was just me.

We came to an intersection where the red in the stoplight was the only color I had seen since we got off the highway. When it turned green, I expected to hear a horn behind us, but there was no one there. This place seemed abandoned. Mr. MacMahon's car moaned while gaining speed and passed black streetlamps, probably about to ignite since the afternoon was growing old. "That's it, up there on the left, that's Evergreen Hospital," Mr. MacMahon said as we took a right. He pointed to what looked like a stone mansion guarded by a tall iron gate and a sloping hill. Because it was around the end of March, spring had begun flirting with the frozen earth, but nothing had come to life yet, and ditches were swamp-like and dank.

Evergreen Hospital looked scarier up close than from a distance. Dead, chipped ivy leaves skulked up its decaying brown stones, and rusty bars blocked the foggy glass windows. The driveway had potholes and was messy with street salt and sand hauled in from the winter storm trucks. The dormant trees were gaunt; I couldn't tell if they were dead or if they would come to life with blossoms in the coming New England spring metamorphosis.

I kept my head down and followed Mr. MacMahon, holding my backpack in front of me like a shield. Just beyond the double doors at the front—the ones that were buzzed open after Mr. MacMahon rang the bell—stood a reception desk. Behind it sat a tall, slender woman who wore wire frames with a beaded string and her hair in a beehive. She was snacking on gummy bears, mashing them with her jaundiced and crooked teeth. "Can I help ya?" she asked in between chews.

"Yes," Mr. MacMahon said, stepping in, "this is Jon. He has an appointment with Dr. Greenstein."

"Okay, right, I have him listed right here," she said. "Have a seat ova there and he'll be right with ya." She picked up the old black phone, dialed a number, waited, and then whispered into the receiver. "Jon is here for his intake appointment." Desperate, I thought, *how did I end up here?*

■ ■ ■

I hadn't been the same since the night in Ocean City with Chad. I remained active in school, but right from the beginning of senior year I began to withdraw socially. I ran farther away from Chad. Sophia had moved on. The melancholia I was prone to turned to dark despair. Something was terribly wrong with me.

Friends began to notice the doldrums and so did my mom. "What can I do, Jon?" she'd plead. There was nothing she could do. I was disgusted with myself for having feelings for Chad and did all I could to stifle them, but like acid reflux, they just kept bubbling to the surface uncontrollably. I was petrified of being found out. What would my dad do if he somehow discovered that I'd fallen for one of his star basketball players, who was also the star pitcher on the high school baseball team? I was the very thing my dad had warned me about so many times. *I'm doomed,* I thought.

I prayed every single night, beseeching God to make it not so. I became a regular at Sunday evening mass at St. Augustine's church and received communion each week, praying the Body of Christ would be digested in my stomach, flow into my veins, and change me, renew me. I did anything I could to be a good boy, a better Catholic, and to make my sinful thoughts disappear. I even went to confession, although I was too scared to mention my feelings for Chad from behind the curtain. I agonized, *What if the priest is compelled to tell someone of my sins?* That confession was just for God right now. *And please help me not be gay. Please help me not be gay. Please help me not be gay.* Never one for subtlety, I figured God was more likely to help me if I repeated it three times.

I did my best to bury my thoughts. I was still good at staying busy, doing homework until the wee hours of the morning, taking on massive projects such as running powder-puff football and student government. I didn't realize it then, but my strategy of distraction only bought me a few weeks at a time. I was also doing everything I could to earn praise despite the devilish secret I was keeping. When those things didn't work, I isolated myself.

But isolating was problematic. The more I pulled away from friends, the more time I had to spend alone with thoughts of my dad and his disapproval looming over me. As my closest friends began imagining their lives at college, outside of the confines of Andover, those thoughts paralyzed me. I retreated to my bedroom. Friends called to cheer me up and tried to peel my limp, soggy body away from my single bed. I'd rise momentarily, for a school dance or a post-football game party, but noticing how much of an outsider I was becoming only made things worse and perpetuated the problem. I'd return home full of despair, oftentimes crying myself to sleep. *I am all alone,* I'd think. *No one is like me. I am sick.* It was a cycle I repeated until I'd had enough.

■ ■ ■

That March, my parents attended baseball week at Rollins College in Winter Park, Florida, where my brother had gone off to play on a full ride—a dream come true more for my father than for Jared. Despite having his shoulder mangled as a high school sophomore during a game of football—a sport he didn't want to play, but that my father made him—Jared still managed to excel at baseball. He had a natural-born gift that he parlayed into a full college scholarship. He broke college records for stolen bases and hits.

Both my parents went to watch Jared play for baseball week. I was left home with Julie, who was working as a nurse at Holy Family Hospital. She was busy and her schedule was hectic, but I was old enough and independent enough to be left on my own. And my parents knew that I wouldn't be having any big parties; I was, after all, the head of Growing Up, Taking a Stand (GUTS).

My outlook grew drabber and more confining. I was depressed. Teachers started to notice that I wasn't myself and asked if I was okay. It was a just reminder to me to keep up the fake smile so no one might suspect what was going on inside me.

Mr. MacMahon was fully aware of the troubles at home. He had been Julie's guidance counselor from her junior year on, and he was also very close with my brother. In some ways he'd become an expert in our family saga and dynamics. And, like many people, he seemed to think I had it worse than my siblings because of my father's reaction to my rejecting sports, and his rejecting everything about me. It's no surprise, then, that Mr. MacMahon was worried about me.

I didn't know whether he knew what else was causing my anxiety and depression. I didn't want him or anyone else to ever know. Other than Sophia—who now knew that I worried I might be *asexual,* and Samantha, with whom I was so symbiotic that she probably had known since I was eight—I had confided in only one other person, my friend Meredith, about my state of confusion.

"Meredith, do you know anyone who's gay?" I asked, as nonchalantly as I could.

"Nope, why?" she asked unfazed, but with interest.

"I don't know. I was just curious."

I convinced Meredith to come along with me to Memorial Hall Library after school one day to do homework and study for a history test together. I also told her I wanted to research how a person becomes gay. "Is it that one makes a choice, or are we, um, is someone born that way?" I asked her. I was so scared to research this. It was as scary as kissing a boy or a girl; it would no doubt yield answers that I needed but didn't want to know. They'd be more concrete answers than I'd gleaned that night in the storm, next to Chad.

Meredith could see I was trembling. I didn't have to tell her I was exploring this question for a science or social studies class; she knew it was for me. She reassured me that she would be there for me no matter what we discovered.

In quiet corners of the library, we huddled over many different books, but didn't find any definitive answers. Then we came across an edition of a popular weekly news magazine—I think it was either *Time* or *Newsweek*—that had a picture of a baby on the cover under the headline: "COULD THIS BABY BE GAY?" Meredith and I looked at each other, grabbed the magazine, and rifled through its pages. We found the article and read it together.

It reported on a scientific theory that sexual orientation is genetically determined, something you're born with. Meredith kept pointing to the page. "See? It isn't something you do or did, or something you think that makes you turn gay," she said. "You just are!"

I was relieved at first. *Maybe God did make me this way,* I thought. It all made sense—my overwhelming feelings for Chad, my lack of desire to snuggle with Sophia on her couch while watching *The Bodyguard.*

It isn't my fault, I told myself. I had always known that I wasn't waking up in the morning and jumping out of bed deciding, "Today I am going to fall for Chad and reject Sophia!" I didn't "choose this life-style," as so many adults at school and church put it. I'd eventually grow to loathe that phrase.

I begged Meredith to never tell anyone about the article we found. I wasn't sure what to make of the information we'd just uncovered. I wasn't like other gay people out there, as far as I knew. Few people had come out in the '90s. I didn't relate much to Elton John, and I didn't have crushes on other guys besides Chad. Maybe I had simply fallen in love with Chad? Come to think of it, not only hadn't I had crushes on other guys (unless that was a crush on Brandon back in elementary school?), I never had them on girls, either.

"I wonder if I'm just asexual," I pondered aloud.

"Is that possible?" Meredith asked. "I love you no matter what, Jonny Boy."

After Meredith hugged me in front of the big glass doors at the entrance to Memorial Hall Library, she walked off to her SUV. She waved sweetly as she looked back at me, still staring off in a daze. I looked up at the sky and asked God how I could go home to my father knowing what I had just learned. What if the magazine article was wrong? *What if YOU actually made a mistake by making some of us gay?* I asked The Almighty. Even if it was genetic, it was still a defect, an imp inside me that had to be stopped. I had to keep trying to suffocate it. I had to keep trying to swallow it. But no matter how many groveling prayers I offered, no matter how hard I tried to suppress it, it was always there inside me.

If you can't change me and make me not be gay, I asked God, *then why don't you just make me die?*

I started thinking about killing myself.

■ ■ ■

Julie was working late. Mom and Dad had been in Florida for a few days and would be gone until Sunday. I was in a dizzy state of desolation. I had thought about suicide many times before that year, but after that visit to Memorial Hall Library, my fate seemed settled. I hated what God had created in me. I hated this part of myself so much that I had to get rid of it, whatever it was. Suicidal ideation filled my mind now all day, every day, until I had enough and was ready to do something about it.

I obsessed gloomily for a few hours about my lack of a future. Then I moved catatonically into slow-motion action. I didn't prepare a note—I wanted to just disappear for good.

I grabbed the keys to my Bronco and headed to the basement stairs toward the garage. The plan was to turn on the car with the garage door shut and asphyxiate. Deep down, I was afraid of dying and I didn't want to suffer. I thought falling asleep inside the car would make it a painless death.

I began to cry uncontrollably. As I struggled down the stairs, the past *and* the future flashed before me. The Mr. AHS Contest. The school yearbook I was editing. Tennis. College. The chance to leave home once and for all. I thought of my friends' faces: Samantha, Meredith, Chad, James. Then Jared's and Mom's—*Oh, my God, Mom,* I thought, *I love you!*

Julie. *Julie!*

What was she doing home? Just as I reached for the basement door leading into the garage, Julie opened it first, from the other side. The Bronco's keys in my hand, tears streaming down my face, I knew my plan had been foiled and that nothing would ever be the same. I couldn't harbor my secret anymore.

"What are you doing, Jon?" she asked. "Are you okay? You look awful. Why are you crying? Where were you going?" I collapsed to the ground at Julie's feet, convulsing in hysterical tears, muttering, screaming so incoherently, even I could barely understand what I was saying.

"I thought you were going to be later!" I shouted. "I hate myself,

Julie. I hate myself so much. And everyone's going to hate me when they find out anyway. I can't live anymore. I can't live like this anymore! I'm disgusting." Julie got down on the cold, ceramic tile floor and held me. You could see it in her face that she knew she had stopped something catastrophic. "Oh, Jon, there isn't anything about you that would make anyone hate you!" she insisted, crying too. "What is it? You know you can tell me anything. It can't be so bad that you'd want to do this."

I took a deep breath and prepared myself for rejection. Julie got me some water and some crackers and she called Matt, her kind and gentle fiancé, to come meet us at my parent's house. After he arrived, we went into the family room, and there, on the floor, crying again and hyperventilating, I told Julie and Matt as much of the truth as I could handle.

"I think I might be gay," I said, sobbing in disbelief myself at the words I'd just uttered. "I can't handle the thought of it being true, so I figured I'd sit in the car and end it all." I felt pathetic. They hugged and consoled me. They promised to keep my secret for as long as I asked them to.

"We will always be here for you," Julie said.

"We will, Jon," Matt chimed in. "We'll never abandon you."

But there was a condition. "You need help," my sister said. "I couldn't live with myself if anything happened to you. We need to get you some help."

The next day Mr. MacMahon called a meeting with my sister and a couple of my teachers who'd recognized my decline. It was decided: Mr. MacMahon would take me to Evergreen Hospital. Feeling defeated and desperate, I didn't know what else to do.

■ ■ ■

Mr. MacMahon directed me to sit down in the wooden chair. I kept twisting and fiddling with the gold Mickey Mouse watch on my left wrist. I had never been to a psychiatrist before, the ones who can give you medicine. I thought psychiatrists were for crazy people. *Maybe I am crazy.*

After I waited for thirteen minutes (according to Mickey), which felt like hours, Dr. Greenstein's nurse invited us to walk back to his office. I looked back to make sure Mr. MacMahon was close behind me.

Dr. Greenstein's office was in a part of the hospital compound that looked like a rambling, dilapidated old mansion—it looked like a haunted house really—filled with well-worn furniture. As we walked the orange industrial-carpeted halls, I noticed that several of the offices had fireplaces and leather couches.

"Welcome, gentlemen," he said, shaking Mr. MacMahon's hand, and then asking him to wait outside in his private waiting lounge just around the corner. Then he shook my hand and told me to have a seat. We were alone now. I looked around and there was a large, brown leather couch and one leather winged-back chair with an ottoman. I didn't know where I was supposed to sit, so I chose the couch. I thought maybe I would disappear in its vastness and Dr. Greenstein would forget about me. Dr. Greenstein walked behind his mahogany desk, sat down at his chair, and reclined, putting his hands comfortably behind his head. "So, what seems to be the problem, Jon?" he asked. I didn't really know where to begin. I wanted to say, "Do you have six days?" Instead, I spaced out for a minute.

Dr. Greenstein was chubby, with a black mustache that matched the color of what hair was left on his head. He wore a green V-neck sweater with light khaki pants. His burgundy penny loafers, with an actual penny in each shoe, stuck out from underneath his desk.

I tried to scan his office without being discovered. He had shelves and shelves of books. Freud, Jung, and Klein were some of the authors' names that I could see. A lot of the books had the words *diagnostic* or *psychopathology.* I had no idea what they meant at the time. On his wall were three different diplomas. He had a stained-glass lamp on his desk and a bulletin board behind him. On it were kids' drawings of rainbows and rain clouds and stick figures with curly blue crayon hair.

Dr. Greenstein took a silver case out from his top desk drawer. From it he pulled a long clove cigarette and lit it with an old-fashioned Zippo lighter. A plume of light gray smoke billowed as he inhaled deeply, the way my mother smoked; it was almost as if they couldn't live without the toxic fumes. I always found it odd when doctors smoked.

I was shaken from my reverie by his voice. "So, Jon, I'll ask you again, what brings you here today?" I started to open my mouth and let a few words free when I noticed Dr. Greenstein wasn't listening. "Ah ha, ah ha, ah huh," he was mumbling as he was writing in what was probably my patient chart. It didn't even seem like he was interested. "Ah huh, so why did you want to kill yourself?" he asked in a matter-of-fact tone. "Things must be awfully terrible for you to want to kill yourself. Is that true, what Mr. MacMahon told me, you wanted to kill yourself?" he continued.

"I hate who I am, okay?" I blurted out.

"And who might that be, Jon?" he asked.

"I don't know!" I responded defensively.

"Well, you must know something about who you are, if you are driven to think about suicide to rid it, yes?"

"I guess." I didn't want to commit.

He asked confusing questions in a condescending tone. "Well then, let's just start with the basics. How were you going to kill yourself? Wasn't it your sister who realized that something was wrong?" I tried to answer, but he didn't seem to be listening; he kept on smoking his cigarette and drinking his cup of black coffee, writing in the folder.

Finally, I explained to him the story of planning my death for when my parents were in Florida visiting my brother at his college baseball week. My sister was a nurse, working a later shift, and wouldn't come home until late.

After forty-three minutes of aimless, awkward bantering and questions, Dr. Greenstein leaned forward in his chair, rested his large arms on his desk, intertwined his hairy fingers, and looked straight into my eyes. I was hoping we were at the end of the session.

"Do you masturbate, Jon?" he asked.

I was appalled. How could he ask such a personal question? We hardly knew one another!

"What?" I responded, in shock.

"Do. You. Mast-ur-bate?" Dr. Greenstein prodded rudely.

"I don't feel comfortable answering that question," I said hesitantly.

"Well, I'm asking for a reason," he explained. "You see, Mr. MacMahon thinks that you may be questioning your sexuality. He said he thinks you might be gay. Do you think you could be gay?"

I squirmed in the leather as it honked around me like a sea lion's call. I was furious with Mr. MacMahon. Why would he make such a terrible assumption—*what a dick!* "No, uh no, I'm *NOT* gay. I'm just confused about things. I'm a late bloomer, I guess. I don't know. Maybe I'm asexual," I stumbled.

"Well, then, do you masturbate?" he persisted. I was silent. "Or let's just assume that you do, because we all do once in a while—it's normal."

"No, it's not," I protested. "My dad says it is a sin. And I have to talk about it at penance."

"So, when you do, and before you ask God for forgiveness for your sin, do you think of girls or other boys?"

"No!" I said affirmatively. "I don't think of anything or anyone."

"So you do masturbate. You just don't think of anything. Ah huh. Interesting. Do you look at pictures?"

Now I was really uncomfortable. Dr. Greenstein was really scary! "No, I just told you that I don't think of anything. . . . I actually don't masturbate much at all," I said with firmness.

"Not much?" he asked. "No? Why not?"

Why is he asking me these awful questions? I wondered. "Because I'm afraid that masturbating will make me gay!" I said. "Masturbation, like homosexuality, is evil; that is what my dad taught me, and after-school Catechism, too, so I thought if I stopped whacking-off, these feelings would stop! Okay? Satisfied?!"

Dr. Greenstein took off his glasses, tossed them on top of his desk, and stared at me as if he had been successful getting out exactly what he wanted. He lit another cigarette. "Huh, interesting," he mused. "I can see why you would be confused and frustrated and angry. But what your father is telling you is not true; none of it." He stopped there.

The smoke from his cigarette made me sneeze, but that didn't deter him. The topaz-colored ashtray held at least twenty half-smoked butts. I was embarrassed and angry at myself for saying too much. I sat there, closed-lipped, and stared at the second hand of my watch for the rest of the remaining minutes in the hour. We sat there in silence. I was staring at my hands folded and he was staring at me. "Well, Jon, if you aren't going to talk, we'll just sit here until the end of our hour together."

Then, exactly at five minutes to six o'clock, Dr. Greenstein picked up the telephone on top of his desk and told someone to summon Mr. MacMahon back into the office. Dr. Greenstein instructed him to sit down on the couch next to me and proceeded to tell him that he thought I was having some problems dealing with adolescent transitions. He didn't think I was a danger to myself or others. He prescribed twice-weekly outpatient therapy with him at Evergreen. My heart plummeted. I did not want to see Dr. Greenstein twice a week. I didn't want to see him ever again! I began to protest.

In the car ride back to Andover, Mr. MacMahon assured me that therapy was the best thing for me. I knew that therapy was probably what I needed, but I could not go back and see that jackass. And I was so upset that Mr. MacMahon told him that he thought I was gay, but never asked me about it beforehand. I didn't talk the entire way back to AHS.

When we pulled up next to my car in the school's parking lot, I was nervous about being seen getting out of Mr. MacMahon's car. Everyone knew that if you were with Mr. MacMahon, something had to be wrong. *I am supposed to have it all together,* I told myself.

As soon as I got home, I saw that my father's car was in his garage stall, and my heart immediately got heavy. I opened the door at the top of the stairs from the garage and walked by the kitchen, then directly upstairs to my room. I had to come up with a way to assure all of the people in my life (and maybe even myself), who were now worried that I would kill myself, that I would not—that *I was okay.*

I would do anything and everything I could to avoid going back to Evergreen and sitting on the couch in that horrible man's office. After negotiating with Mom, she finally agreed I didn't have to see Dr. Greenstein, but only if I saw Mr. MacMahon multiple times a week at school.

"Fine, Mom! I'll do it! I'll do anything!"

I buried all of my emotions and put on a brave face to ensure everyone that I'd be all right.

I opened my books and began studying for the next day's English test. I wrote in my journal and plotted how I would convince everyone I was fine. I needed to prove that I wasn't gay. "I wish I never said anything to Meredith or Julie or Matt!" I wrote. I needed to prove to them and everyone else that I was normal again. I needed to focus on my senior year and making it to graduation. I needed to get my class rank as high as I could. I needed to avoid Dr. Greenstein and I did everything to show Mr. MacMahon and Mom and Julie that I was getting better.

After the difficult conversation with my mom, I realized I was hungry. I hadn't eaten much all day. But, I thought, *there is no time for food. And maybe I need to punish myself without dinner, the way my dad often has.*

I dialed Sophia's phone number.

"What are you doing this weekend?" I asked, as casually as I could. We made plans to go to a movie, and I felt a little bit hopeful. Maybe now, after this ordeal, I'd be physically attracted to her.

I looked down at my desk calendar and saw there was so much to do for the Pre-Prom Fashion Show, for student government, for preseason tennis workouts. I opened all of my books and spread them out all over my desk. It felt good to have all those distractions before me, under the bright desk lamp light.

Every time I had a thought about being different, being confused, being gay, or that dreadful Dr. Greenstein, I locked myself in my room. I stopped eating dinners downstairs. I was imposing a self-inflicted exile, much like my father had imposed on me throughout my life. No food, no fun. I just stuffed my face into books and read the same line over and over again, obsessively, like the way I prayed to God.

✳

Chapter 10

To Bates and Back

I was standing on the stage looking out to a vast audience. My gown was iridescent blue and the gleaming gold sash around my neck heralded my making it to the top of my class. *Dad has got to be proud of me now,* I mused under my cap. The blue square hat sat crookedly atop my full head of Sun-In bleached blond hair. I was honored to be standing there in front of my senior class. We'd achieved so much together.

Our high school commencement had to be held inside Merrimack College's hockey arena because of the downpours sopping Lovely Field at the high school, and there was no other space large enough indoors to hold the crowd.

My classmates' gowns shimmered, too, in the arena's lights in front of me. I wasn't the valedictorian or even the salutatorian; I just wasn't that smart. I had painstakingly worked my way up from the freshman-year ranking of thirty-nine to graduate at number nineteen. I'd just barely made it past failure in my father's eyes the year before when I was inducted into the National Honor Society. I had to fight for every A I earned, and logged hours upon hours studying late into the night under my desk lamp to get to where I did.

At the graduation ceremony, as student council president, I stood tall, despite my short stature, next to Charlie, one of my closest friends since we met freshman year, and we alternated reading each of the nearly three hundred students' names as they crossed the stage and received their diplomas.

■ ■ ■

For most of my friends, senior year was everything they'd imagined it to be. We were an unusually tight group, both boys and girls, who were respected by our peers. We weren't the coolest group in our class or in the school, but we were leaders. Whether musicians, politicians, athletes, thespians, scholars, good citizens, or even partiers, we seemed to be liked by most and had few enemies. We had been affectionately dubbed "the English Family," although a few kids on the outside of our group would eventually come to use that name to make fun of us.

We got the name because most of us were either on student government or captains of sports teams or ran major school events. We set a good example and invoked a deep school spirit and pride at AHS. That afforded us a bit of what some saw as a "royal relationship" with the faculty and administration of our school. We weren't a bunch of Goody Two-shoes, but we were certainly liked by the adults in the school. And in return for our good deeds and leadership, we were sometimes treated to some special leniencies, such as not being challenged when we asked for bathroom passes, asked to get out of school early, or were absent every now and then. The faculty always assumed it was for a good reason.

By our senior year, some said we "ran" the school, like the royal family once ruled over the United Kingdom. In some ways we did. We had one of the only student-run student governments in any high school across Massachusetts. And it was governed by a real constitution. We had the authority to write new laws and amend old ones. Because so many of us were elected to student government posts, we had significant influence.

To most who did not know me well, it looked as if I had it all going for me. That was the image I was taught to uphold. But the truth was I was terribly lost, and without the English Family and their families, I would've been more lost than I already was. The English Family became my true family. By the time senior year rolled around, Julie and Jared were out of the house. I was alone with my parents, who were stuck in a miserable marriage. My friends often provided an escape for me from what went on at home.

The English Family spent many weekend nights having get-togethers at each other's houses and sleeping over. I think I was one of the first to start the boy/girl sleepover trend. It may be surprising that my father, who said God would punish us for premarital sex, allowed such a thing. However, at that point in my life, he was doing pretty much anything to encourage me to interact with girls, and not just as friends. I capitalized on the lesson learned that having many people in the house at the same time meant that my father would be on his best behavior. Everything my dad did was designed to ensure we lived up to the image he wanted everyone else to believe, so he rarely, if ever, acted up in front of groups of friends at our house. I took advantage of that.

I adored my friends. I loved what they had to say and what they taught me. I loved that they thought I was funny and fun and that they respected me. I wanted to be around their way-more-normal-than-mine families. I would spend hours with each of them on the phone, listening to them lament about boy problems or girl troubles. I'd do just about anything for any one of them.

And yet, all the while, I was alone, without a mate, without a real date to the prom—a date for whom I didn't pick out the dress, that is—without a date with whom I'd dance and get all tingly inside. I went all four years of high school without ever kissing a soul.

Despite my efforts to keep secret the question of my sexuality, and my tremendous anguish around it, my closest friends knew that inside—beneath the alleged layers of fat my father constantly ridiculed me for—something gnawed at me. They were the ones who knew I was prone to real lows, some pretty scary. We didn't yet know to call it depression, but that's what it was. Sometimes, even among the swarm of the English Family, the feeling of being singular, and the loneliness of being different, were unbearable.

The girls considered me their best guy friend, and when I found the nerve to ask one of them out, they always said that it would be like dating a brother. By senior year, because I always showed a lack of desire, the boys left me out of most of their adventures that involved random hookups with girls. While Charlie and Chad were getting "double whammies" (handjobs by the same girl at the same time), I was sitting at home listening to Barbara Streisand or writing poetry about being the only one like me.

That's exactly what it was. I felt like there was no other kid at AHS or in all of Andover who was going through what I was. No one in the group had grown up in a house like mine, and while my friends were supportive and always there for me, they couldn't possibly fathom the darkness. It was a loneliness that was isolating and inconceivable to anyone who knew me. How could someone who had appeared to have all the friends in the world and who had achieved so much at school be so lonely? *What is wrong with me?* I wondered. None of us could really make sense of it.

Staying focused, I prayed to God at night for the strength to get through the last year I would have with this group of people. I had the foresight to know that after graduation things would never be the same. I had to enjoy this special time while it lasted. That became even clearer to me after my foiled suicide attempt. I promised myself I would not let the demon growing inside of me take over again. Not yet anyway. Not this year.

So as senior year progressed in all its glory—parties, football games, coed sleepovers—I did whatever it took to stuff the darkness inside me deeper and deeper. Chad fell further away from the English Family, a change that was partly my fault. I would get mad at him over nothing. I made a big deal of small things. I was very deliberately pushing him out, not only socially, but in my mind. During Spanish class, I pushed out every fleeting thought of Chad that fluttered into my mind faster than our teacher could roll her letter *R*s. Every smell of his clothes that would waft my way from his locker, I'd exhale out harder than a sneeze. Every butterfly that levitated in my stomach when I saw him, I stuffed down with another Quarter Pounder with cheese, a bowl of creamy macaroni and cheese, or a plate of my mom's meatloaf. This particular coping mechanism came at a high price; as I distracted myself from thoughts of Chad, I added to the layers of fat my father berated me for.

No one else seemed to notice I was gaining weight, or at least no one mentioned it, except for Dad. As captain of the tennis team, I was working out on a daily basis. When I look back at photos now, I can see that I looked strong, just as a senior boy should. But I was putting on the pounds and it wasn't muscle. During senior week, it was hard for me to button my white-and-blue-striped shorts, and to get into the matching short-sleeved sweater vest for our boat cruise in the Boston Harbor. I refused to swim when we spent the day at Eastover, a retreat site, because I couldn't bear the thought of taking off my shirt in front of my classmates.

I remember, as editor in chief of the 1994 yearbook, looking at pictures throughout senior year and getting upset about how round my face seemed in so many of the photos. It was unsettling. When I saw myself, I saw fat.

I'd always felt uneasy about my appearance, always felt as if I was chubbier than most of my friends or classmates. But as senior year progressed, I began to loathe what I saw more and more in the mirror. The more I struggled with my emerging sexuality and feelings for Chad, the more I obsessed about the way I looked and how others saw me. Surely, my father's lifelong obsession with appearing perfect had something to do with my insecurities. But looking back, I wonder whether my feelings about my appearance grew worse as it became more difficult for me to suppress my sexual feelings.

For me, the end of senior year meant the end of so many things. Mostly, it was the end of our special friendships as we knew them. We would all be off to college and would meet new people and begin new lives. My English Family was breaking up, and I wasn't ready to let go. They were safe—they knew me and they accepted me. They didn't question my sexuality or push me about not having had sex. They didn't push to find out what was really going on inside for me. They bought my façade. Where would I find people like this again? I was convinced others in the outside world would be able to tell immediately that I was gay. This was clearly the beginning of the end of my being able to hide from my own secret.

It was also the end of being able to protect my mother. I was the last of the three kids to leave home. After the summer, my mom would be left alone with my father, and the thought frightened me. I worried about whether she could handle it. I'd broken up so many fights between them that could have ended badly. I stood up to him so many times, not only for Mom, but for myself and Julie and Jared. I was terribly uneasy about leaving my mom behind. I felt as if it was my responsibility to make sure she was going to be okay.

■ ■ ■

My father's new charcoal gray Lincoln Town Car was so dark and sprawling; it felt like a hearse to me. It seemed the perfect vehicle for transporting me to a place I feared almost more than death: Bates College.

I succumbed to the pressures of applying to the right set of schools my guidance counselor and my father wanted me to apply to. I didn't even visit Bates before I enrolled. I went through the motions of applying to colleges, mostly because I was dreading going at all, perhaps foreshadowing what I felt was the inevitable.

My parents bickered in its front seat as we drove north on 95 toward Maine, where Bates is located. I had on the headphones of my yellow Sony running Walkman, which I'd cranked up to its loudest setting so I could tune out my parents with Celine Dion's "The Power of Love." It became an anthem for me, partly because no one else at the time had the belting voice that could drown out my parents' fighting. Mariah Carey's "Hero" was also a favorite song that year, but it was a bit too soft to compete with raised voices.

Most of my friends were excited about going to Boston College or Providence College or University of Colorado or UMass. They were excited to be starting their lives anew. I dreaded it.

That summer I was still basking in the afterglow of the fact that people had started to notice my voice. I'd snuck on stage (without telling my father) and sang with James at the Mr. AHS contest the year after I produced it. Another time, at our senior assembly, I sang backup for a popular senior rock band. Then, at the end of my senior year, I won another major battle with my father that was on par with the fight over my playing tennis. This one was about trying out for Merrimack Junior Theatre's summer show, *Sweet Charity*, at the encouragement of many people in town. I was cast in the role of Oscar, and spent the summer with many of my best friends who were also in the play. I enjoyed every moment of it and realized that the camaraderie my father derived from sports, I derived from being part of a theater cast. The highs my father got from hitting a home run, I got from nailing a musical solo or comedic scene. People said they were blown away by my performance as Oscar, and I was encouraged by many to pursue singing and performing in college. But Bates wasn't the place to do that.

When we got to my dorm, I asked my parents if I could go to my room first and meet my roommate without them. I searched the halls for my room, and once I got there, I found the door was shut. I knocked. When he finally opened the door, my roommate Stanley looked like a zombie sleepwalking. "Uh," was all he muttered. The room was dark and smelled like the locker rooms I had grown to loathe. He stumbled back to his bed on the left side of the tiny room. This was it? Two desks in between his bed and mine for the entire year? *I'm fucked,* I thought.

Out in the hall, I could hear my father shooting the shit with a few of the jocks. They had their football jerseys on, so my dad could spot them immediately. And they were drawn by his charm, too. The football players and other special groups—my new roommate included—had arrived on campus for early move-in. Since my arrival date was later than theirs, I had already missed a lot of the fun and games.

"Hey, Jon, come say hello to Tyler," my dad said. "He's a red-shirt freshman on the football team!" I obliged and shook Tyler's hand, embarrassed that my father was making this such a big deal.

"Nice to meet you, Tyler," I said, perfunctorily. "Mom, can you come help me unload the car?" I kept my head down, nervous that people would notice me. Mom and I went down the concrete and tile stairs to the first floor, where the car was parked. The trunk was open, revealing my new denim comforter, pillows, tapestries, and everything else I'd packed. I dreaded moving them into the room. I didn't want to be there. I didn't want to share this room with this stranger. "Cheer up, Jon!" Mom said. "This is supposed to be fun! You're getting your *freedom.*" She winked at me. It was ironic, because I knew what she meant. I was getting the freedom that Jared and Julie had each eventually received: a ticket away from Crescent Circle. But at the same time, one of the reasons I felt so terrible was leaving Mom behind to suffer on her own in that house. Who would be there to protect her and to distract my dad from berating her? I felt like I was abandoning her.

Back upstairs, my father now had a herd of athletes around him. It was fine with me, because they kept him out of my way. Quietly, I dropped off a laundry basket full of clothes on my side of the room as Stanley continued sleeping with the covers pulled up over his head. *He's a peach,* I thought, rolling my eyes. Obviously my roommate wasn't going to be my new best friend at Bates.

I had to go the bathroom, so I walked down the hall and found the door marked men's room. Inside was a line of toilets in stalls, and a line of old-fashioned urinals. Toilet paper was strewn all over the floor and the bank of sinks and mirrors was a mess, splashed with spit and what appeared to be puke. *This is nasty,* I shuddered. And then, on the far right of the expansive yet prison-like bathroom, was a room full of showers, just like the ones in the basement locker rooms at Andover High. No curtains. No stalls. Just a wide-open shower room. No privacy. Again, I thought, *I'm fucked.*

This was nothing like the perfection I had created in my room at home, where I had a bathroom all to myself. I was mortified that guys would see me naked in the showers. They'd make fun of me for being chubby, for sure. And the football players living on my floor would make fun of me and bully me, since Jared wasn't there to protect me. This would be worse than shirts-n-skins on the basketball court. This would be all skins.

I went to my mom, grabbed her hand, and pulled her down the stairs and outside to the car again. "I can't do this," I said, collapsing in her arms and starting to cry. "You can't leave me here! I've made a terrible mistake. I can't stay here." I sobbed.

"Jon, you are so smart and handsome and everyone loves you," she said. "You can do this. I know you can."

After a few hours, Mom and I got my side of the room as nice as it could be. She spoiled me by splurging on as many decorative touches as it took to make me vaguely comfortable there. I was all set up and ready to go.

As my dad kept talking with all of the jocks, my mom and I walked around campus. It was a beautiful fall day. We came upon a gathering on the quad, where the dean of students was speaking to a crowd. I stood in the back, hating every moment, wishing I was with my friends, and still in the halls of AHS. I couldn't stop the flow of tears, even though I tried.

Mom began to look worried. She didn't notice the other kids on campus crying like I was. When we met up with my dad, he had no empathy. "Suck it up," he said, dismissively. "We have to get back to Andover for a game. You'll be fine."

As he was leaving, he gave me a rare hug. It was one of the few times I can remember needing a hug from my dad and getting it. I didn't want to let go. I wanted this man who had never protected me—who instead often made me shake with fear—to hold me and to take me away from this place. *Please rescue me, Dad,* I begged in my mind. But then he quickly let go.

Mom, however, held me for as long as I needed. I didn't want to let go and cried into her shoulder.

"Stop babying him, Judy," Dad scolded her. "Let's go. He's gotta grow up some time." I couldn't believe she was really leaving me. The last time I felt this way was when I was three or four and I had to get my tonsils and adenoids removed, and my sinuses drained. Before surgery, I superstitiously believed that if I refused to kiss my mother good-bye, they wouldn't wheel me away into surgery. I was wrong. They pulled me away, and I screamed back to my mom, my arms reaching out for her, "I want to kiss her good-bye now! I want to kiss her good-bye!" They didn't turn around, and the next thing I knew, I was waking up from the anesthesia.

As my parents drove away, my fear rose. *What would I do without my father's strictures and criticisms?* I wondered. *Will the jock guys figure me out?* I was convinced that everyone there would surely know that I was gay. Now, away from my father reminding me to not hold my wrist a certain way or to not prance along to a song, would I be sealing my fate? And my poor mother, how would she survive in that house without me? All of these questions spinning in my head, I ran up to my dorm room, shut the door, and stuffed my face into my pillow and bawled.

For three days, I cried. I'd felt alone my last year in high school, but this was worse. When I wasn't crying in my room, I would pace the tree-lined campus by myself. Occasionally, I'd try to talk with Monica, who'd graduated with me from AHS. She had already made a lot of friends and her roommate was really great. I tried to fake it with them, but eventually I broke down to Monica, too. "I feel like an outsider, an outcast," I cried to her.

"Why, Jon?" she asked. "It's a new beginning here. Just be yourself."

Myself? How could I? I walked around campus, desperately scanning the faces of the students for someone who seemed like me. But there was no one and I felt more alone than ever before.

At night, I'd try calling Samantha or Charlie, but they'd be out taking part in orientation activities at their schools, the very sorts of activities that I kept avoiding out of fear of embarrassing myself. My confidence plummeted more and more with the passing hours. I walked with my eyes facing down, afraid that if someone saw them, they'd spot the gay in me and make fun of me or walk away. I was afraid to meet anyone new because I was convinced they wouldn't like me. I don't think I even saw the inside of the cafeteria. I didn't eat for days.

For three nights I didn't sleep, soaking my pillow with my tears. I wanted to call my mom, but I didn't want to make her worry. I called Jared and Julie, but they just encouraged me to keep going, insisting it would get better. I don't remember much else from those three days other than feeling overcome with grief and fear. It did keep Stanley out of the room, though. He never said anything to me beyond that first "Uh . . ." the morning I had arrived on campus.

On the fourth morning at Bates, I sat beneath a maple tree losing its autumn leaves. I wrote in my journal, "I'm not ready for this. I feel like everybody hates me, like everybody knows my secret. I just want to go home. I hate myself. Why am I like this? Why is this happening to me?" I picked up an orange and yellow leaf and put it in my journal on the page where I'd been writing, now smudged with black ink and salty tears. I walked to my room and called my sister.

"I can't handle it anymore," I told her. She heard the distress and panic in my voice.

I heard her put her hand over the receiver and, in muffled tones, talk to my mom. "Mom will be on her way to get you," Julie said when she got back on the phone. When I hung up, I knew it was over.

I started to remove my Ansel Adams photos, cheaply framed at Prints Plus at the mall, from the concrete walls and throw my clothes back into my duffel bags. I packed up the rest of my things so I could quickly get out of there when my mother arrived.

I heard my father's disappointed voice in my head. "You are a sissy, you know that?" I knew I'd be banished to my room when I got home. But another year of that was comforting in a sick way. Although I had worked hard to escape him over the years, I felt weak and vulnerable so far away. I was dependent on him, addicted to his strictures and denigration.

I walked away from Bates certain that I would go down in AHS history as one of its most colossal failures. But at least I knew that when I walked back into my bedroom at home, under my father's rule, he'd keep me straight for a little bit longer. And maybe, deep down, that's what I really wanted.

✳

Chapter 11

Soup for Lunch

From the time I was a sixth-grader, anxious about having to go shirtless during shirts-n-skins basketball, I never liked my body. That anxiety persisted. In high school, I'd leave my shirt on at pool parties in ninety-degree heat waves, only to suffer jovial but antagonistic pleas to "show my stuff," since I was the only guy with a T-shirt on, and sweating through it.

Sometimes when I watched the guys playing beach volleyball in Ocean City, where I went with Chad's family each summer, or saw my tennis teammates in the locker room without their shirts on, I wished I could be built more like them. They were leaner than I was, with defined, taut sinew—not an ounce of fat on them.

"Come on in, Jon," one of my friends would yell from the deep end of the pool. "The water is so nice!"

"Nah, I'm okay. I'm too fat to take my shirt off. I'm embarrassed," I'd respond, even though I was secretly dying to go cool down in the water. I always talked about feeling fat, even though everyone insisted I wasn't. Some said I was fishing for compliments, but they didn't know what was really going on inside me. It didn't matter how many compliments I received. Nothing changed.

To make matters worse, all my best guy friends, who I hung out with all the time—Chad, Charlie, James, and Vinny—were also built like lean Greek gods. I was the odd man. What I saw in my reflection, and what was forever imprinted in my mind, was a pear-shaped chubby person. I loathed my Humpty-Dumpty figure, the one I'd inherited from my dad—skinny legs and an oversized, flabby torso.

I was afraid of developing man boobs, covered in brown hair, like the ones my father had and didn't seem to be ashamed of when he'd walk downstairs with his shirt off after taking one of his long baths.

The girls I hung out with in high school were also fairly thin. I found them to be gorgeous, even though in my mind I didn't necessarily associate their beauty with their thinness. They were weight conscious and always talking about their bodies in front of me. Being privy to this kind of conversation was another way in which I was different from the other guys. I heard a lot of discussions about wanting larger breasts, thinner thighs, or tighter tummies. Like the girls, I wished for my shape to be different. I didn't want to *be* a girl. But I wished I'd inherited more of my mom's genes than my dad's.

In middle school and in high school, I was always wishing for something different than what I'd been given. My father didn't help, often reminding me that, to his dismay, I wasn't built to be a star athlete.

It didn't occur to me, until after I left Bates and imposed upon myself a yearlong exile in my father's house, that I could *actually change* what I'd been given. Once I figured that out, I started a love affair, an obsession, with habits that would make me thinner, keep me leaner, and ensure I was purer than anything had made me feel before.

■ ■ ■

I'd been a bit dazed since I got home from Bates. "If you want a roof over your head," my father admonished me upon our return, "you have to get a job to earn your keep." He had to have noticed that his youngest son was completely unraveling before his eyes, but he didn't say anything. All he worried about was having to tell people in town that I'd left Bates after just three days. He reminded me how much of an embarrassment I was to him on a regular basis.

My public version of the truth was that I needed the year off to "find myself." What that really meant was that I wanted to face the demon inside of me and deal with it. I feared that outside in the real world, at a place like Bates, far away from my father's rigidness, the "real man" tendencies my father had instilled in me my whole life would disintegrate or break down. Everyone on the outside would instantly know I was gay and reject me.

That winter, I went to visit my brother Jared at his college, Rollins. He lived off campus in Winter Park with one other guy and two girls. The house was cute and fairly clean. It was sunny in Florida and the campus was beautiful. I had actually applied to Rollins because Jared was there and probably to try to win some points with my father, who had attended there as well. *Maybe if I went there,* I wondered, *Dad would finally like me.*

On the visit, even in the Florida sun, my depression didn't lift. I didn't want to do much. I was scared of going to parties and afraid to mingle with Jared's friends when they came to his house. I was petrified that everyone would know what was "wrong" with me, as if some sort of plague was marked on my head or they would be able to somehow see it in my eyes that I was gay.

Jared told me he was worried. He didn't think it was normal for me to want to be by myself all the time. Over the years, Jared had stopped asking me about girls and if I was getting any action. When I was in middle school, and when I was a freshman in high school, he and his friends would gather in the basement and talk about their conquests and about how far around the bases they had gotten with their girlfriends. I always thought it was rude and disrespectful that they talked about girls that way, and I'd usually leave and walk upstairs to avoid the discussion.

I'd worried prior to arriving in Winter Park that he would try to set me up with someone, so I pre-empted that possibility. "You know," I told him on the phone before I went, "I'm not really interested in having a girlfriend during my year off. I'm trying to find myself."

The trip turned out fine. I always loved being with Jared. He tormented me when we were young, like when I was in the third grade and he'd pin my elbows down with his knees while pounding on my chest. But he made up for it all later by protecting me from bullies in high school and from the big bully at home, our dad. That's when his older brother instinct starting kicking in, like the night he knocked my father into the closet after he had broken down our front door.

When I got back to Andover, he called me. "I know what's going on with you and I want you to know that I love you no matter what," he said with conviction.

"What do you mean?" I asked. "I'm fine, Jared."

"No, you're not," he said. "I can see it in your eyes, how sad and lonely you are. How alone you must feel. I think you're gay and you don't want to be." My heart palpitated. *How did he figure it out? See, people can tell!*

"What do you mean, I mean, how did you . . ."

"Jeremy got that sense from you," he explained how his roommate said something to him about it. "At first I was pissed at him, and I pinned him against a wall and told him to never speak about my brother that way again. But then I calmed down and heard what he was saying. It all became crystal clear. It all made sense."

I started to cry. "I hate myself for this, Jared. I don't want to be gay, but no matter what, I can't seem to change that."

Like Julie and Matt before him, Jared said it wasn't something I could reverse. "That's how God made you and there's nothing you can do to change it," he said. "I love you unconditionally, Jon. I always will, no matter who you love." He wanted me to accept who I was, but I wasn't ready to. I still saw it as a quiet curse I'd kept to myself, that was now starting to leak out of me. My greatest fear had been that my gayness would become more and more evident to others around me, and that fear was being realized.

I knew now that I wouldn't be able to hide it from anyone anymore, least of all myself. I finally had to face the fact that the "demon" inside indeed was homosexuality. I believed I needed to rid myself of it, at any cost.

Dieting and exercising to the point of nearly starving would become my singular method, my only focus. I'd already started changing the way I ate. That began shortly after I got home from Bates and I started a new job.

■ ■ ■

The first few days at home, I didn't leave my room and barely got out of bed. On the fourth day, Mom brought the classified section of the *Andover Townsman* to me. She knew that in order to keep my dad off my back, I had to get a job. With me lying down, and Mom sitting at the edge of my bed, we thumbed through the help-wanted section. There was one opening for a teller at the Andover Bank. It paid above minimum wage and seemed to be something I could do. How hard would it be to count money and cash checks for people? It seemed easy enough.

I got the job.

When I first started, townspeople would open the large, fifteen-foot front doors and whisper and point at me as if I were an animal in a zoo. Standing in a three-piece suit behind the counter at Andover Bank, I had become the talk of the town. People were shocked to learn that I'd left Bates so quickly. "What went wrong?" I'd imagine them asking. "How did one of Andover's most well-rounded students become such an immense failure in just a matter of weeks?"

Incongruously, at a time when I had an emerging desire to disappear, in more ways than one, I had a job that put me right out there in the public eye. This grand old bank, where I stood behind the counter every day, was where most people in town came to withdraw or deposit their money. ATMs were much less prevalent then, so people interacted frequently with the bank's tellers—meaning me.

All of my fellow tellers were women, and they were very nice to me. They told me I was cute and funny and charming. I enjoyed joking and laughing with them on breaks and in the lunchroom downstairs underneath the huge vault. Most of the time they all brought their lunches, and sometimes, maybe once a week, they'd go out. I noticed that all of the women talked obsessively about their weight and dress sizes. As in: "I have to get down to an 8 before the holidays!

That way there's room for me to eat, and I won't be busting out of my 10s. But if I start out where I am now, I'll balloon!"

Someone among them was always trying a fad diet, joining Weight Watchers, or eating a Lean Cuisine for lunch. Regardless of the particulars of their regimens, they always ate salads with the dressing on the side. "Did you know that the dressing you're using, Jon, has like forty grams of fat?" Surprised, I thought, *there must be so much fat in my brown bag lunch!* The bulging brown bag lunches Mom packed for me every morning were a bit embarrassing. Inside were chips and Ding Dongs and big ham and cheese sandwiches. When I looked down at my belly fat and the rolls that would be there when I sat at my bedroom desk at night by myself, it dawned on me that there had to be a connection. I needed to make some changes.

"Hey, Mom," I asked one evening after work, "do you think that instead of chips and cookies you could put apples and celery in my lunches?" And so she did. The sandwiches she sent me with were still big and layered with Italian meats, cheese, and Miracle Whip, but I took dieting one step at a time.

Then one Saturday morning, I was watching MTV's *The Grind* when the show's host, Eric, told the live audience how he got his amazing abs. I perked up because in all of my life I'd never seen even one of my abs and his were like six large mounds. I wondered how I could see all six of my abs and have the six-pack that Eric did. *Dare to dream!* I thought. "I eliminated fat from my diet," he said on the air. "That's my big secret." He said it was what kept him "lean and buff." I wanted to be lean and buff, just like Eric.

As time went on, my senses and mind began to hone in on everything having to do with fat grams. I started out by going grocery shopping with my mom and studying food labels. Then I examined the labels on the boxes and cans in our pantry at home. I became conversant with which foods had the most grams of fat—such as cheese, my favorite, and butter and whole milk. I gained an encyclopedic knowledge of all the foods that were low in fat or had zero fat, such as fat-free yogurt, fat-free cheese, pretzels, potatoes, and other vegetables. I paid no attention to carbs or sugar grams. All I knew was that Eric had eliminated fat, so that was what I was going to do.

At first I reduced my daily intake of fat to twenty grams, then fifteen, then ten, then five, then finally zero. In my mind, at that point, anything above zero was failure. It wasn't long before this little hobby that kept my bored mind occupied became a full-blown obsession. I discovered some good-tasting foods that had very low fat content. For example, sugared cereals, the very foods that my father had banned from our pantry, actually only had a couple of grams of fat. Some even had zero fat and still tasted great. I could have sugar cereal with skim milk without ingesting a single gram of fat. Ketchup on baked potatoes? Zero fat. Mustard on pretzels? Zero fat. Progresso fat-free soup. Jell-O fat-free pudding. *Yum!* I figured out all the tricks and combinations that would be satisfying, but contained no fat grams—pickles, gummy bears, diet sodas, pasta with fat-free tomato sauce. My new diet was perfectly timed; it was the beginning of the fat-free craze of the 1990s. SnackWell's cookies were fat-free. They even made fat-free Fig Newtons. The possibilities were endless. Maybe getting "healthy" wasn't so bad after all.

But in a short time, fat-free wasn't good enough. I started eating less and less of my fat-free portions. My big brown lunch bags were shrinking. I brought smaller and smaller Tupperware containers of fat-free cottage cheese and celery. It wasn't long before it was just soup for lunch.

■ ■ ■

Then I started running. When I began running late that winter, I had no idea that I was launching a war—on myself and my body. At first, I couldn't even run a mile. I was never one of the fast ones when we took those fitness tests in high school—the fifty-yard dash, the mile. The first time I went outside, in the raw, late-March wintery mix of rain and sleet and snow, I could barely move my heavy, untoned body for more than ten minutes. The cold air burned my lungs and made me cough. I'd never run long distances before, but something inside me made me get on the road.

At first, a mile took me twenty minutes, then fifteen, and then twelve. I ran every day with determination, and when it hurt, I knew it was working. Eventually, one mile became two, then five, then eight, and then ten. I also knew from reading an article that the longer I ran beyond twenty minutes, the more fat I burned. When I noticed that my suit pants for work were becoming looser around my waist, I made the connection that it was the result of running and controlling what I was eating. *It's working!*

The inner dialogue began in my head. I wondered how many miles I could run without stopping. *How little can I eat,* I wondered, *without running out of energy on a run?* I wondered how few fat grams I could consume and still run six miles. Half hours extended to fifty minutes. Fifty minutes grew to an hour. An hour became seventy-five minutes. I'd run in the rain, during thunderstorms, at five in the morning, and at eleven at night, oftentimes both. It didn't matter, nothing could stop me. I never missed a day. As I soldiered on, something happened to me: I came to feel like a superhero.

As it got warmer, then hotter, whenever I could, I ran in the middle of the day. I needed to burn as much fat as possible, and I knew the best time to do that was in the noonday heat, especially in the summer. Stride after stride, I made my way through the winding roads of Andover, pounding the pavement with my feet, fighting the fat from forming in my belly.

Push-ups became part of the routine, too. The asphalt on High Plain Road was too hot to touch, so I did them on the lawns along the way. In the middle of July, the midday sun was scorching and the humidity so high that perspiration bubbled from my forehead even when standing still. On my long runs, the heat radiated from the pavement into my sneakers and up my legs, which eventually were mere muscle upon bone. I could even feel the rubber soles of my Nikes melting. I got sunburned, and the sweat made it sting. I welcomed that discomfort, though, because, masochistically, it inspired me to go farther.

My nylon shorts were as wet as they would've been from jumping into a pool. My tank top stuck to my body as if the sun had turned it to wax, and the beads of sweat were the wax dripping off me. I developed a pilonidal cyst on my tailbone from running too many miles day after day, and I could feel it growing. But the pain on my tailbone was evidence that my punishment was working, so I kept going. My chafed nipples, which had scabbed over just the day before, were bleeding again, staining my shirt with red lines from the middle of my chest down to my waist.

My ankles were swollen from the banging. The greater the impact of my feet landing on the blacktop, the harder I knew I was working to eliminate the possibility of the fat multiplying. Staring at the double yellow lines on the road, determined to never look up, I was hell-bent on burning off the fat I'd grown so afraid of. Never mind that by the end of the summer, that fat was virtually nonexistent. Still, I imagined it was there, and that it got bigger with every tiny bit of food that I allowed myself to eat. It was impossible to put on weight by eating just the nonfat yogurt or the fat-free hard pretzel I had the day before, but I wasn't thinking straight.

When this obsession first started, my runs became something I looked forward to in my otherwise dismal days. The winter doldrums had taken their toll on me, especially that winter, when I felt stuck at home while all my friends were having a blast at college. My life was even more depressing now than when I'd come home from Bates. *This wasn't the plan,* I admonished myself. I wasn't doing very much to "find" myself. I didn't travel cross-country as I had dreamed I would spend my adventurous year off. I did manage to visit my friends at various colleges, but was dismayed every time I discovered there were only group showers like at Bates, and disgusted each time I'd have to use the bathroom and find barf on the toilet. Eventually, I stopped visiting and just stayed home all the time.

The inner dialogue about fat grams and running became more obsessive and possessive. I wanted only to be with my runs. I wanted only to be without food. There was something freeing yet shackling about it all. Once I began a run and set a goal of ten miles, I felt free; no one could stop me or tell me no. Simultaneously, I felt like I had to finish or else I was a failure. In essence, I was a slave to the road, to the sun burning my back like a whip. By reducing my fat intake to zero and running for an hour at a time, I knew that I'd destroy every fat cell that existed in my body. I had commenced an all-out attack on the feelings I still harbored for Chad and the demon inside me that made me feel that way. With the strategy that combined running and starving, I was sure to waste away.

It was incredible to witness my body evaporating. My work suits hung on me, and having achieved that made me feel powerful. I felt as if I was in charge of my own future—even if that future was death. For the first time since I was a child, my pectorals were flat. The fat rolls that had once layered upon my torso were now absent. When I used to sit down at my desk to write, my belly fat hung over my shorts or my underwear. Now, a small, thin line around my stomach was all I had left to burn; I was determined to make it perish. So much of my body had already wasted away and with such little effort. Getting rid of what few fat cells remained would no doubt be easy. Run by run, broccoli spear by broccoli spear, I was winning the war I'd launched a few months earlier against my body. Slowly but surely, I was disappearing.

On the road, I could also achieve asexuality. I didn't have to describe my feelings of despair to anyone there. I didn't have to worry about the depression that had overtaken me. I didn't have to think about being different. *I am a sinner and this is my penance,* I told myself. *Keep running, you faggot!* I just kept running, sometimes aimlessly, sometimes endlessly, away from what was going on inside me. If I missed a day, I felt incomplete. I felt as if I were doomed and God was going to punish me even more. All the while, as I obsessed about the running, I became more intent on eating nothing more than just soup for lunch.

Unlike most of the women at the bank, for me, it was never about the numbers on a scale or the size of my waist. I didn't really know much about what would be a healthy weight, and I hardly got on a scale anyway. The only numbers I cared about were those indicating the fat grams in foods I considered eating.

■ ■ ■

By the time of the mid-August heat waves, Mom was pleading with me every day to eat something more substantial than a small microwaved baked potato with ketchup. Despite her years of never cooking, she asked me each day what she could prepare for me for breakfast, lunch, and dinner. "I am NOT hungry," I would bark at her. I was irritable and angry all the time.

Eventually, she just started making my favorite things, and she'd put out plates of food for when I got home from the bank. She'd leave cute little notes of encouragement, too. "Dear Jon, You must be starving after such a long day at work. Enjoy! Love, Mom." I'd look at the plates and the notes with envy and rage. She was trying to set me off my rails, I told myself. I wondered what her offerings tasted like; it seemed so long since I'd savored the heartiness of meat loaf or the zesty cheese and cream of chicken divan. Despite the temptations, I wouldn't eat. I'd walk upstairs to my room, close the door, and do one hundred sit-ups to self-flagellate for even considering eating. Surely I was stronger than these primitive temptations! I had to rid myself of all of these earthly pleasures.

I had to cut out relationships, too. Because with laughter and friendship came drinks and food. I couldn't put myself into situations where the lure was so irresistible. For the first and probably only time in our relationship, I stopped talking as much to my mom. Her nagging about my eating less was grating, and worse, it was having a negative effect on my battle plan. I needed to stay focused. I had stopped believing in family meals long ago because we rarely sat down to eat as a family, and when we did, like Thanksgivings, it was a disaster. I stopped believing in *meals* altogether. I had theorized that humans had become too obsessed with food and that when Neanderthals roamed the earth, food was not plentiful. We Homo sapiens had enjoyed too many years of excess when it came to food—at least I did, and I didn't deserve it. I thought I needed to struggle for food, to work to be nourished. In my mind, I did not deserve the goodness and abundance of food, and the jovial spirit that went along with feasting.

Instead, in the early mornings before my parents would wake, I would measure less than a cup of Special K, pour it into a coffee cup, and eat it dry. The chalky taste wasn't pleasant, but it was all I believed I merited. A few months before, when I first started running that early spring, I would eat a heaping bowl of Golden Grahams with skim milk, but even that was too decadent now. Now, for lunch, I would usually steam a handful of broccoli crowns in a small saucepan on the stove, and for dinner, I would have the coveted hearty meal of my day: a baked potato with ketchup.

I always made sure our refrigerator was stocked with potatoes. I would grab one out of the fresh foods drawer and stab it with a fork, put it in the microwave and nuke it until it was soft. I would cut it open and watch the steam rise. Then, I would squeeze the ketchup down into it. I decided I was only allowed two squeezes. My favorite part was the skin, so I usually ate the center part first with a fork and saved the skins for my hands.

I became very strict about sticking to my new way of eating. I didn't want to find myself in situations where it would be difficult to adhere to it, and I also didn't want people to notice and remark on it. Eventually I scheduled my long runs at times that would ensure I could avoid all social occasions and interactions. By the end of the summer, I was running at least two times a day. On the rare occasions I saw friends—rarely, if ever, in situations that involved meals—they would issue statements of concern. "Jon, you're losing too much weight!" they'd say. "Are you eating enough?" I'd attribute my weight loss to simply eating healthy foods and suggest they should, too.

My first run of the day, in the morning, tended to be a shorter one of forty-five minutes to an hour. The length of the longer one, later in the day, depended on how many fat grams I'd consumed that day or the day before. Each run's purpose was to burn calories and fat consumed, and also to get my body to start eating itself. The more my body feasted upon itself, the more it would get to the core, to the center, to the demon. If I slipped up and had too much Special K or too much ketchup, I simply went for a longer run. It was difficult to quantify my weight loss. Because I didn't focus on the scale, I didn't remember what I used to weigh when it all started, and worse yet, I didn't know what kind of numbers I was heading toward. All I knew was that I was shrinking, and the more I shrank, the better I felt.

An insatiable demonic persistence took over my mind. It was never enough to lose another inch or two. I set more goals than I could keep track of—about my waist size, the amount of squeezable fat in my belly or in my ass, the degree to which my cheeks sunk. None of the goals were attainable, because nothing was ever enough. I just had to keep going. I no longer recalled why I had launched the war in the first place, nor for which cause I was raging. There were too many battles going on at once and too many voices in my head launching new attacks—against my father, against my body, against my sexuality. It was a full-time assault that required 100 percent of my mind, body, and soul to execute. I would retire each night around seven or eight, long before the sun set, praying to fall asleep. At least during sleep, the demands and the orders quieted.

There were times when I felt myself getting weak, and felt I no longer had command of all that was going on. I would turn to God. *Dear God, please help me kill the fat, please help me not eat any more broccoli, please help me run a few more miles.* As in the past, He didn't seem to listen; I knew because I'd screw up. I remember one night the numbness in my stomach had temporarily lifted and I felt like I was going to black out from hunger pains. I snuck to the drive-through at McDonald's late enough at night to be sure no one would see me. I ordered a cheeseburger and a diet soda. Once I had the crinkled bag in my lap and the diet soda in my console, I sped off to the parking lot next to Sanborn School and shut off my headlights. I sat there in the parking lot and ate the burger in a matter of seconds and washed it down with gulps of diet soda, filling my mouth with as much as I could and then swallowing it down hard and fast. At first, the pleasure of tasting the charred meat, the tangy mustard, the sweet, sugary ketchup, the spicy onions, the creamy cheese, and the fluffy bun was so overwhelming, so delicious that I felt the pleasure in my groin. I hadn't felt anything like that in months.

But afterward, I felt as if I had just lost a major battle, and had perpetrated a horrible act—a sin, in fact. I couldn't go home with the McDonald's wrappers, so I drove to the high school, found one of the green barrels for trash, and tossed it all from the car. I looked around to see if anyone noticed. I didn't want there to be any evidence.

The next day, I awoke with a pit in my stomach. I was so ashamed. I had succumbed to the pleasures I had promised to avoid for so long. I needed to be punished. I needed to keep those calories and fat grams from settling on my body. So I skipped my first two meals, and then, just after noon, I ran fourteen miles under the raging sun.

Step after step, as the sweat poured out of me and onto the ground, I envisioned the fat from the cheeseburger still sitting in my belly, dissolving off me. I needed to get it out of my body, and I wouldn't stop until I believed it was gone. I went to bed without eating the baked potato that night, more punishment for my bad behavior.

■ ■ ■

One of my goals for my year off was to do more theater, and to take acting and singing lessons. I wanted to finally do all of the things I hadn't been allowed to do as a kid. Looking back, I wonder whether that entire year off was about trying to make up for a lost childhood, maybe even physically. By starving myself, was I trying to regress?

Before I could achieve my goal of performing, I had to get around my dad. He'd agonized, knowing about my performing the lead in *Sweet Charity* the summer before going off to Bates. This summer, the local theater company was doing *Once on This Island*. All my friends were planning to try out, and encouraging me to do so as well.

"I don't know, guys," I said. "My dad will probably freak out."

I auditioned without even asking him and was cast in the lead role of Daniel. I was thrilled, not only because I loved getting to play the part, but also because it felt like a triumph, and an act of defiance against my dad.

Even though I was living under his roof and I followed most of his rules, we rarely spoke. I don't think we even said hello or good-bye to one another the entire year I took off from college. The sight of him, the sound of him, the smell of him, the feeling of his presence in the house had all been so oppressive for so long that I'd grown to absolutely despise him. Maybe, at least for a time, I'd just given up on trying to please him or get him to love me and realized those efforts were futile. If he hated me now because he saw me as a failure for leaving Bates, and a "faerie" for doing musical theater, he was going to want me dead when he found out who I really was.

Over time I came to hate him as much as he hated me. I wanted to look nothing like him. It made me angry when I glanced in the mirror and saw anything resembling flab hanging below my chin. *I refuse to grow a double chin like him,* I resolved. I was determined to *be* nothing like him, too, and did all I could to kill off any part of him that existed within me, one fat cell at a time.

■ ■ ■

Another thing that would add to my dad's hatred of me, if he knew about it, was my secret ritual for measuring my weight loss progress. In my old bedroom, now the guest room, my mom had filled the closet with her overflowing wardrobe. In there I found the sea-foam green sequined and beaded dress she wore to my sister's 1993 wedding. When I spotted it, I remembered everyone raving about how beautiful my mom looked in it. The dress fit her like a glove, outlining the straightness of her rail-thin body. Not only did people rave about how stunning she looked, but they commented on how thin my mom was, and to my state of mind, that was a good thing.

As I looked at the dress, I thought, *I wonder if I could actually fit into this?*

One day, when Dad wasn't home, I decided to find out. I went to the closet and pulled out the dress. I lifted the plastic dry cleaner wrapping, and then took the dress over to the mirror, where I held it up to my neck as I studied my reflection. I unfastened the hook and eye at the top of the back and lowered the zipper. I removed my shorts and shirt and stepped into the dress. It felt scratchy and heavy with all of its beading and sequins. I thought of Katie, my playmate at Hudson Country Day. I hadn't put on a dress since preschool.

My face was gaunt. My hair was short and blond from the bleaching spray I was using. I got the dress on, but I couldn't quite make the small metal buckle fasten on the back. I was still too big. But in the mirror, reflecting back at me was my mom. I didn't see my father anywhere in there. I was achieving my goal.

I kept running. I stayed focused on my prayers for the strength to not slip up like I had that night at McDonald's. If I did slip up, I'd wind up being more like my dad than my mom, and I didn't want that. People began commenting on the size of my wrists. "They're so little," they'd say, "Your face has gotten so thin." "You're wasting away." The comments, mostly out of concern, backfired and further fueled me. The more people commented, the more encouraged I felt. I could eat less and less, and run more and more, and people would keep complimenting me. I wanted that, and I was going to do whatever I had to, in order to keep it coming. My willpower was unstoppable. It felt dangerous, and I actually liked that.

Rehearsals for *Once on This Island* were progressing. One night we were rehearsing the scene where Daniel gets into a car crash. For days, Ti Moune holds vigil at Daniel's bedside. It was my job in this scene to pretend to be close to death from the accident. My cast mates kept commenting that it wasn't far-fetched for me, because of how much weight I'd lost. They said I looked like I actually could be dead. I dismissed their comments as evidence of envy. When I lay on the hard, wooden stage, however, I could feel my spine and my tailbone scraping it. It was agony. I didn't say anything because that would be admitting that they were right. I had to keep going.

Keeping up with my two runs, work, and rehearsals was getting hard, but I had no choice. I was no longer in charge; something else was working inside me now and I couldn't stop it.

The cyst on my tailbone eventually got so large, and was protruding so far, that the pain became intolerable. Before I could perform onstage, I had to go to the doctor to get it drained. Through the blur of that summer, I hadn't been on a scale in a long time. When the nurse weighed me, it read 1-1-8. I almost collapsed when I saw it. I got scared for a moment, trying to recall what I'd weighed when I started the offensive on myself so many months before.

But as I lay on my stomach waiting for the doctor to remove the fluid with the large needle, the entity in charge of my mind took over again and saw the draining of the cyst as an opportunity to lose even more weight. I couldn't wait to get on the scale when I got home. Sure enough: 117 (though this may have just been a difference between the scales). And now, the show could go on . . .

My Grandmother Youngdahl, my only remaining grandparent, came opening night. I hadn't seen her for several months, and I was excited that she was coming to see me perform. The show went off without a hitch.

After the show, at the dressing room door, many friends and family showered me with flowers and cards and gifts congratulating me on my performance. I could see my mother off in the distance, walking slowly with my grandmother in front of her. As she was leading her to me, my grandmother nearly walked by me. "Oh, Jon, I didn't even recognize you," she said when I approached her. "I couldn't find you on the stage. I had to ask your mother where you were about halfway through the show, I was so confused. Are you okay?" She began to cry and gave me a hug. "You are skin and bones, Jon. What's wrong with you?"

There was nothing wrong with me, I assured her. I was strong. I had stamina like never before. People were just jealous that I'd mustered so much willpower and looked so good. The comments made me feel triumphant. That, and finally working my way into my mother's size two dress, after many secret attempts to close the back. I was thin and beautiful. People started remarking how much I resembled my mother. I no longer resembled my father and I was determined to keep it that way.

■ ■ ■

Jared graduated from college that June. He hadn't seen me since my visit to his school earlier that year. "Holy shit," he said when he saw me. "You look like a different person!" But not in a good way, apparently. He and everyone else were worried, including the therapist that I agreed to see once a week to allay Mom's, Julie's, and Jared's fears.

There was no way I'd go back to Dr. Greenstein, so I agreed to see someone else. Jeffrey was nice enough and kind enough, but I didn't want to be helped. I wanted to die. So I didn't tell him much of anything. I suspected Jeffrey was gay, too, and that made me uneasy. It wasn't that he did anything inappropriate; he just talked with the lisp that my father had tried so hard to remove from my own speech. In some ways, seeing this effeminate man every week gave me additional willpower to destroy the very thing I was determined not to become.

I kept running and cutting food from my diet. Oftentimes, when I'd run endlessly, suffering with determination, I would think about my father. I wondered if he would be sad if I collapsed on the side of the road. I wondered if he ever regretted calling me a "sissy" or a "pussy" so many times. I wondered if he'd still think I was a pussy if he realized I was running more miles than he could ever imagine running. I believed myself to be stronger than he was, but in truth, emotionally, I was at my weakest. In the hot sun, I was dropping fat and calories and sweat, instead of shedding tears.

Sometimes, people asked where I was getting the energy to run so many miles. I always knew I was being fueled by a force from deep within me. It was a power from my center that propelled me into doing what was expected of me; I was simply following the orders that had been given to me as a child. This force inside of me, the commander in chief that was in charge of this war I was waging, was not me, but was actually an extension of my father. From deep within me, as he had since I was a child, he was ordering me to starve the *faggot* inside. At my foundation, conscious or unconscious, I knew that my father would rather I be dead than be gay. There was nothing I could do but obey the orders I was given until I disintegrated into nothingness. I was getting closer to completing that mission. Nothing and no one was going to stop me.

Chapter 12

He's Under the Bed

It all seemed so different the day before—so exciting, so amazingly hot, and unbelievably sexy. Paul had been irresistible. Our afternoon and evening together leading up to it may as well have been foreplay. From nearly the minute we were introduced, we couldn't keep our eyes off each other. Later it was our hands we couldn't keep off each other, then everything else.

I was visiting Bianca at Emerson, an arts and communication college in Boston, during the early spring thaw of that year I'd taken off. When I got there, Paul was standing outside Bianca's dorm with her and two other friends. He was handsome enough, with dirty blond hair, blue eyes, and chiseled cheekbones. He wore a fitted shirt that traced his arm muscles and his rounded, firm pectorals. It wasn't just his appearance that caught my attention. There was something else, although I couldn't put a name to it.

"This is Jessica, my roommate, and these are my friends, Paul and Mark," Bianca said between puffs on her Parliament Light. She grabbed me by the elbow and led us to the cafeteria for a bite. The four of them filled their trays with chicken cutlets, macaroni and cheese, pizza, and burgers. I got a diet soda.

"Aren't you hungry?" Bianca asked. I shook my head. In truth I was famished, but I wasn't interested in eating. I was too busy enjoying the feeling of emptiness in my stomach, the concaveness of it. I took great pride in my willpower not to eat. "You're so skinny, Jon, it's like you're disappearing," Bianca said, genuinely concerned, on the way to our table. I had to keep from smiling. I derived a sick satisfaction from her observation. At the time I visited Bianca I was on my way down from 170, eventually toward 112, but hovering around 140 at the moment. I'd been restricting my fat intake for a few months at that point. I'd somehow stopped being able to tell whether I was skinny or fat, and now Bianca was telling me what I wanted to hear—that I was noticeably skinny.

"How the hell are you losing all that weight, anyway?" Bianca added, as if to lighten the mood. I just smiled at her and rolled my eyes. I wasn't up for explaining that I spent my nights and weekends running to burn fat, trying to disappear, trying to numb myself, trying to escape being gay.

"Well, whatever your secret is, I want to know it!" she said, with a laugh.

We all settled into a booth. Paul sat quietly across from me. He kept looking up at me. At one point, he looked directly, intensely, into my eyes, and I had to look away. No one had ever looked at me that way. It made me nervous, although I couldn't really say it made me feel bad, exactly.

Suddenly five people barged into the cafeteria, singing and yelling. One of the guys was wearing a royal blue velour sweat suit with white stripes and a matching sweatband pushing back his long, corkscrew blond hair, the tendrils spiraling out like curly fries. Another had huge, round silver sunglasses and matching silver platform shoes. "Hey girls, what's cooking?" he asked animatedly, with a heavy lisp. Bianca introduced me to the group.

"Honey, you're cute!" said Shawn, the one in the sweat suit, pointing at me. "Damn, Bianca, why didn't you tell us you had a cute-ass friend coming to visit? I would have put on my makeup!"

Everyone laughed, but I was mortified. My face was redder than the Coca-Cola fountain cups we were drinking from. "Did I embarrass you, honey?" Shawn asked. "I'm sorry! I thought you were . . . are you . . . ?"

"Shawn, stop that!" Bianca interrupted.

"Just ignore him," Paul mouthed to me.

This was what I was afraid of, what my father had warned me about. To Dad, Emerson was the land of "fairies, freaks, and misfits with purple hair," a place I was to avoid at all costs. I didn't know whether to feel terrified or hopeful. I was so afraid of being gay, trying so hard not to be, and here were these over-the-top reminders of everything I didn't want to see in myself. On the other hand, if I had no choice but to be gay, here was a place where I'd be accepted.

Bianca's invitation to come visit her at Emerson was actually part of a not-so-subtle campaign on her part to get me to go there. She knew I loved theater and that I could sing, but that my father wouldn't let me have anything to do with any of that. She knew I didn't belong somewhere like Bates College in the middle of nowhere Maine. My biggest concern at Bates had been that people would instantly uncover the big secret about my sexuality; at a place like Emerson, I wouldn't have to conceal it.

"I know what's going on with you!" Bianca said when we spoke on the phone. "If you were at Emerson, you could be who you are, no matter what, I swear! They encourage people to be themselves. Come here and I'll show you!"

I pretended not to know what she was referring to. I was still trying to reject what was "going on" with me. But I promised to visit.

A visit to Emerson I could get away with, but not enrolling there. I'd brought it up once when I was applying to schools the first time around, but my dad quickly, angrily shot it down. My guidance counselor, Mrs. Haverford, discouraged me, too, without even asking why I was interested in Emerson.

Mrs. Haverford seemed to have walked out of a time machine. She wore polyester pleated skirts with floral silk blouses buttoned all the way to the top. I often wondered how she didn't choke.

"You are too smart for that school," she insisted. "It's really not the best for what you want to do. I mean if you want to be a writer or a singer or an actor, or even a newscaster, yes, but that is not what you want to do," she informed me. "I see you becoming a doctor or a lawyer." I didn't see myself becoming those things. I saw myself on stage or behind a desk writing. Even though I was never encouraged to sing or dance, or to try out for the plays at school or through the local community theater group, still, I imagined myself on stage. I had played out scenes or lip-synched songs in front of my bedroom mirror for as long as I could remember.

But I listened to Mrs. Haverford. She wasn't just my guidance counselor, but my National Honor Society advisor, too. I figured she knew what she was talking about, and that she had my best interests at heart. I never brought Emerson up again, and just did what was expected of me. For a long while, I'd found a certain comfort and safety in doing that. As I discovered in those three miserable days at Bates, though, there was a limit to that comfort and safety, and I'd reached it.

In the two weeks between making plans with Bianca and going to see her, I dropped into the high school and paid another visit to Mrs. Haverford. "I'm seriously thinking of applying to Emerson for next year," I said.

She looked at me like I had three heads. "But you're so smart," she whined. "You were at the top of your class. You could go anywhere you want." She threw out the names of a few small liberal arts colleges and Ivy League schools.

I couldn't leave my future in her hands anymore, though. I went ahead and applied to Emerson, to the honors program, on my own, and didn't tell anyone but my mom. My father would freak when he found out, but I hadn't been accepted yet; I'd worry about that later. In the meantime, I'd check out the school while I visited Bianca. Dad was probably only too happy I was going, hoping I'd get lucky and hook up with her, maybe even end up dating her.

Even though Boston was only a half hour away from Andover, I'd never driven to the city by myself before. I threw a couple pairs of khakis, oxford shirts, and sweaters into my backpack, and tossed the bag into my car, the old Bronco II that kept getting handed down from one person to the next in my family. The traffic made me nervous. I was used to driving in the suburbs; in the city, cars weaved in and out of lanes, speeding up and slowing down, beeping. I had no idea what I was doing, and got lost. *Maybe this is a sign I shouldn't be here,* I thought. *Maybe I should go home.* But I kept going. I turned off 93 South and took the Storrow Drive exit. The road curved along the Charles River. People were running along the paths, rollerblading, and riding bikes. The sun was beginning to set, and in front of me, off in the distance, was the blinking CITGO sign, with some of its lights burned out. Just off the Back Bay exit ramp was a tall ten-story building with a bunch of kids my age smoking in front of it, some with their hair dyed green, orange, and blue. I wasn't in Andover anymore. I finally got to Emerson, only twenty-five minutes late.

■ ■ ■

I couldn't tell whether or not Paul was gay. Outwardly, he didn't seem it, at least not compared to Shawn, the loud guy in the sweat suit in the cafeteria. I still had the impression that gay people were all like him, or Elton John, flamboyant and fluorescent with feather boas. That they inappropriately flaunted their sexuality in public at all times, as my father had suggested when he brought me on that business trip to San Francisco.

Shawn was what I feared I'd become, but Paul didn't fit this stereotype at all. It seemed to me that he talked like a straight guy, if straight guys talked a certain way. There was a certain confident, declarative quality to his speech, and there were no sharp, lispy *s* sounds. (If we'd met years later, I'd know in two seconds that he was gay. But back then, I even wondered whether he was Jessica's boyfriend.) Then again, as the day progressed, Paul's attention seemed more and more focused on me.

That evening, we had all seen a remarkable student production of *Merrily We Roll Along* at Cutler Majestic Theater at Emerson College. Bianca took us backstage to talk to her friend, Melissa, one of the stars. As we all crowded around her, I suddenly felt a hand on my shoulder. It was Paul's.

"What did you think, Jon?" he asked, warmly. "Did you enjoy the show?"

"I was blown away," I said. "I can't believe how professional it was. I can't believe you can major in this in college."

Afterward, we all piled into a cab to go to a cast party at another Emerson dorm called Charlesgate. The party was crowded. A cloud of smoke hovered despite the open windows. Bottles of beer were left half full, some of them with cigarette butts swimming inside. In the corner I saw a guy and two girls huddled close together on a couch, sucking out of a tube.

"What are they doing over there?" I whispered to Bianca.

"That's a bong, Jon," she explained, trying not to laugh. "They're smoking pot."

I'd never seen a bong before; I'd never tried pot or any other drug for that matter. Actually, I'd never even had *a beer.* I'd been pretty popular in high school, sure, but I was part of the good-kid crowd. We were student leaders, academically inclined and involved in extra-curricular activities. We weren't nerds, but we also didn't party—not like this. Some of us were, after all, the founders of GUTS, and we'd all signed a pledge that we wouldn't drink until we graduated. There was likely another unconscious motivation behind my sobriety during high school: I feared that if I took anything to alter my mental state, I might lose control, and with it my ability to hide my gayness.

As we got deeper into the crowd, I could hear Madonna playing. A small group was singing along and dancing together in a way that seemed choreographed. Paul joined them, and a few minutes later waved me over. I went, and he introduced me all around. His friends were so warm and friendly. They welcomed me as if I were already one of them.

"I just applied for the fall," I told them, and they were all very enthusiastic. Bianca's roommate Jessica was particularly animated—that or hammered beyond oblivion. She jumped up from the couch and screamed, "YOU HAVE TO COME HERE!"

Bianca and her friends made me feel important and wanted. Paul made me feel that at a whole new level. He didn't take his eyes off me for more than a few seconds at a time. He assumed the role of host even though Bianca was right there, making sure the conversation kept including me and that I was having a good time. I felt so attended to.

"Do you want a drink, Jon?" he asked. "A beer maybe?"

"Oh, I don't drink beer," I said. "Is there anything else?"

He pointed to a huge gallon of red wine. There didn't seem to be any Diet Coke, my beverage of choice. I nodded my head. Paul poured some of the wine into a small cup and handed it to me. I brought it to my nose and smelled it first, hoping no one would notice this was my first taste of wine. I brought it to my lips and sipped a tiny bit. It was bitter and tangy.

"Thank you," I said to Paul, smiling, pretending to enjoy it.

By two in the morning the crowd had seriously thinned. Paul and I sat on a mothball-scented couch. We talked and talked, connecting in a way I hadn't ever connected with another guy that quickly before. He was clearly attracted to me. And maybe it was the wine, but somehow after years and years of suppressing my attraction to boys, I let myself acknowledge that I was attracted to him. When he spoke, I couldn't stop noticing his eyes, and his lips. His nose moved up and down in this adorable way as he talked. His fingers were thick and smooth, slightly tanned. I wanted to grab them and hold them, put them to my face and kiss them, but there was no way I was going to do that. That would require a huge leap since I had never touched a guy before in an intimate way—nor a girl for that matter. I knew I was one kiss—with either sex—away from confirming my greatest fear about my sexuality. If I kissed him and liked it, my life would be over.

And yet here I was in Boston, full of desire for a man I'd just met, allowing myself to want him.

Paul and I were deep in conversation about, well, *everything* when Bianca made her way over to us.

"I'm ready to go," she said. Paul looked at me. His expression told me he didn't want the night to end. I didn't either. Bianca knew without either of us having to say anything.

"But Jon, why don't you stay out with Paul?" she suggested. "Seriously, don't worry about me. You have a good time and I'll see you back at the dorm in the morning."

She said it like it was no big deal, but my heart began to race. Did this mean that I was going to have to stay with Paul overnight? I couldn't do that!

"I don't know," I said. "I should go back with you, Bianca." Paul looked disappointed. "Don't you want to stay and talk?" he asked. "I mean, you'll be leaving tomorrow and we're just getting to know each other."

I was deeply conflicted. I felt guilty about making Bianca walk back to her dorm by herself. Worse, I was scared of what might happen if I stayed. She assured me she'd walked the streets back to her dorm alone thousands of times before and that she'd be fine.

"Stay, Jon," she said. "You should totally stay."

I gave her money for a cab and walked her downstairs to the street.

"Bianca," I admitted, "I don't know what to do."

"Just be yourself," she said. "That's all people want from you. Just be yourself. You deserve that, Jon."

Back upstairs, with disco in the background and stale cigarette smoke in the air, Paul and I talked for hours—about our families, our experiences in high school, what we knew, what we wanted to know. I was floating above us looking down in disbelief. This beautiful guy was clearly interested in me! I couldn't take my eyes off his moist, soft lips and his milky skin. At one point we stopped talking and just stared at each other. In the awkward silence, he just kept smiling at me.

He must have sensed my fear, because he reached out and laid his hands on top of mine, holding them down, as if to settle them, to calm me. I couldn't believe what I was feeling, just from having his hands on mine. Chills, everywhere! They branched out from my hands to my heart, and traveled throughout my body in what seemed like less than a second. I couldn't believe I was doing this, but I responded by squeezing his hands. But now I was in trouble; that simple touch brought me so much pleasure, I felt myself begin to get an erection. I tried to downplay what was going on, but Paul could tell. He stood up and asked me to follow him, his hand behind him, gesturing for me to take it. I grabbed it and went along.

We walked out of the dorm suite and down the stairs. The streets were quiet as we walked. It was 2:30 in the morning. No one seemed to be out in the whole city. No one but us. I had no idea where we were, or how to get back to Bianca's if I had to. But I didn't care.

"May I hold your hand?" he asked. I looked around to see if anyone could spot us. The darkness helped me feel safely hidden, but I was still worried about being discovered. I agreed but was afraid and let go after only a few seconds.

Paul's single dorm room was small but cozy. The twin bed had a dark quilt on it, and pictures and posters covered the walls. His lava lamp had already been on, and the orange, melted glow permeated the room. Paul lit three white pillar candles and put on Sarah McLachlan's *Freedom Sessions*. The music was eerie but beautiful, and even though I was excited, I began to feel uneasy again.

I had no idea what to do. I was having a hard time believing what was happening. What was I doing with another guy, *in his room?* Was I about to sleep there, *next to him?* Or was it understood that I would sleep on the floor? How did this whole thing work? My mind flashed to my father. "What are you doing?! Are you a queer?! How can you do this to me?!" I wouldn't be able to do anything if I couldn't get his angry voice out of my head. Had I invoked him as a way to stop myself?

But Paul came in close and looked at me with yearning eyes. His eyes were one of his sexiest features. He opened his arms to me. I hesitated and shook my head no.

"Come here; it's okay," he said with assurance.

I moved closer to him. He enveloped my entire body, my arms down by my sides, and began swaying us to the music. After a few minutes like that, I could no longer resist, and I pulled my arms out and wrapped them around him. We kept swaying like that. It was so tender. It was so nice being so close to someone else. I wondered if this was how my guy friends had felt at the school dances. I had never felt like this when I danced with girls.

Something was unleashed in me. I couldn't just be passive anymore. I needed Paul closer to me, as close as possible. I pulled him in tighter. He put his cheek against mine and moved his head up and down. It was the first time I had felt another man's stubble against my own.

I couldn't help it. I got aroused. I was embarrassed because I knew Paul must have felt it against him as we were standing so close. He ran his hands over my back. I did the same to his. I couldn't believe how natural this all felt, how much my body and my mind just knew what to do. For so long, through most of high school, I had worried so much about how to touch a girl and how to be with a girl. But this just seemed so natural.

I felt a rush of adrenaline, and probably a whole backlog of hormones I'd been damming up since the onset of adolescence. I was suddenly in some kind of altered state—deeply intoxicated.

My hand moved to the back of Paul's jeans and I felt the smooth skin of his upper bottom. It was soft and firm at the same time. I turned my head toward his and looked into his eyes. He looked into mine and smiled.

Holy shit, I thought, *this is going to happen.*

I couldn't believe I was doing this, but I pressed my lips gently against his. Our mouths started doing an instinctual dance together. I naturally opened my mouth just slightly at the very same moment he did. My eyes closed, and our lips moved in rhythm. His tongue entered my mouth ever so slightly, gently, and mine touched his. The experience was very erotic and I was shocked by how liberating it felt.

Here I'd been thinking all along that I didn't know how to kiss. I was reminded of all those picnics at the wishing well in Andover with Sophia, tossing pennies, silently wishing, "Please let me want to kiss her. Know how to kiss her! Please!" No, I knew how to kiss! I instinctually knew! It felt so good to discover it. It was as if I'd been Pinocchio all along, and now, finally, I was a real boy. Well, a young man.

Paul unbuttoned my shirt and removed it. I panicked.

Uh-oh, I thought. *He's going to see my belly and think I'm fat.* Of course, I wasn't fat, but starving isn't known for imparting clear thinking.

Years of pent-up lust prevailed, though; I quickly forgot all the insecurities I had about my body and didn't fight him. I let his fingers touch my virgin skin, and it made me quiver. I unbuttoned his shirt and then his button-fly jeans. My belt's buckle crashed to the floor as he pulled it through the loops, while kissing my neck. I let loose, touching every inch of his body—his stomach, his chest, his biceps, his forearms, his shoulders, and the small of his back. I even loved feeling the pronounced veins in his arms.

I don't remember when his jeans and my khakis came off, but there they were, crumpled on the floor, while we rubbed up against each other. I could feel the hair on his legs, the muscles in his thighs, and then the bulge in his underwear. My knees buckled, so I pulled him down and we fell onto his narrow bed. He pulled the comforter down and we got under the sheets. They smelled, delightfully, I thought, of his skin.

He wore red briefs. When he reached inside the back of my underwear, I got goose bumps all over my body, almost begging to be handled and touched. I wanted to touch him, too.

Who am I right now? I wondered.

We entangled like laces of a shoe and kissed for an hour. Several times I felt like I was going to come, just from being so close to him.

Paul whispered in my ear, "May I take off your underwear?" I didn't answer, I just moved his hands to the band now below my hipbones, and he pulled my briefs down. Straddled above me, he pulled his down, too. I became so aroused I did the unthinkable: I began to pleasure him with my mouth.

How do I know how to do this? I wondered. *I've never done this before!* But just as with kissing, I instinctually knew.

I massaged him with my lips and tongue, caressing him every-where I could.

In hindsight, considering how obsessed I was with my weight and with the potential fat content of everything I took in, it's almost hard to believe that I actually swallowed. But I was so turned on, so enrap-tured, that I just fell back onto Paul's pillow, wiped my mouth, and took in gasping breaths, one after the other. I moaned, laughed—and then I cried.

Did this really just happen? I wondered.

I was overcome with emotion: elation, joy, excitement, relief, but then sadness, remorse, shame, and grief. I laid there in disbelief. Paul was gorgeous in that moment of utter vulnerability. We stayed there, naked together, holding each other in the single bed, and I fell asleep with his arm across my chest.

■ ■ ■

When the early morning sun peeked into Paul's dorm room from behind the old white shade, I was startled and, for a second, couldn't remember where I was.

Then I looked at him as he slept and remembered. For one mo-ment, I thought of how beautiful he was, how beautiful the evening had been.

But as I came to full consciousness and looked at the door to the hallway and recalled where I was and what I'd done, something in-stantly changed. Still tucked in beside Paul in his twin bed, my body still entwined with his, I suddenly felt sick and scared. I stared at the ceiling for an hour, pinching what little fat remained on my stomach as I imagined what my father would do to me.

That's when I started checking under the bed, certain that he had been in the room all this time. Next I imagined my father break-ing down the door, swinging his arms, yelling, "You faggot!" I almost thought I saw his massive shadow through the space underneath the doorway. The room began to spin. Then, when I realized what was in my stomach, I was overcome with nausea. I had to get rid of it, get it out of me. Would it damn me to hell? *Could one blowjob seal my fate?* I asked God, or myself. *And God, how many grams of fat did I just ingest?*

And with that insane thought, I was off and running—away from Paul, away from reality.

✳

Chapter 13

The Mornings After

he good news: I'd been accepted to the honors program at Emerson, with a scholarship! The bad news: Now I'd have to convince my dad to let me go there.

I lobbied my mom, my brother, and my sister to help me with Dad. I needed to prepare a set of arguments explaining to him why Emerson would be good for me. I mentally prepared myself for the all too likely possibility that that he'd try to shoot me down. I was going to go to Emerson anyway, despite his calling it a place for derelicts, purple-haired freaks, and tattoo artists, and the rest of the family was going to back me up. Challenging his rule had consequences. Knowing that, it took balls for me to audition for Emerson's musical theater program behind his back. I figured that if I got in, I'd deal with it later. And then I got in. I wasn't going to let this opportunity pass me by just because it wasn't part of my dictatorial dad's plan.

Like the time we'd all gathered to tell Dad we wanted him to move out, I made sure everyone was nearby when I approached him.

"Dad," I said, "I have good news," even though I knew he wouldn't think it was good. When I finished telling him, he went berserk. "You'll never amount to anything if you go to an arts school!" he insisted. "You're throwing everything away!" What he didn't understand was that if I *didn't* go, I'd feel as if I was throwing it all away. All he cared about was that he would have to tell people in town that I wasn't going to an Ivy League college, but instead studying musical theater.

Mom yelled back, "Will you leave this kid alone for just a second? Will you let him do what he wants for once? Jesus Christ!"

Dad paced back and forth, visibly angry. It was almost as if he was trying to figure out what he was going to do to control me. He didn't chase me out of the room as he'd done so many times before, which was progress, but he kept screaming. "All this work I put into you for nothing! All this time and you're just going to end up a failure!"

Then Mom pulled a surprise card from her hand. "What about Leo?" she asked. "He went there. And look at him today!"

This was the one argument Mom used in the thirty-minute screaming match that Dad actually heard. Leo, his cousin, went to Emerson and did very well there, and in life. Leo was a radio and marketing major when he attended the college in the '70s, and had been very successful throughout his career. First, he was a sports radio announcer. Later, he thrived as a professional sports marketing executive. It was shrewd of Mom to recognize Leo as a device for disarming my father. *Nice one, Mom,* I thought. It worked. It calmed Dad down. He became somewhat rational. I'm sure Mom had to endure many more private conversations about this and coercions over time, but we won the battle. I was going to Emerson despite my father's disapproval.

That summer before I entered Emerson, I had no life. I'd pretty much given up everything for my runs—any resemblance of a real life, that is. In the middle of that summer before Emerson, I was exhausted each night by eight o'clock and asleep by nine. There was no time for any other pleasures. There was no time for meals or drinking with friends. I avoided all outings, especially parties, because I didn't want people to notice that I didn't eat the chips and dip, or the cheese and crackers. I didn't even make time for Mom anymore.

There were those rare occasions, like the secret McDonald's run, when I'd slip up and let too many fat grams pass my lips.

It was a hot summer night when Dad ordered a pizza. I'd had a handful of steamed broccoli spears that night. When he left the house for a baseball game, I slithered to the kitchen like a sneaky serpent, trying to be undetected. When it was clear I was alone, I opened the oven door where, inside, the pizza was still sitting in the box, forbidden-looking, but so desirable. I pulled the box out of the oven and put it on top of the range. When I opened the box, the smell of the melted cheese made my mouth immediately water. Salivating, I picked up one of the three remaining slices. It was warm and tender in my hands. I brought it to my nose. It smelled sweet, and somehow evoked family—the kind I always dreamed about anyway.

That's love, I thought. The slice of pizza reminded me of the things that used to bring me joy: gooey melt-in-your-mouth mozzarella, soft but crusty dough, sweet marinara that Mom made sometimes on weekends. I trembled just holding the slice in my hands. I wanted to bite into it, shove it into my mouth, all at once. I could feel in every cell in my body the urge to move my hands to my mouth and indulge. It was like the moment right before that first kiss with Paul in his dorm room. It bordered on erotic, the enticement of this amazing indulgence that I knew would be bad for me. I wanted it to happen but was afraid of the consequences. How would I feel afterward? *You'll regret this,* my anorexic voice told me.

I disobeyed that voice. I shoved half the slice into my mouth as quickly as I could. The faster it disappeared, the sooner it would be gone and I could forget this ever happened. I chewed furiously. I chewed and chewed and chewed. I was on autopilot, but euphoric. Then something short-circuited the euphoria. It was as if the fat had been absorbed in the inside of my mouth and went straight to my brain, like an ice cream headache, but this was worse. Suddenly I couldn't swallow. My body went into fight mode and I started to gag. I ran to the sink and spit out the few bites of pizza still in my mouth into the garbage disposal. I spit and spit, purging every last morsel from my lips. I frantically cupped water from the running faucet and shoved it inside of my mouth, swishing it all around to vanquish every speck, every fat gram that may have been hiding in between my teeth. I switched on the disposal, pulverizing what had been in my mouth into nothing I could retrieve.

When the panic dissipated, I turned away from the sink and caught a glimpse of myself in the reflection in the microwave oven's door. I hated what I saw. *You're a failure. You suck.* I was so ashamed of what I had done.

On a daily basis, I loathed what I saw in the mirror. I couldn't stand the sight of myself. I began avoiding mirrors at all costs. I even kept my head down when I passed shop windows on Main Street in Andover. All I saw was an ugly, disgusting, hideous, obese, and grotesque man. All I saw again was my father.

■ ■ ■

By the time I was getting ready to go to Emerson, as far as I was concerned, I still had too much skin on my belly, and it disgusted me. I was pissed at myself, and humiliated. *What if I have to stand naked in the group showers?* I was worried what everyone would think about my fat belly. If I was going to get any acting roles at Emerson, then I had to lose the fat that still marred my body.

Paul was now an upperclassman and he hung out with a different bunch of kids, because he wasn't in musicals. I avoided him as much as I could after the first week or two of school. I think he was crushed that I didn't pay attention to him, but in my mind, what had happened between us was an accident, a mistake, my mistake.

During orientation week, I was cast in the *New Student Review,* a showcase that put the new freshman talent on display, as Hugo, Kim's love interest in *Bye Bye Birdie.* At the performance, my flailing, puny arms seemed ill fitting for the manly part I was playing. But it didn't seem to matter. The director of the fall musical approached me after the show and said that he'd hoped I'd try out for the production of *The Best Little Whorehouse in Texas.* I didn't think I was as good as the other guys in the freshman musical theater class. They'd been doing theater all their lives. They had parents who encouraged them and told them they were the best, and they soaked it all in. I didn't have nearly their confidence, and often wondered how I'd gotten in.

I was also suspicious about why some of the guys in school were interested in me. I didn't see what they saw. The attention I began getting from boys was confusing. I didn't see myself as a sexually attractive being. I didn't see myself as *sexual*. I'd pretty much been chaste my entire life except for that one experience with Paul, which seemed to set me off even more on the course of self-destruction. After that, I tried to be asexual, and more or less committed to a vow of celibacy.

Meantime, there was a lot of hooking up going on at Emerson. Boys with girls. Boys with boys. Girls with girls. And even all of them at the same time. I'd see classmates making the walk of shame as I walked to my early morning class. I was scared of all of it. Maybe I was scared by how alluring it was. So I tried to keep to myself as much as possible.

It wasn't always easy. I was a young adult male, a jumble of hormones and curiosity. There was one guy who had captured my attention during the *New Student Review* our first week of school. He had been given multiple solos for the show, and people were blown away by his talent. It didn't hurt that he was also handsome. He had jet black, thick, wavy hair and dark olive skin. If he'd had an accent, you would've thought he'd just gotten off the plane from Spain or somewhere in Latin America. But he was from New Jersey.

I had mastered falling for people who were unavailable, and Enrique was clearly taken. He and his boyfriend, Sam, couldn't keep their hands off one another, or stop their lips from locking. I was embarrassed for them at first. They made out constantly. At every rehearsal they made out, and whether they were standing or lying down, it was always in public. I'd see them outside the Brimmer Street Theatre building groping one another, and my eyes would widen. I'd never seen two guys make out before, as my dad had warned me I'd see in San Francisco a few years before. At first I was startled and thought that their hand-holding and making out was strange and unnatural. Then I found myself lingering and watching them longer than I should have. I was watching Enrique more and more.

Then I felt that twinge of jealousy, that tug on my heart that seemed strangely familiar. I realized it was the same feeling I had felt when Chad would go out on dates with girls like Maria. *Wait,* I wondered, am *I crushing*? I was. It didn't matter, though, because Enrique and Sam were hot and heavy, smooching and petting constantly, and becoming the gay "it" couple on campus. Furthermore, Enrique barely talked to me during rehearsals; he hardly knew I existed.

Despite my unrequited crush on Enrique, things were going much better at Emerson than they had at Bates, right from the beginning. For one thing, I'd gotten a single dorm room so I didn't have to worry about an antisocial roommate. Even better, we had private single bathrooms so I didn't have to worry about group showers. Those two things alone made my start at Emerson a good one. With Bianca there, a year ahead of me, I was introduced to all the right people. She watched out for me the way Jared had watched out for me my first year in high school. Getting cast in the *New Student Review* enabled me to make some good friends on my own. My classes were decent, too. My professor for my honors seminar was a hippie poet who I thought was so cool. Then I learned you could major in poetry. *You can major in poetry!*

At first, I didn't think many of my friends or classmates knew what was going on with me. I did a good job of putting on a smile. I didn't want anyone to think that I was as crazy as I felt inside. A couple of weeks after the *New Student Review,* I ended up auditioning for the main stage musical production with a few friends. If I was going to be at Emerson for musical theater, then I had to start trying out.

The fall musical was *The Best Little Whorehouse in Texas*. The director of the show was always a senior—an assignment for the course in directing musical theater. Dwayne was a fun-loving guy with wild, curly blond hair. I always got the sense that he was hot for all of us freshman boys. During the auditions, he smiled at me when I sang. One of the advantages I had was that I was coordinated from all the sports Dad had made me do. And because I had watched my sister do cheers and dances my entire life, I was able to pick up on choreography quickly. When it came to the dance tryouts, I must have stood out. I was one of five guys cast as part of the ensemble and a Texas Aggie. When I saw the cast list posted on the fourth floor of the

Brimmer Street Theatre, affectionately known only as Brimmer, others congratulated me and told me that it was quite a feat to make the main stage musical as a freshman.

The majority of my rehearsals were dancing and ensemble singing. Everything was going well. I was paired up with this great senior for many of the dances. She was short like me but strong, and a powerful dancer. She took to me and coached me along. I had never taken a dance lesson in my life, so I didn't know any of the terminology associated with choreography. But Jessica stayed late after rehearsals with me in the dance studio and walked me through anything I might not have picked up as quickly as the others. The director and choreographer liked me because I worked hard and was a perfectionist. I wanted to get it right.

Being in the main stage musical at a school as small as Emerson, I met a lot of people quickly. I was clueless about it at the time, but a bunch of guys had asked me out on dates. I was either oblivious to their overtures or in denial about them, and mostly turned them down. I was still fighting against my sexuality, hoping it wasn't too late for me to become straight, despite what had happened with Paul the prior spring. Although I tried to keep my head down most of the time and not even look at men, a guy named Cristian, a dancer and actor, finally caught my attention. He was cute and blond, and kind looking. He was intense like me, and he pursued me hard and persistently. It took me a while to fully realize that he was interested in me in *that way*. I liked him, too. There was a story of gentleness that the lines around his eyes told. I wondered if he would be warm and patient with me as I struggled to accept my sexual orientation, even though I didn't really know that was what I needed at the time. He seemed like someone I could talk to.

Then one night after a rehearsal, Cristian was waiting for me outside of the dance studio. "Jon, do you want to have dinner?" he asked. "I'd love to get to know you better." And despite two of my biggest fears at the time—food and dating guys—for some reason, perhaps an inner hope that I could do it, I accepted.

We went out a few times. We'd go out and I'd even drink a little bit, but then I would eat more than I wanted to, and later punish myself with starvation and punitive exercise. But while we were out, I was careful not to let Cristian get a glimpse of my eating issues. I didn't want anyone to know about them. With alcohol in my system on those dates, my inhibitions collapsed. Afterward, we'd find ourselves in my single dorm room making out. I loved it at the moment, just like I did with Paul, but when it was over and we'd awake intertwined in my single bed, I'd have recurring paranoia about my father barging in the door and finding me lying with another man. To make matters worse, when I woke, I'd remember that I'd had drinks and fattening foods the night before. Those mornings after were horrible, like a bad hangover.

Even though I wasn't, I felt as if I was starting to expand. The combination of letting fat into my body and letting a man touch my body had that effect on me. For most of my friends, the mornings after nights of great food and drinks and hooking up came with a blissful afterglow. For me the mornings after were pure hell. If I'd hated myself the day before, I hated myself even more on those mornings. I tried not to let it destroy things for me with Cristian. I tried to enjoy our relationship, whatever it was, but ultimately I couldn't handle it.

As I'd done with Paul, I soon pushed Cristian away. I told him I was too focused on the fall musical and my grades to have a boyfriend. That wasn't a complete lie, but the greater truth was that I wanted more time to devote to running and withholding food, especially after I went on dates. Catholic guilt for being with a man was getting the best of me. It drove me toward staunch penance. I banished myself to my single dorm room, without food for a couple of days. I ran for longer and longer. I eliminated all men from my life. And my new obsession became fat burners.

I'd first heard about them on an infomercial. Then I saw them on the shelves at drugstores in big, brown plastic bottles—models with Herculean, fat-free abs posing on their labels, under the words FAT

BURNERS, all caps. Since I was convinced I'd hit a plateau in my quest to annihilate the fat on my own stomach (a delusion for at that point it was really just skin), I thought I could use the help of these magic pills. I thought they'd eat away at any remaining fat on my body. I also thought that on any occasion when I consumed too much fat, I could undo it with the fat burners. In my mind, they'd make my transgressions go away.

I hesitated at first before buying them, because they were expensive. But finally, I succumbed.

The pills were huge. They were light beige speckled with brown spots. I imagined the speckles were some sort of microscopic fat-eating bacteria that would release once you downed them with water. They smelled horrible, like days-old urine in the alleys of Boston. But I didn't care. If they would help me on my fat-burning mission, then I was going to take them. The warning label cautioned that these pills, essentially a stimulant/diuretic combination, could cause dizziness, elevated heart rate, frequent urination, and high blood pressure. I read that, but ignored it. Clearly the fat burners weren't good for me, but I didn't care about that; I cared about destroying the fat, and maybe even myself.

I was trapped in a cyclical conundrum. Guys at school found me attractive, which I couldn't comprehend. They asked me out. For a while I tried to avoid them, and the running and anorexia fulfilled me. But then I'd get lonely in my room after rehearsals, all by myself while the others would go out and party. The loneliness would remind me how nice it was to have someone like Cristian or Paul sleeping next to me, and then I'd want to try again. So we'd go out and have drinks and a meal together. We'd sleep together. And I'd awake filled with that morning-after doom in my heart and mind, and start the cycle all over again.

At first I'd take the recommended dosage of the fat burners after a date, or after I'd eaten a meal with friends. (Of course, what I called a *meal* and felt was a huge binge, others considered hardly eating.) But soon I found myself taking the fat burners by the fistfuls.

As the first semester at Emerson rolled on, my body took a beating. I wasted away to nothing and *still* felt fat and gross. I was exhausted from classes all day and studying all night, but couldn't allow myself to score anything less than an A. Long runs demanded more of my time, even though my studies and rehearsals left little time to squeeze them in. Rehearsals ran all night as we got closer to the show's opening. All the while, my calorie consumption diminished and my intake of fat burners increased to a dozen a day. On top of it all, I found out from our director that there was a locker room scene when "the Aggies" would go shirtless. I panicked. *Shirtless? Skins? Oh my, God, I agonized. I'm fucked.*

■ ■ ■

By November, the red under my alien eyes started to get people's attention. Cast mates and friends couldn't help but notice that I barely ever ate in front of them. Hell, I barely ate at all. My wrists were as skinny as broomsticks. My cheeks were sunken like the funny fish face I used to make when I was little. The most I'd eat each day was a plain, untoasted bagel with multiple diet sodas to wash down the fat burners. I felt guilty that my meal plan was a complete waste of money.

But if I was going to have to be shirtless in that scene, then I was certainly not going to be fat doing it. How many times had I heard my father tell me I had fat rolls every time he'd see me with my shirt off going into the shower? Too many times to count. It was branded in my mind. There was no way I was going have even an ounce of fat on my body. Not if I could help it. I became even more disciplined, more determined, if that was even possible. It *was* possible, and through determination and discipline, I eventually achieved what I had been subconsciously shooting for the entire time: to be destroyed.

It was an unusually warm early evening. I wanted to get in a long run before rehearsal, so I left my dorm just as the sun was going down. It wasn't an unusual time for a run. I had the same energy I always did. I didn't go any faster or any slower than normal. My runs were pretty much ritualistic, so at any given point along my path, I could guess the time that I was there down to the second. I felt good, strong, determined.

When I got back to the dorm, I did my stretches on the steps out front. I said hello to my dorm mates going in and out of the building. I took the elevator up to the seventh floor, walked to my room, turned the lock, grabbed my toiletries bucket and towel, and headed for the bathroom to take a shower. First, though, I had to urinate. As I peed, I looked out the window, which overlooked a big alley. Peeing hurt. *How strange,* I thought. I turned my head toward the toilet and saw that the water was bright red, as if I had emptied a bottle of food coloring into the bowl. I stopped my stream of urine and screamed. But the pain from blocking the urine hurt more than peeing, so I let it go. The stream of pee was blood red. My heart began to race.

When I was done, I fell to the floor and called for one of the three girls in the triple room next door to me. No one answered, so I got up myself and walked to my room and called my mom. "Get to the hospital," she yelled. "You need to get to the hospital!"

■ ■ ■

At the time I went to the hospital, I was told I weighed 112 pounds. Days earlier, despite the pain in my flank, I didn't dare stop my long run. My T-shirt was stuck to my chest, the sweat dripped off my nose like a leaky faucet, one consistent droplet after another. My legs were numb from running for two hours without stopping. I started near 100 Beacon Street and pounded over the Massachusetts Avenue Bridge to the outskirts of MIT. Despite how frail I'd become, my fortitude was as stubborn as concrete. I wouldn't let go of my long runs. I couldn't.

I ended up at the emergency room, where the doctor assigned to me was a Harvard Medical School intern. When my mom arrived, her wrinkles looked different to me. They hung heavier and looser. With IV fluids going into my left hand, Mom holding my right, and doctors scrambling to figure out why I was pissing red, I wondered if I had actually succeeded in my mission. *Did I finally do myself in? I thought. Maybe I'm not a pussy after all.*

I was freaking out about how much fat was in the intravenous fluids they were giving me, but ironically, it never occurred to anyone to ask whether I had any kind of eating issues. It probably never occurred to them that a male could be anorexic.

After hours of tests and an inconclusive diagnosis, I was discharged from the hospital. The Harvard intern wanted me to see a specialist, a urologist. It wasn't kidney stones or an infection. I hadn't been in an accident so it wasn't trauma. Or maybe it was. The doctor and nurses made me feel as if I was crazy. None of them asked why I'd dropped so much weight. Even though I told the doctor I was running twelve miles or more a day on a bowl of cereal or a bagel and a handful of fat burners, he never asked about an eating disorder. And so I didn't acknowledge it either. It had to be something else. So what was it?

Mom took me to a top urologist to find out. I endured test after test and probing and prodding, one invasive procedure after another. MRIs, CT scans, X-rays: they showed nothing. Then I had an intravenous pyelogram (IVP) and a cystoscopy, where they send a microscope up your urethra and look inside your kidneys, your bladder, and every channel to and from. I had to be put to sleep for that one. And other than having a major reaction to the anesthesia (I was so little, my body probably couldn't handle its potency), the test showed nothing.

I felt as if I were eighty years old. I was exhausted and weary. What was this all for? It had to be a message.

Is God warning me? I'd allowed myself to engage in the behavior I was told all my life was sinful. I had gone on dates. I let food pass by my lips—food that could put back on my body the rolls of fat my father always chastised me for. I drank a little bit too much on some nights. On those nights I had hooked up with guys. Maybe it was that night that I got a little passionate with Cristian, and I had too much fun? Was my bleeding penis a sign from heaven to stop? Was this some sort of new STD that hadn't been discovered? Was this another message from God that I was experiencing His wrath? All these questions and no answers. Instead, a deep pain in my side flank that would never go away.

The discomfort reminded me that I was a slave to my own actions. I couldn't stop them even if I wanted to. I was running a fever in my mind, unable to stop the burning. Had the obsession turned into a disease that was killing me? *But isn't that the point?* was my answer. I recalled feeling the flank pain on my long runs and actually missed it while being hospitalized. *I deserve this pain,* I reminded myself. I created my own hell on earth. And if running was going to kill me, then I was going to just keep running.

✳

Chapter 14

Going Outward to Go Inward

H ere's what my days were reduced to that first year at Emerson: I hid out in my dorm room, avoiding all social interaction, especially interactions that would involve food. I left my room only to attend classes or rehearsals, to run obsessively, and to pick up more fat burner pills at the pharmacy. It wasn't much of an existence.

Clearly I needed an intervention. I may have even known that, may have hoped someone would intervene. But none of the adults in my life—not my parents, not my teachers, not my doctors—did. To be fair, I don't think anyone knew what to do for me, not even Mom. My self-loathing and self-destructiveness were at an all-time high.

I was lost, deep in the rabbit hole of my obsessions. But even though I was deliberately, systematically destroying myself, there was a small presence of myself that wanted it all to stop—the self-flagellation, the penance. I'd had enough.

It was going to have to be up to me to make it stop. I'd have to try to save myself. At some point in my desolation, I remembered the trip my friend Charlie took in high school to Hurricane Island, Maine, with an organization called Outward Bound that took young people on empowering outdoor survival adventures. I recalled how Charlie's experience solidified his resilience. Troubled by living with diabetes since he was just eleven years old, he was determined to prove to himself and to others that he was no different than any of us. And he did. He left that summer a teenager. He came home after fourteen days, his skin golden, and his hair yellowed from the salty ocean and sun, a young man. He was stronger and better after his adventure, and hearing about his experience moved me.

I wondered whether Outward Bound could help me, considering my deeply depressed state. Nature had always brought me some semblance of peace when I was conflicted. Maybe spending many days out in the wild, challenging my mind and body to survive, would shake me. *What else is there?* I knew it had to be something extreme, like Outward Bound—or the hospital.

I signed up for a twenty-one day, multi-element program that included a land excursion with canoeing, backpacking, and mountain climbing, and a sea excursion that included sailing to Hurricane Island off Maine. Dad was against it because he said it was dangerous. I didn't understand why he cared about my safety; he didn't seem to care much about my well-being at all. He didn't understand why I would put myself through such "torment." He didn't like anything about being outside unless it was for organized sports. He hated camping and loathed bugs, which made this another opportunity for my father to be confused by his youngest son. How could this prissy kid suddenly have such an avid appreciation for the wilderness? It was yet another thing we didn't have in common.

I was drawn to nature my entire life. For me, it was solace, escape, peace. When I went skiing as a kid, my friends would make fun of me because I wanted to enjoy the views from the top of Loon Mountain. Creeks, lakes, the ocean, forests, and mountains always calmed me.

Mom asked, "Do you think this will help you, Jon?" I told her I prayed that it would. "You're strong; I know you can do this. You should do this," she assured. "I'll get your father to pay for it. Go and do this and get better."

■ ■ ■

In the middle of May, after barely surviving my first year at Emerson, Mom drove me four hours north to Rockland, Maine. The day before, she had helped me pack my new REI backpack with the very specific items I was allowed to bring. My gear was minimal—a couple of shirts, long johns, water-resistant hiking boots, a hat, a sweater, underwear. I had to leave many of my comforts behind except for a blank journal and a pen.

When we arrived at the base, I could see a few other people roaming around and wondered if they would be in my group. Then from one of the buildings, one of our two instructors emerged. "Hi, I'm Merrill," she said. Her hair was gray, frizzy. I wasn't used to seeing women who didn't use product. The lines on her tanned face were deep, I imagined from squinting on hikes or swims in the open ocean. She wore shorts, a fleece vest, ankle-high socks, and hiking boots. Her legs were strong but laced with varicose veins. She must have been in her late sixties.

"Hello, what's your name?" she asked.

"Jon. I'm Jon."

"Well, Jon, you have to take all of those things from your beautiful new bag and transfer it all into this." She handed me a smaller, used but more sophisticated backpack. *My first challenge?*

"Okay," I said with reluctance.

Once Mom helped me repack everything in the given backpack, I was instructed to say good-bye to her. She hugged me and held me tightly. "You are so strong, Jon," she said. "It's so brave of you to embark on this journey. I know it will be great for you." As I watched her drive away in her SUV, kicking up the rocks and white dirt, I felt a pit in my stomach. It would be the first time in my life that I wouldn't be able to talk to my mom whenever I wanted to. I didn't know when I would be able to call her on the trip, but they promised that we'd be able to check in about halfway through the program.

Merrill called our group together into a circle on the lawn outside of the school's headquarters. She introduced Pedro, her co-instructor. He was a short guy with short black hair and a black mustache. He, too, wore shorts with a long-sleeved shirt and a fleece vest. He was short, but stocky and strong. "Yo, great to meet ya'll!" he said. "It's gonna be an adventure together!"

Merrill then asked us to go around in the circle and introduce ourselves. We had to say where we were from and why we were doing Outward Bound. Our group of eight was six men and just two women. A couple of the guys had been on previous adventures. One of them, Aaron, wearing cargo pants with a spiked belt, said he was sent there because he was always getting in trouble. When it was one of the women's turns to talk, she burst into tears and said she couldn't do it. She walked away from the group and ran into the school crying. Merrill and Pedro let her go. "Okay, so who's next?" They didn't acknowledge what had just happened. I wondered how many people took off like that at the beginning of each excursion. The second woman told us she was from Florida and she was on the trip for vacation. Merrill giggled and said, "Well, guess what? You're going to need a vacation from your vacation." Everyone laughed.

"Hi. I'm Jon," I said when it was my turn. "I'm from Andover, Massachusetts. And I'm here to . . . to . . . get better, I guess, to get stronger." But there was more to it, even if I wasn't ready to acknowledge it, even internally. Maybe I was also there to prove to myself and to my father that I could do this—that I could finish something that a "pussy" would never finish. Maybe I was trying to prove I was a "real man," despite now majoring in theater and doing musicals against my father's wishes.

Whatever the reason, I was desperate for an epiphany, some sort of spiritual shaking, like the inner shift Charlie had experienced. As we prepared to embark on our journey, Merrill asked us to take a moment of silence to think. I closed my eyes and prayed to God. "Please help me get better," I asked. "Please help me finish this. Get me through this."

The twenty-one days started out on land. An oversized white, rusty-around-the-wheels van carried us farther north from Rockland to Moosehead Lake. The long drive marked the last time we'd see cars or roads or hear a radio for the duration of the trip. I didn't know to savor these everyday things we took for granted. I had no clue what was to come.

The van dropped us off; its brake lights were the last we'd see of something shining in the dark, other than a campfire or a star in the pitch-black sky. We were in the middle of nowhere. There was nothing but tall evergreens and vast grasslands, still brown from the harsh winter. Everything was muddy from the recent thawing. It smelled like muck. But it was unpolluted muck. The air was fresh and crisp, thinner up there, easier to breathe. The nothingness in the air was loud. The silence startled me. It made me feel small and insignificant. It put me and my being, my humanness, immediately into perspective. In the vastness of the scene that stood before me, behind me, above me, and all around me, I had my first spiritual moment.

Right away I became a good soldier. I did what I was told, I did it on time, and I did it right. I volunteered for the manly tasks, like starting the fires at night or helping the remaining woman on the trip by carrying her backpack on top of mine when she cried from exhaustion and pain. I was intent on making the members of the group like and appreciate me. At first, I thought that meant suppressing my sexual orientation. *This is my chance,* I thought, *to not be gay, once and for all.*

For what seemed to be weeks but was only several days, we portaged our heavy red canoes across open fields to waterways that would take us south toward our starting grounds. Aaron complained about the gnats that swarmed around our heads so they could take in the carbon dioxide we exhaled. He made jokes and often disobeyed Merrill and Pedro. He was a distraction to some. In the beginning, I did my best to ignore him, but by the time this endeavor was over, he'd become one of my favorite people in the group.

Every morning Merrill and Pedro would wake us at sunrise and gently force us to jump into the water as our shower—our "dip," as they called it. We weren't allowed soap or shampoo, so it was the only way to sluice the sweat and earth from our bodies. The water was so cold I wondered how it wasn't iced over. On the first morning, when they told us about our daily mandate (we were not allowed to start our days until every single person dipped), I was hesitant and was one of the last to submerge myself. I'd never been afraid to go into the ocean or a lake, even in Massachusetts or New Hampshire, but that was usually in July and August when temperatures were higher. This frigid Maine late-May/early-June water could send one into a state of panic. When I finally took the plunge, I lost my breath and forgot how to catch it. My body flailed and convulsed. I looked up at Merrill in very much the same way I'd look to my mother. "Just try to calm yourself and focus," she said. Within seconds my heavy breathing slowed. I could see plumes of my breath hitting the cold spring air. "You're doing it, Jon!" Merrill cheered. In the beginning, I dreaded every sunrise because of the dip, but eventually I got used to it and looked forward to the fresh feeling the crystal clear water gave me. Most of the group seemed to feel the same way. Some needed two dips a day!

My role in the group was very much in keeping with the role I played so many other times in my life: I went out of my way to be "good," to do everything that was asked of me perfectly to make up for the secret I was keeping about my sexuality—my worst demon. I never mentioned to anyone in the group that I was even questioning my sexual orientation. I still hadn't honestly confirmed with friends at Emerson that I was gay, or even within myself. I was still confused, or hoping that there was a way for me to become straight. I wasn't about to tell a bunch of strangers in the middle of the woods the one thing that had brought me the most angst in all my life.

I kept my head down when we hiked up mountains. I kept my arms strong above my head when we portaged the canoes. I did all I could to help set up the camps at night and I paddled as strongly as I could when we were in the swiftly moving rapids. All of my father's "training" toward how to be a real man was certainly paying off, and I don't think anyone suspected the secret I was carrying.

Naturally, in this group setting, food was a challenge for me. I had to avoid the gorp, the mixed nuts, raisins, dates, chocolate chips mixture they had by the buckets—big white ones with metal handles. Nuts had a ton of fat, and fat still scared the shit out of me. I did eat the unrefrigerated fruit and vegetables. I knew that unless I fueled my body sufficiently, I wouldn't survive in the wilderness, our grueling daily tasks, and the freezing late night temperatures in my tent with my thin sleeping bag. It was hard to resist the urge to starve, but for the first time in a long time, I began to notice what it felt like to be hungry.

Although this adventure was strenuous, painful, and challenging, I was surviving. It was my cardiovascular stamina and my willpower that made me a leader in the group. Did I hate having to brush my teeth with baking soda and brown iodine water? Yes. Would I wake up in the middle of the night in the tent scared that a bear would claw it open any moment? Absolutely. Did I feel at times that this was the most ridiculous thing I'd ever signed up to do? For sure. But the resolute determination I'd honed over the prior two years helped me soldier on.

I was one of the few in the group who never lamented about the journey's physical demands. Despite the daily challenges and my ongoing anguish, it felt good to be doing something other than running or starving. All the while, I knew I was burning fat and that kept me sane. By the middle of the trip, I was beginning to remember what hope felt like. But the toughest part was yet to come.

■ ■ ■

The sun had gotten stronger over the course of the first ten days, and the winds crossing into Maine from Canada were beginning to die down. The warming marked the start of June in northern Maine and also the halfway point of the trip. It was time for our solos.

Anyone who'd heard about Outward Bound heard about its biggest challenge, the solo, a three-day period that each participant spent in isolation, fending for himself. And here it was. The night before, we gathered on a small, treeless bank that led down to the water of Moosehead Lake. Our guides gave us our final instructions and laid out our plans. One by one, they were going to canoe us out to our own individual spots on the opposite shore of the lake. They planned to leave us about three miles apart from one another with just a tiny, rectangular bug tent, a journal, a bag of gorp, a bag of celery, and a bag of carrots. No watch. Absolutely nothing else.

"Do not wander far from your designated campsite," Merrill instructed. "Every day we'll canoe by each of you. If you're okay, raise one arm. If you need help, raise both. But you have to *really* need help to raise both."

"Keep track of your thoughts in your journals," Pedro added.

The next morning, I woke with a racing heart. I rose as soon as the sun peered through the tent's zipper. I wasn't sure how I'd do out there on my own. I was nervous that I'd have to raise both arms, but I desperately didn't want to. I wanted to prove I could do it solo.

After our morning dip, Merrill and Pedro canoed members of our group out to their spots. The rest of us waited anxiously for our turn. When it was my turn, they paddled me out for about forty-five minutes. Because I was one of the last to go, my location was likely the farthest from the base camp. Our canoe slid up onto a little shore, and we bumped up against a small stretch of sand and dirt. Beyond it, the forest was thick and endless. Looking out at the place they were going to leave me, all I could see were pine trees. We unloaded the sparse amount of gear, and both Merrill and Pedro looked at me with encouraging smiles. "Good luck, Jon," Merrill said. "We'll check on you every morning just after sunrise," Pedro said. "You can do this." *Did I have a choice?*

I surveyed the plot of land. I looked around it and became instantly familiar with north, south, east, and west. I found a tree that looked big enough to serve as a base. Without thinking, I began to create a shelter. I was like a primitive animal creating my nest to protect me from whatever it was that was looking at me, or getting a whiff of me, from afar. I cleared crusty leaves and other brush at the bottom of the tree, on the side of it away from the water, perhaps to conceal myself from any predators. Then I began to gather large sticks and twigs and brought them to the tree. I piled them up, bunch by bunch, until they towered up to my waist and spanned about the size of my lying-down body. That's where I hung my bug tent, between the pile of sticks and twigs and the large tree. It took me hours to build this nest that was to be my home for the next couple of days.

Time got heavy and slow. Everything dragged on like Sundays when I was a child. I made it through the first night, getting into the bug tent just as the sun was setting. I prayed, *Dear God, please help me fall asleep fast so I can't hear any of the creatures around me.* I was scared that a bear would find me, even though I had concealed myself as best I could. It must have been early when I fell asleep. I seemed to sleep through the night—I don't remember waking up or being scared alone and in the dark, which I would have been.

I didn't do much during the next day. I took my morning dip, carefully following the rule not to go in beyond my waist. It was a rule that Pedro and Merrill emphasized over and over, because some poor soul who did Outward Bound before me drowned while on his solo.

I raised my one arm when Merrill and Pedro passed shortly after the sun came up. It was an especially warm, clear day, and I wanted to take advantage of that rarity. I spread my clothes on the sun-drenched rocky beach. It was the first time they dried completely from the rain and the cold since the trip started. I, too, laid there for much of the day absorbing the UV light into my pale, chilled, and sun-thirsty skin. My body may have been worse off than my clothes.

Now recognizing hunger, I spent a lot of time thinking about how I'd ration the food. Because I was an expert at controlling my intake of food already, I'd measured out small portions of bites from the bags. I had a system: a dozen pieces (mostly the raisins) from the gorp, a celery stalk, and a carrot stick. Three times a day, I'd prepare my meals on the stump of a fallen tree. It was the most regularly I'd eaten since I'd launched the battle against myself a couple of years prior.

I spent a lot of time sitting by the tree, writing. My thoughts weren't always rational, and as the time droned on, my imagination began to wander into the depths of the pines. I wondered if I could climb the tall trees and perch within their branches. I fantasized about having bionic strength, like Steve Austin on the *Six Million Dollar Man,* a TV show I'd watched back when we lived in New Jersey. Perhaps it was a defense mechanism. Maybe I needed to think about being bionic in order to imagine handling the challenges I knew were certain to come in my future. I thought about coming out to the group and wondered, *will they reject me the way my father certainly will?*

On the second day, I created a musical production in my mind. I designated some of the trees as actors with me, the leading character, and other trees as the audience. I sang songs I'd learned at Emerson at the top of my lungs. I knew no one could hear me because the day before I'd screamed to see if one of my comrades would scream back. "Hello! Can anyone hear me?" All I got back was the echo of my voice. I read that in the solitude and starvation of the solo, some had been known to hallucinate. *Was this it?* I wondered. *Had I lost it?* I just kept writing in my journal, keeping track of all the thoughts, fleeting and lingering alike. All the while, I came back to the question: *Should I tell the group the truth?*

On the final morning of my solo, after my dip, I began to remove the branches and brushwood that had become my shelter. I took down the bug tent and made sure that I combed and smoothed all of the areas where I'd slept, marched, and danced, so they looked undisturbed. When I was packed up, I sat down on the shore, the sun high in the blue sky and shining on my face. It dawned on me how close I was to finishing the solo, something I'd never thought I'd be able to do. I was filled with pride, without qualification, without remorse, without shame, without question. And yet, I was the same person I'd been three days ago. So what was different?

I was seventh to be returned to the group's base camp. Everyone was commiserating about their time alone in the woods. Aaron joked about how, against the rules, he'd wandered away from his site and found Mark. He begged us not to tell Merrill and Pedro when they returned with the last of the bunch. Others mentioned seeing moose and hearing coyote. Some described hallucinations. No one had encountered a bear.

Merrill and Pedro prepared a bigger than normal dinner that evening, which we'd have around a campfire as we debriefed about our solos. We were each to describe in detail a moment on our solo that changed us.

As we made our way around from one to the next, I looked at everyone's faces, glowing orange, in between shadows, reflecting the fire's dancing flames. People shared intimate stories about their paths of recovery, or forgiveness, or moving forward. One said he was going to reconcile with a sibling. Another talked about needing to give up using drugs. They were moving stories, and the group was incredibly supportive.

By the time it was my turn, I was enveloped by everyone's stories of courage and hope. I felt compelled to tell my truth, out loud, to this group of people who had gotten to know me for several days before the solo, and to whom I wanted to prove that I was the same after it. Maybe I needed to prove it to myself. I picked up my journal and read to them a letter I'd written to them at some point in my nearly seventy-two hours of solitude. As I began to read the letter aloud, my voice shook, and cracked. Tears dropped onto the page, making my inked words blurry. As I continued, a few of the guys got up and walked behind me. One of them began rubbing my back in reassuring circles, encouraging me to continue.

I told them about my self-hatred, and the torturous ways I'd been treating myself for the last two years. I told them why I hated myself. I told them I was gay, and hoped that wouldn't change anything. "I don't want you to hate me just because I'm gay," I said. "I'm still the same guy you got to know before the solo." I wanted to prove to them that I was the same Jon who did rugged things, and helped others, and carried heavy canoes. I wanted them to like me just the same. I supplicated them to accept and embrace me. And at that moment, the entire group, mostly straight guys, made me stand up. They hugged me, one by one, and told me it would be okay. They promised me it would be okay. I listened to their promises next to that burning fire. The acceptance of my Outward Bound comrades, who were once all strangers to me, resonated through me like the wind off Moosehead Lake. It's something I still remember to this day.

■ ■ ■

We'd been on the sailboat for five days when we docked in Camden Harbor. We were there for our day of service, another element of the trip. We hadn't seen civilization or boats or cars or houses for nearly sixteen days. I was at my wits' end.

I had thought the sailing part of the trip would be the best part, but I was wrong. Instead, it was the hardest. The boat we sailed on was really an oversized canoe with a single sail. If there wasn't enough wind, we were forced to row the boat with giant wooden oars. Worse yet, at night, we had to set up a canvas tarp from the bottom of the boat up to the center of the boat to create an enclosure to keep us warm in the still chilly dark. Night after night, setting it up was misery. The ocean water was salty and frigid, which made our hands red and cracked and numb with pain. We would untie the oars that were in the center of the boat and lay them out across the hull. On top of the oars, we laid our thin yoga-like mats, and those were our beds for the entire sailing part of the excursion.

In the front of the boat was what Merrill and Pedro called "the head," a small wooden structure underneath which was a yellow bucket. If you had to go number two, you had to go in the yellow bucket in front of everyone. When we sailed out of the harbors from island to island, it was someone's job to dump the bucket off the side of the boat. We weren't allowed to dump in the harbors for pollution reasons. I did my best to hold it as long as I could.

If the sailing part of Outward Bound was bad on sunny days, it was much worse when it rained. I don't think I was dry or warm until we finally landed at that harbor where we were doing service, and the sun was out. I was so excited to have a real bathroom to use. To sit on a real toilet and use real toilet paper—who knew this could be thrilling?

The plan was for us to go to Camden high school to play with children who had intellectual disabilities while their parents attended a conference. Our job was to entertain the children and play with them in the gym. It was a rewarding day of service, but the best part was having the ability to eat in the cafeteria. Since I'd developed my eating disorder, one of my staples had become any kind of cereal with zero fat and skim milk. It's all I'd been craving since starting the excursion—that and dill pickles. So at lunch, I ate two bowls of Special K with skim milk. It was as delicious as I remembered. And I felt only minimal guilt. I was getting used to the idea of nourishing myself—well, within reason. I wasn't anywhere near up to indulging in the sandwiches, lasagna, cheeseburgers, and chocolate cake the others were scarfing down.

While everyone stayed at the table to finish lunch, I excused myself to go to the bathroom downstairs. Once down there, I noticed a payphone. As I relieved myself in the men's room, I wondered if I could sneak in a call to my mom, whom I'd missed so much. I wanted to tell her I'd made it so far. I wondered for a moment whether I'd already done enough. *Should I call her and have her come get me?* The idea of getting back on that oversized canoe to sleep in the chilling temperatures at night on oars, and to have to take another shit in that horrible bucket with nine pairs of eyes watching me . . . hadn't I been humiliated enough? Hadn't I proven that I'd conquered so many of my fears, even telling the group that I was gay? And they didn't hate me. They didn't shun me the way I thought they would. *Now's my chance.*

I picked up the payphone and dialed home using our calling card number, which I'd memorized since high school. Mom answered the phone, "Hello?" Her voice sounded like heaven to me. "Mom, it's me! I'm in Camden on the day of service and I'm not supposed to be calling you, but I wanted to tell you that I love you and I've made it." But then there was another "Hello," in my dad's voice. He'd picked up another extension. My heart sank. "Jon, is that you?" I imagined he was on the phone in their master bedroom, and Mom was probably all the way down on the first floor by herself, watching television.

"Yes, it's me, Dad."

"What are you doing? Where are you? Are you okay?"

"Yes, I'm fine," I told him. "It's been a huge challenge, but I've made it through so much. I think I'm ready to come home. I don't know if I can get on that boat for another five days."

"But Jon, you're only a few days away from finishing," Mom interjected. "Keep going. You can do this!" Dad cleared his throat and interrupted Mom.

"We'll come get you, Jon," he said. "I've been worried about you, not knowing where you are in the middle of the woods. This has been agonizing. I'll send a helicopter up there to get you if I have to. You've made it farther than I ever would. You've been more of a man than I ever could have been on that crazy trip." *Did he just say that?* I wondered. *Did I hear that right?*

"No," I insisted, "Mom's right. I can finish this. It's going to be hard, but I can do it. I'll see you in a few days in Rockland. Can you bring me Special K and skim milk and maybe my favorite Vlassic pickles? I love you, Mom."

I slammed the phone down on its receiver. Dad's words repeated in my head, sending a jolt of adrenaline through my veins. Had I really become the man he always wanted me to be? Whatever he meant by those words, they gave me the strength to stomach five more days on that boat—five more days of pooping in that yellow bucket; five more days of my bloodied, cracking, red hands; five more days of jumping in the polar-like Maine ocean every morning. And five more days of showing myself, and perhaps my father, too, that I was more of a man than either of us had ever thought I was, or could be.

✳

Chapter 15

Letter from "the Castle"

After Outward Bound, my mom came to me worried. I think we all thought that I'd return from the woods and ocean of Maine a different person. And though I had been moved by the experience, depression still seemed to be sticking to me like a creepy crawler on a wall. It clung to my insides. She asked me what was going on with me, and during a walk around our neighborhood, I told her the truth. "I think I'm gay, Mom," I said. "I don't want to be. I've tried not to be. But I can't help it." My mother burst into tears. She cried and cried. After a while, she stopped and turned to me. "Are you sure? Well," she said, "I don't completely understand it, but I will never stop trying to. I promise you that." She said she loved me no matter what, but asked me to promise her one thing: "Never tell your father. Just promise me you'll never tell your father."

■ ■ ■

Outward Bound had indeed changed me. Although I was still unsure of my future, it instilled in me a kind of confidence I never knew I could muster. Having conquered that three-week challenge in the summer after my freshman year, I felt I was ready for another challenge: my first trip overseas. After three weeks of survival training in the Maine wilderness, I figured traveling to Europe for Emerson's study aboard program in Holland would be a cakewalk.

And so, in the fall of 1996, I found myself about to board a chartered bus from Emerson in the Back Bay for Logan Airport. You'd think my roughing it in the woods for three weeks with the contents of just one backpack would have influenced my packing choices, but apparently that was one area in which Outward Bound hadn't rubbed off on me. I overpacked and wasn't allowed to take it all with me. I was a clotheshorse, after all.

"What do I do, Mom?" I asked, panicking.

"You've got to figure it out for yourself, Jon," my mother said. "You're a big boy!"

I frantically stuffed my small roll-neck sweaters and size 28 corduroys from my second bag into the massive hockey bag that had already been swollen to capacity. Packing for an entire fall and winter away in Europe was a very stressful challenge for me. So many different fashions to consider! But something else was probably at the root of my meltdown: I was anxious about leaving Mom alone with Dad, and being on my own so far away from her for the first time in my life. So much farther than even the woods of Maine.

When it was time to go, I held on to Mom for several minutes. I kissed her good-bye and handed her a bag of the extra clothes I was leaving behind.

The flight was long, but the excitement kept me awake. So did the heavy cigarette smoke in the back of the plane where my seventy fellow classmates and I sat on our way to the medieval castle Emerson owned and operated in Holland.

When we finally arrived, I found I was mesmerized by Kasteel Well (Castle Well). It was magnificent—this huge, ancient edifice of brick and stone, protected by two moats, complete with lily pads. Its towers stood proud and tall. The grounds were green and lush, tended by gardeners and historians dedicated to preserving the Castle's splendor. The interior was worn, with cracking walls and creaking floors. It was surreal—a time warp. The place held the spirits of centuries of inhabitants and visitors, some of them major figures in history, including Napoleon, we were told. Chandeliers hung from the vaulted ceilings. Winding staircases seemed to appear at the end of every corridor, leading you to five floors of guest rooms. In these rooms, for four months, the Emerson students would sleep and dream about their adventures, as they studied abroad in Well, The Netherlands.

The place was affectionately known among those fortunate students as "the Castle." It was nestled in a small farming village near the Holland–Germany border. With nowhere else to easily get to, we were left to make our own entertainment inside the Castle. We'd have poetry slams in the wee hours of the morning or talent shows in the middle of the day. You'd always hear amazing stories back on the Boston campus about people's adventures outside of the castle, too— such as hopping a bus from Well to Nijmegen, Venlo, or Venray for a day of visiting coffee shops, bars, and theaters.

Strange things happened inside the Castle. Some spoke of ghost activity—books flying off desks in the middle of the night, lights flickering on and off. I never saw Sophie's actual silhouette in the room called Sophie's Lounge—my favorite room—but I am sure I felt her presence at the Castle, especially there in the room where she was said to have been hanged.

Sophie's Lounge was a grand room with some sort of special energy to it that seemed to bounce from wall to wall. Maybe it was Sophie's spirit. In the middle of the wide-paneled old hardwood floor sat two big sofas, two wingback chairs, and some ottomans. In another corner of the majestic room, a grand piano sprawled the entire length of one of the walls. When music filled the building, it was easy to imagine you were living in the Renaissance. The walls had moldings and designs you'd only expect to see in the palaces of England. At times it was hard to believe that what you were seeing was real, that living in the Castle was just another part of the curriculum.

Emotions at the Castle were acute and boundless. You heard someone crying to a Mozart symphony coming from the stereo in the Vigil Lounge. There was hysterical laughter at two in the morning. And when feelings of love arose at the Castle, there was no escaping them. It was the essence of romance there. It was easy for many of my classmates to fall in love—sometimes with people who weren't in love with them, which led to much writing of poetry in journals about love and sex.

While my friends and classmates were taking chances with their hearts and their bodies, not to mention legal-in-Holland marijuana, I remained abstinent and chaste. There was no one there to whom I was drawn, but even if I had been, I wouldn't have allowed myself to indulge and relish in any kind of romance. I was distracted by my obsession, my addiction to running and starving, which still lingered. Although I'd drawn strength from coming out to my Outward Bound comrades, I still lacked the courage to tell my father. It was a huge hurdle and obstacle for me. Knowing my sexuality was still a secret to him and believing that my father would reject me if he found out made me very apprehensive about getting involved with anyone.

Back at Emerson during my second semester, freshman year, I had tried to be in a relationship with Enrique, that gorgeous, brown-eyed, Spanish tenor from the *New Student Review*. When he told me how much he liked me and gave me a thoughtful, well-crafted mix tape, I pushed him away. I regretted that decision often when I felt alone and depressed at the Castle, and I'd call him to tell him so from the tiny pay phone room in one of the winding staircases. I was too late; he'd already moved on.

Despite my loneliness, I managed to make the most of my semester at the Castle. It gave me the opportunity to travel. Monday through Thursday, we had classes, taught by professors who'd traveled to the Castle from all across central Europe. Then Thursday night, after school, my friends and I would board trains for Copenhagen, Rome, Prague, Paris, Madrid, Budapest, and the other cities I'd previously only dreamed of visiting. We'd awake each Friday morning in a different sprawling train station with arched ceilings, in a new city in another part of the world. Cathedrals, towers, rivers, mountains, museums, paintings, and sculptures we'd only read about in textbooks came to vivid, three-dimensional life. There I was, visiting Big Ben, the Baltic Sea, the Swiss Alps, the Mediterranean, the Sagrada

Familia, the *Mona Lisa,* Michelangelo's *David,* Van Gogh's *Starry Night.* The Eurail became our moving hostel. *This is unreal,* I said to myself at every sight. The world suddenly became a much more interesting place, a richer fabric of people and places compared to homogenous Andover and even once-exotic Emerson.

No matter where I'd decide to go, it would be somewhere I'd never been before. And I was doing things I'd never done before—in Budapest, for instance, getting wasted on wine and walking the foreign streets into a Puccini opera for only seven dollars. *Where am I? I wondered. Who am I?* But I now felt more like me than I'd ever felt before. I wondered, *Could I finally be exactly who I was meant to be?*

Even though in Europe I tended to get tipsy more often—tipsier than I ever had before—I deliberately never allowed myself to get drunk enough to act on the desire to go home with a random stranger or a guy from a club. Only twice I allowed myself to walk into gay discos, and I convinced myself that I was more interested in the music and the dancing than the guys. In retrospect, it would've been wonderful to allow myself the freedom to be who I was not only inwardly but outwardly. But I couldn't let go of the hope that I could still change the compass inside my belly and become the man my dad wanted me to be.

I did get tipsy enough, though, to let more fatty and fattening foods past my lips than I normally would have. This happened mostly when I'd had a little too much Amstel beer. Ironically, beer and wine were probably adding to my caloric intake, but I was obsessed specifically with fat grams, not calories. I didn't know a lot about calories. In hindsight, considering my consumption of zero fat and very little food in general, I was probably taking in no more than 1,000 or so calories each day. I had no idea that a glass of wine or two got me substantially on the way to my usual daily total.

There were consequences. I'd wake up the next morning feeling as guilty as I did when I kissed a boy. That guilt led me to find the bike path along the winding river that passed the village of Well. It went on for miles. As I ran, huge, flat barges would sail by me carrying train cars or cranes or other machinery. Miles and miles of farms with evergreen grass rolled along the river, pastures dotted with cows made the run smell of manure. I got used to it.

On those mornings after, I'd also pop fat burners. Fearing the food at the Castle would be traditional European fatty fare, and knowing I would be traveling to other cities with many culinary temptations, I'd had the foresight to pack several large bottles of them.

Keeping up with the long runs was tough, and taking fat burners was a chore because they were so hard to swallow, but I didn't have a choice. I wasn't yet in control. Something else in my brain was.

Aside from the occasional buzzed indulgence, the food in Europe was completely wasted on me. As students we were offered three meals a day that we ate in the Castle's dungeon, each catered by a celebrated local hotel and restaurant, De Grote Waay. And our weekend travels allowed us legendary delicacies in one city and then another. My classmates were in heaven, from one meal to the next, but eating with people—let alone eating in general—was an even worse nightmare for me in Europe than it had been at home. Main courses at the Castle consisted of fried cheese puff pastries oozing with melted Velveeta-looking cheese when you broke into them. Students devoured Nutella and peanut butter sandwiches, one after another. Breakfasts overflowed with pastries, hard-boiled eggs, meats, and jams. They didn't have skim milk, they had *extra-fat milk*; it was thicker than any cream I'd seen in the States.

Meal times scared me and I did what I could do avoid them. But I was being watched by my roommates, Tom and Michael. They'd both seen me struggle with my eating and running back in Boston, so they were on high alert. "Time for dinner, Jon," Tom would encourage me. I was also being watched by Helga, the Dutch woman who lived with us. She had an apartment right over the Castle's main archway, and she was like a mother to all of us—from the moment we arrived at the Brussels airport until the moment we boarded our planes to go back home to Boston. Helga was something of a legend among Emerson students. We'd all heard of her long before arriving at the Castle. I'd imagined her looking like a typical Dutch woman, complete with clogs and a knee-length skirt with matching apron. Instead, she was stylish, wearing fitted jeans, flowing roll-neck sweaters, and funky boots. She was tall and full-figured, radiant and plump. Her hair was dark and straight with severe bangs cut just above her eyebrows. She laughed loudly and smiled often, revealing dimples.

Over time, Helga and I found ourselves growing close. We played pool at the Vink, the local café where the students spent most of their time and money on sweet Holland beer and greasy fries, or *frites*. It was with Helga that I most often found myself eating fatty foods.

■ ■ ■

Early on, a bunch of us decided we'd go to London for an upcoming weekend. Tom and Michael would come along with a few other kids from the Castle. Some of us theater geeks wanted to get to the West End in London, and I always wanted to see where the Queen lived.

Seeing Big Ben and Parliament and Buckingham Palace was surreal. Then we walked to Westminster Abbey. Inside the massive church we heard a choir practicing. It was so moving. Tom, lover of musical theater, nursery rhymes, and fairytales, wanted to go to Kensington Gardens to see the statue of Peter Pan. Something came over me. I was overwhelmed—so moved by everything I'd seen so far, and so grateful for the opportunity to be there. I was happy, but also solemn. I felt compelled to sit down, pull my journal from my backpack, and write the way I had during Outward Bound. This time, I wasn't writing to come out to my friends. I felt I needed to tell my father the truth. Underneath the statue of Peter Pan, I sat down and began to write him a letter.

As I sat there, I played my mother's words over and over in my mind. "Never tell your father. . . ." But for some reason, I needed to tell him. I knew in my heart that he would reject me, but I guess I also hoped my father, the man I was supposed to look up to as a hero, would come through and save me. I thought blood had to be stronger than his biases against anything I could tell him about myself. I also knew that after surviving Outward Bound, no matter how bad my dad's reaction would be, I could survive it, too.

Under the statue of Peter Pan, writing down my truth and losing whatever innocence I had left, I explained to my father in seven pages why I'd contemplated suicide, why I'd starved myself, and why I wanted to disappear.

Over the next several weeks, I rewrote the letter many times. But then, in Barcelona, after traveling to Olympic Park and being inspired by the beauty and by what had gone on there, I found the courage to actually mail it. My mother had warned me. My sister and brother had both warned me when I called them from the Castle to talk about this. But I didn't listen. I couldn't live with the lie. Despite their contention that Dad wouldn't handle it, I needed to tell him. The prospect of living without my father was better than the prospect of living a lie. I licked the foreign stamps and placed enough of them on the envelope to carry it across the Atlantic Ocean and into the mailbox at Crescent Circle. I knew that letting the letter go into the mail slot at the post office was going to change my life, but it was essential. I let my confession slip out of my hand and into the slot. And with that, there was no turning back.

■ ■ ■

A few weeks later, in early December, when frost appeared regularly on the Castle's lawn, I called my sister to see if she knew whether my father had gotten the letter. There was a long pause. "Yes, Jon, he did get it," she said, glumly. "He opened it and . . . he stopped reading it after a few sentences. He said he knew where it was going, and he was disgusted." He apparently carried on, calling me a coward for not telling him in person. My sister asked what he would have done if I had indeed told him in person. "I'd probably throw him out the window," he told her.

"I guess it was pretty smart of you to tell him with an ocean between you," she said.

The news of my father not even reading my letter through—the letter in which I poured out my feelings and bared my soul about my struggle with my sexual orientation—exacerbated my feelings of self-hatred. I found myself wondering, *Am I not even worthy of his reading my letter?*

With that news, the final days at the Castle were ruined. I called my mom. "I knew he would react that way," she said. "This was why I didn't want you telling him—I didn't want you to be disappointed." She was heartbroken. I was too. I descended into a dark place, a depression the likes of which I hadn't experienced since leaving Bates in 1994.

On one of the final nights at the Castle, the night we were to have our group photograph taken, I hid in my room and took dozens of fat burners. In slow motion, I took one at a time with water, swallowing each one of the large pills until the bottle was gone. I didn't know what would happen to me if I took that many, but part of me was curious and didn't care about the dangers. I wandered out of the Castle and down to the river by myself. I'd later find out that Michael searched the entire castle for me so that I could be in the picture, but I was nowhere to be found.

I sat on the river's bank contemplating whether I should just walk into it and drown. The rejection from my father, although predictable, still hurt more than any physical pain I had experienced in the past. None of my broken bones on the football field were a match for this pain. Any hope I'd had that my father would welcome me home with open arms as a young, gay man was shattered. What I'd feared my entire life had come to fruition. I assumed my father saw me as so repellent that, in the way I'd once been banished to my room for hours without food, I'd now be banished from our home, forever. I wondered whether walking into the river would be easier, simpler, not only for me, but for Mom, Jared, Julie—and most of all, my dad. *Would I have to make the ultimate sacrifice of myself to make everyone else's lives easier?* I wondered. Under the dark Holland sky, the river rushing by me, fresh manure in the air, I sat and wondered beneath the stars.

■ ■ ■

What saved me was Dad's thick layer of denial. Saying he didn't read my letter past the first few sentences meant, technically, he was never told I was gay. Therefore my coming out to him never happened. His denial was just that—a powerful defense mechanism. Anything could be swept under the rug, like his knocking the front door off its hinges, or anything else for that matter. Our family's rugs were forming mountains beneath them. But if it weren't for my father's willful denial, I wouldn't have been able to return home at the end of my semester at the Castle.

I had no idea how he'd greet me. I was scared. It helped that I didn't show up alone. One of my two roommates, Michael, wasn't able to get all the way home to Dallas on the same day we were to arrive home to Boston. I called my mom and asked if Michael could come stay at our house for a little bit before he went home to Texas. In hindsight, I think it may have also been a self-preservation tactic to have someone there so my dad couldn't flip out on me. It was a way to test the waters and ease into being around him following his reaction to my letter. For much of the two weeks before I was to return to Emerson for the spring semester, Michael was my human shield.

While I was beginning to admit my homosexuality to myself and to others, my father's rejection allowed me, at times, to claim to just be confused or asexual. Other than Paul, and a few hookups here and there, I'd really never been in a homosexual relationship of any duration. Girls at the Castle wanted to hook up with me, and I'd thought about it. Michael and I even tried to have a threesome (or a two-on-one really; Michael was straight and I wasn't interested in hooking up with him) one night with Amanda, a girl who'd been begging to hook up with both of us the entire semester. Michael, being the good friend and roommate that he was, wanted to help me figure things out. So he arranged for the three of us to try one night in our room. But when I saw Amanda's breasts in front of me, I had strong gut repulsion. I ran out of the room as fast as I could.

After Michael left my family's house for Dallas, I still had a few days before returning to school, and I pretty much spent every moment at Samantha's house or Charlie's or Meredith's. I did what I could to avoid my dad, and he did the same with me. We barely even said hello or good-bye, and when he did, he could hardly lay his eyes on me. We just co-existed. And while I struggled with knowing that deep down he knew the truth and that the worst was yet to come, he was living in complete and utter denial that his youngest son, tortured and tormented for so long, was dying inside just because he was gay.

✳

Chapter 16

Laxatives, and the Moment of Truth

The semester before I left for the Castle, a guy in my Intro to Psych class piqued my interest. At first I noticed Andy because of what he wore to class—when he showed up. He had an intriguing style that combined things like ragged boot-cut corduroys with a hip, high-end, tight black leather jacket. His russet brown hair, parted in the middle, long enough to frame his face, was the perfect contrast to his blue eyes—eyes that usually spent most of class fixed on the ceiling. He was skinny—*skinnier than I am,* I lamented—and walked like a high fashion model, but those more feminine characteristics were counterbalanced by his pronounced Adam's apple. It was confusing, and in trying to make sense of it, I became fixated on Andy. One day in class I tried to get him to see me, too.

"Hey, nice boots," I said.

"Thanks," he responded, sounding annoyed and rolling his eyes before walking back to his seat in the back of the class, where he tried to be unnoticed by the professor.

He probably thought I was annoying because I'd taken to psychology and I participated in class. You know the type, the one always raising his hand to get the professor's attention. That was me. When I wasn't answering the professor's questions, I'd look back at Andy, especially during films that the professor showed. He'd always be writing in some book that looked like one of my journals. I was dying for him to look at me, but he never looked up.

At the end of the semester, during our final class, I got up the nerve to ask the girl who always sat next to Andy, "Hey, are you . . . or is Andy going to the Castle?" He wasn't, so I had to let my crush simmer for the year. I probably wouldn't have done anything about it anyway.

When I returned from the Castle for the second semester of my sophomore year, in January 1997, I felt as if my experiences there had ripened me a bit. Just as all the students who had gone to the Castle before us had promised, I'd returned stateside a more evolved young man. At least that's what I'd hoped. My crush on Andy hadn't disappeared, and I felt ready now, and was eager to find out whether it could actually turn into something. I looked everywhere for Andy. I'd see him standing, smoking a cigarette at the front stoop of 100 Beacon Street, his dormitory. I'd see him at Zero Marlborough, the Back Bay side of campus's café, getting a diet soda. It seemed he barely remembered me from psych class. He was aloof, at best.

Then one night I was with a few girlfriends in the dining hall in the new Little Building at 80 Boylston Street on the other side of campus next to the Boston Common. The cafeteria had a series of booths on one side of the room and a slew of four-tops in the middle of the room. Suddenly, Andy approached our booth under a bright iridescent light and slapped down a flier. It advertised a protest against the *Berkeley Beacon,* Emerson's newspaper, for running a photo depicting gay marriage in a negative way. "This one's just for you," he said as he slid it across the table with his hand and let it go in front of me. I was stunned.

What was on the front of the flier may have been provocative, but what was on the back shocked me: he'd written his dorm room phone number. *Oh my God!* I thought, trying not to let on how excited I was. After he walked away and was out of earshot, my girlfriends at the table squealed, "What are you going to do? He's so cute!"

"He is cute, isn't he?" I heard myself say, not really believing those words had come out of my mouth—out loud. Through the period I preferred to think of as one of "confusion," I didn't comment on guys much. I continued to try to appear ambiguous, at least for my father's sake. I thought that if I didn't talk about it much out loud, then maybe there was still a chance I could fall for a woman. But it was getting harder not to act on my urges. "I guess I'll call him," I said. "He's too cute to let slip away." I ended up allowing myself to fall for Andy. *I guess the Castle did change me,* I thought to myself.

Andy wasn't like the other guys I had been attracted to in the past. First and foremost, he was available. Also, he was an activist. He was the head of EAGLE (Emerson's Alliance of Gays, Lesbians, and Everyone), he helped run Boston's Pride Parade, and he was an advocate for equal rights and treatment for gays and lesbians. He was a true leader, but about things my dad wouldn't have approved of, things I didn't yet approve of. It made me nervous that he was so involved in the gay community, but I was also drawn to it. I was jealous of his ability to be so open about his sexual orientation. I'd seen him holding hands with his ex-boyfriend a couple of semesters before, near 100 Beacon. I told him, on our first date, that I'd never hold his hand in public. He asked me why and I told him that I didn't believe in "flaunting" my sexuality.

Over time, my relationship with Andy grew to be like the tide on Cisco Beach in Nantucket, where I first learned to body surf as a kid. It was beautiful and breathtaking at times, flowing in with huge waves of passion tumbling against the sand. It was strong and overwhelming, but the undertow and riptide were fierce and drowning. The ebbs and flows were exhausting, mostly for Andy, I'm sure.

The relationship started getting serious at the beginning of the summer, coincidentally just when I needed to find an apartment. I was anticipating being completely excommunicated by my father. Logically, I was sure it was coming; *it would only be a matter of time,* I theorized. He was notorious for pulling the plug on funding for college if you screwed up. He'd done it to my sister a couple of times— once for getting a C and another time because she moved in with her long-term boyfriend, whom my father called a "hoodlum." Worse still, to him, they weren't married, so he didn't talk to Julie for months. He'd also threatened to pull Jared out of Rollins if he didn't maintain a certain batting average, or if he struck out too many times. Being gay was my big screw-up.

Even though Dad said he never read my letter from the Castle, I had a sinking suspicion that he had. Maybe not when I sent it, but eventually. He made it clear that he didn't like who I was becoming, just by the disdainful way he looked at me the few times I saw him after I'd returned from the Castle. I made sure it was obvious I was becoming someone different, returning from Holland with my hair flowing nearly to my shoulders, hoop earrings in both ears, and a hemp necklace around my neck. It was a huge risk, but one I needed to take. I got in trouble for all of it, mostly through his usual mode of telling me that only losers have long hair and earrings. Other than that, Dad didn't talk too much that unbearable time that I was home, let alone even look at me. When he did, you could just see the disgust in his expression, the same look he wore years before, when I told him I liked to wear girl clothes in preschool. Even though he was giving me the silent treatment, I heard him loud and clear. I was certain he'd completely lose it eventually and cut me off altogether.

During my time at Emerson that semester, I avoided calling the house when I knew he was home. And I didn't visit at all. Instead, Mom would come to the city to visit me. We'd have coffee or simply sit on a bench in the Boston Public Garden together. While she'd smoke cigarettes and I'd sip my diet soda, Mom and I would have intimate conversations about my emerging sexual orientation. As I tried to learn to accept it within myself, still a deeply challenging struggle, she tried to learn to accept it. I later learned from Julie that, unbeknownst to me, Mom attended Parents, Families, and Friends of Lesbians and Gays (PFLAG) meetings. She tried to persuade my father to try to understand and to accept me, but instead he sent messages to me through her indicating he wasn't interested. He was in denial and remained staunch in his insistence that no son of his was gay. It was as if she were an envoy between two conflicting nations. He only wanted to know how I was going to change it—to make it not so. He wanted me to turn to the church. He wanted me to turn to doctors, psychologists. All with the purpose to change me. To him, if it was true, then I was a deviant, a derelict, a sinner, just like the men he'd described to me in San Francisco.

My father's disapproval was branded in my mind and haunted me twenty-four hours a day, seven days a week. I thought about him when I went to sleep, and when I woke up in the middle of the night, my stomach clenched and my shoulders tightened. I was petrified he would see me walking to dinner with Andy. I worried about him showing up, out of the blue, despite his lack of interest in my life at Emerson, just to make sure I knew he didn't accept who I was. I worried he'd call me names in front of everyone and disown me. My anxiety was at an all-time high. I wasn't sure I could make it on my own. He was good at making us all feel like we couldn't survive without him, even though he'd never been there for us, emotionally. Ironically, we all fantasized about life without him, but were afraid of it, too.

That's why I didn't tell my mom about Andy. It was one of the only secrets I'd ever kept from her. I was afraid of giving her information that would get her into trouble with my father. I was scared of him finding out through her. And then who knew what he'd do to either of us.

To deal with my fear of being around my father when I was growing up, I would try to appease him; now my strategy was to keep my distance from him and from home. Maybe the self-preservation skills I had learned at Outward Bound and the experiences at the Castle were sinking in. Maybe I was beginning to take care of myself by staying away.

Since I believed Dad would cut me off as soon as he understood that I really was gay, and that I couldn't change, I decided to get to a place where I didn't need to rely on his support or his money. I took eight classes in just two short summer terms, which gave me the excuse to have to get an apartment in the city. I'd gotten a job at the Continuing Education office at Emerson when I decided to take the eight courses. *Yes, eight, you can do it,* I told myself. That meant I'd graduate from Emerson in three years instead of four. Between my honors program scholarship and working at the Continuing Ed office, I was able to pay for all those summer classes. Mom committed to getting me the rent money, and since I was still barely eating at the time, I wasn't spending much on food.

I found an apartment on Beacon Street—a studio with a loft at the top of an old, decrepit five-story brownstone in the Back Bay. The bathroom sink's drain was rusty with age and neglect, and the tile floor in the kitchen was cracked, but it was more spacious than anything else I'd seen. The loft had dingy wooden slats that overlooked the main living space and a plywood floor, but it could fit two beds so it was perfect for two people. If I could find a roommate, my rent would only be $450 a month, and Mom promised to help. It was cheaper than room and board at Emerson, and I could stay there not just for the summer but until I would graduate the coming May.

At the same time, I made the decision to take on a psychology minor. My psychology professor from Psych 101, Dr. Feinberg, had pulled me aside after our last class and told me that I had a gift for writing and for understanding human behavior. She had encouraged me to keep taking psychology courses and to consider a minor. I took four different psychology courses that summer.

One of them was with Dr. Carbalatto, the chairman of the department. Dr. Carbalatto was a short, older Italian man who wore tailored pinstripe suits and iridescent ties with Windsor knots to class every day. He had a full head of gray hair, slicked back with lotion, and thick hands that he used when he talked. He reminded me of my dad's dad, my Grampy Emilio. I was scared to meet Dr. Carbalatto at first because I'd heard he was demanding and assumed that, like my Italian dad, he'd hate me because I was gay. But after a couple of classes, I saw a softness about him that drew me in. He had a wonderful sincerity, an empathy evident in just his expression, even at first glance. The wrinkles on his face told a long history of experience. *He's seen it all,* I thought, and I grew to feel as if his acceptance of me would be unconditional.

It helped, too, that he was slowing down a bit. I later learned that he had congestive heart failure, which would explain his frailty. He relaxed with age, the way everyone always said my father would, but never did. Dr. Carbalatto's mind, however, was strong. He knew theory inside and out. He pontificated about deep questions and he worried about human suffering. He loved reading our papers and he said they made him smarter. He said he learned something new from every student paper he read and that they kept his mind sharp and engaged.

I started to relate my own life and my own upbringing to what we'd discuss in class. Understanding psychology, understanding human behavior helped me to understand myself.

With Mom's support, I'd also been seeing a therapist once a week in Boston. Katherine's office was a few blocks from the apartment on Beacon Street. She witnessed my self-loathing for being gay and many relapses of the cycle of bingeing, purging, starving, and punitive jogging. I now really wanted to get better so I let her see it all.

Being in psychology classes while I was in therapy was an important intersection for me. The theories I learned in the classroom would sometime spill over into the work Katherine was doing with me. It gave me insight that I'm not sure I would have otherwise gained. I could now look into the future and imagine myself worrying about something other than getting fat or being despised just because of my sexual orientation. It was far off in the distance, but I could at least see it on the horizon.

■ ■ ■

I now needed that roommate to help with the rent, and Andy just happened to be taking classes that summer, too, and he needed a place to stay. Moving in together seemed like the easiest solution. That's how I presented it to him and how I justified it to myself—as a solution. I needed a roommate and the most convenient roommate just happened to be the guy I was sort of dating. Since the loft in the apartment was big enough for two double beds, I invited him in as long as he understood he'd have to have his own side of the sleeping loft. I didn't want any of my family or friends to suspect that we were *living together,* living in Catholic sin, that is. Even though I had created distance from my father, I still feared him and struggled against his omniscient presence in my battered head. If I kept Andy a secret, then maybe I could keep my homosexuality at bay, even though it was getting harder and harder to do so. It must have crushed Andy's heart to have to be a secret.

Living together, nonetheless, revealed things that I didn't necessarily care to see about Andy and about me. I now understood why he was so skinny. He ate less than I did, and he ran almost as much. Oftentimes, we fed off each other instead of feeding off real food. There was a subliminal competition that happened between us—who could go the longest without eating, who could run more miles. Other times, however, at moments of celebration and passion, we'd indulge in a good meal, a bottle of wine, and sex. Afterward, I'd ask him to leave my bed and go to his own. Pathetically, even though we were in our private cocoon in the apartment, I never stopped being petrified my father would find out, or worse yet, that he already knew.

On one of those nights of fervor, while kissing passionately on my bed, a family photo that I kept near my bed crashed to the floor. I seized. Instantly, convinced that it was God (or my father, telepathically) crashing it down to the ground in disapproval, I pulled away from Andy. I demanded he go to his own bed. He slowly dragged himself out of my bed, respectfully obliging, but also with remorse and sadness. I lay awake on my back, with my hands folded across my chest in the prayer position, horrified about what I had done with Andy. Then I freaked out about what we had eaten beforehand. I prayed all night for forgiveness until the darkness in the skylight above my bed started to turn to light blue from the rising sun.

This disequilibrium in our relationship went on for weeks. Without fail, the next morning I'd hate myself for eating more food than I really wanted to, and both of us, for having sex. I'd punish myself and Andy for it. I'd ignore him or pick fights for stupid things and I'd try to purge the calories I'd eaten the night before by running longer and longer.

Then I discovered something new: I found a box of laxatives that Andy kept in our medicine cabinet. I read the directions on the box and popped a couple in my mouth. Quickly I became hooked on this new way to try to disappear.

Even though I liked Andy, I secretly hated him, and who we were together in that apartment. I was no longer the only target for my homophobia. Andy was, too. I know I hurt Andy and he resented me for it. And I resented him for being so free and positive about his gayness, but at the same time I was attracted to him for that. Living together made it worse. Every morning when I woke up, everywhere I'd go, I'd see the "sin" right in front of me and all around me.

As time went on, the resentment outweighed the attraction and I fell out of love. *I want to be in love with him,* I thought. I wanted to make it work almost as much as I wanted to make it work with Sophia in high school. I'd invite him into my bed to try one more time, but I'd always end up kicking him out. Even though we were clearly in some sort of relationship, I never liked to admit it to anyone. I kept Andy away from my friends in the English Family. Andy knew this and would ask me why I wouldn't invite him to parties at Boston College or Providence, where my friends went to school. The truth was, I was embarrassed, not so much by Andy, but that I was engaging in this kind of lifestyle. The moving forward and pulling back went on and on for months.

We went forward and backward until Andy went to an LGBT advocacy group summer party in Cape Cod and met a nice, young, well-adjusted gay guy named Josh. I wasn't supposed to find out about Josh. I accidentally learned about him when one of Andy's friends left a congratulations message on our answering machine in the apartment. Instantly, I was engulfed with jealousy, even though I realized I had no right to tell him who he could or could not date since I always said that we weren't really together. I wonder if I would have felt jealous if we weren't living in the same apartment together.

Then one night Andy went out on a date with Josh. He came home later just to pack a bag so he could spend the night with him. I didn't say anything and lay in my bed alone, feeling dejected and desolate. I was so alone and scared that I was letting this wonderful man, who cared so much about me, out of my sight and out of my life. When the door closed and he locked it, I could hear the jagged key slide out of the hole in the lock. I hated what I was feeling inside, I didn't know what to do with myself except scream into my pillow and cry. Then, suddenly, I knew what I had to do. I got up and even though I hadn't eaten much that day, I took a handful of laxatives.

I had already been taking several laxatives a day, but never a handful all at once. I had been quite sick that summer. My kidneys ached constantly. I was urinating blood on a regular basis, all while running miles a day and taking multiple classes. But as I took more and more laxatives, they became less and less effective. I was sure I was gaining weight, so I would binge and then use the laxatives, exacerbating my bulimic state. My face was bloated and puffy. My hair was long and tangled. I wore clothes that were messy and too big for me to hide my ailing body underneath. I felt crazy at times. I'd watch the other kids in the dining hall eating chicken fingers and fries and taking pieces of greasy pizza from the pizza trays without a care in the world. They stuffed ice cream sandwich after ice cream sandwich down their throats and washed them down with whole chocolate milk. I was furious at the injustice. While kids were out buying groceries and treats for their dorm rooms, I was hoarding laxatives and fat burners. I was a mess and Andy had reached his limit. One night, he was on the phone with one of his best friends and I heard him call me the "Cancer Kid: He's just so toxic and crazy." When I heard him say that, I lost it. I picked up the other extension. "Do you know what it is like to absolutely hate who you are and hate everything that you are becoming?" I screamed, trying desperately to explain myself to both Andy and his friend. "I fucking hate myself!"

Andy packed his clothes and his stuff in trash bags and left. I waited up for him that night, and the next night, and the night after. He didn't come back for several days.

When he finally did come back to pack up the rest of his stuff and a couple of pieces of furniture, I knew it was over for good. I felt empty and didn't know whether to fill the void by eating everything in sight, or relish the emptiness and eat nothing at all. It was exhausting, all of it, and I hated myself for falling for someone who represented so much of what I hated inside myself. Having his persona in front of me every day made me angrier and angrier that this is what I'd become.

Nobody knew what I was going through. I was alone and wanted to die. After starving myself a couple of days after Andy left, I actually felt hungry. Probably more than anything, I needed something to bring me comfort, to fill my psychic emptiness.

I went to the convenience store close to my apartment and looked for the most fattening foods that I could get my hands on: Ring Dings, potato chips, corn chips, and chocolate chip cookies. I stuffed it all in my backpack, ran to my apartment and up the five flights of stairs, locked the door behind me, and tossed all of the food onto my bed. The array of wrappers and colors and textures was beautiful. One after another, I tore them open, and started to eat. Bite after bite, I must have inhaled hundreds of grams of fat and thousands of calories. The instant pleasure of eating everything brought on a euphoria like I'd felt while having sex. Exhausted from the exercise, I fell to my bed, the sugars going straight to my head. *The fat,* I thought, *is going straight to my belly.*

Suddenly as I lay down, the guilt rushed over me as fast as the sugar high had. The pleasure turned to dirtiness, the euphoria to despair. *I have to get this out of me,* I told myself, but I couldn't make myself throw up. I ran down the stairs of the loft and into the bathroom medicine cabinet and grabbed the box of laxatives. My body had developed a tolerance to them since I'd been using them so much. To get rid of everything I'd binged on, I thought, *I've got to take them all.*

One by one, I swallowed them in a catatonic-like state, six, seven, eight . . . fifteen, sixteen. That was all that was left in the box. I walked upstairs in a daze, dizzy from the sugar and at some level anticipating the misery that would come in a few hours. I crashed onto my bed and fell asleep.

At four in the morning I woke with an agonizing pain in my stomach that radiated all the way into my back. The cramps would come and go at first, but then they just came and stayed. The churning in my belly was epic with a keeling-over kind of pain that I knew would be relieved only by the release that I prayed to God would come soon. I was moaning out loud, but no one was there to hear me. I tried lying on my belly to stifle the pain, then I turned onto my back, but nothing worked. My heart raced, sweat gathered on my forehead. I felt like the flu had descended upon me in an instant.

Then it finally came. I ran to the toilet and the release was exhilarating. But the relief didn't last long. The cramps came back and I began to scream in agony once again. I'd take deep breaths, thinking the air would help make the pain go away. But it didn't stop. I spent the next thirty minutes in the bathroom.

When I was finally able to get up and out of the bathroom, I started to make my way back to the loft and my bed. Wobbling toward the steps, I stopped at the kitchen counter, spinning. I started to see different colors and my head got heavy. Things went dark. I panicked. I felt like I was about to pass out, fading in and out. My heart raced and pounded and I couldn't slow it down. I suddenly felt feverish and broke into a cold sweat. I wondered, *Is this it?* Was this how I was going to die? Alone in my apartment at the mercy of a bunch of little chocolate-flavored tablets? *This can't be happening.* I felt like this was the end, and that's when I realized I didn't want it to be. I freaked out. *I don't want to die.* I fell to the floor on my back. I repeated over and over like a mantra. *I don't want to die.* I crawled over to my desk and reached for the phone. I pressed 9-1-1 and screamed. "My heart is pounding and I am spinning; the room is turning colors!" I yelled at the operator. "I feel like I'm going to pass out. I feel like I'm going to die. Please help me! I don't want to die."

"Calm down, calm down," she said. She wanted me to tell her what happened.

"I took like fifteen or sixteen Dulcolax."

"Okay, Jon, okay. You aren't going to die. They won't kill you. They've made you very, very sick and you are very, very dehydrated. Stay on the line with me. Listen to my voice. Listen to what I'm telling you."

She told me to drink water. I went to the refrigerator and got the plastic gallon jug of water. "Sit down and drink it," she said. "Just drink it all and stay on with me. Stay with me, Jon. You're not alone. Stay with me. . . ."

■ ■ ■

The morning after I overdosed on laxatives, I called Mom and confessed what I'd done. I told her everything—even about Andy. "I really thought I was going to die," I said. "I can't bear the suffering any longer. Enough is enough!"

I didn't want to die. What I really wanted was some peace. Peace within myself, peace within my mind. That night on the phone with the operator, I figured out that there was a difference between the two. When I was faced with the moment where I actually felt closest to death, I knew I had to alter my thinking, alter my actions, and change my way of being.

When I told her about the laxatives, Mom begged me to go into a clinic or a day program for eating disorders. She even called a couple to do some research, but I was too ashamed, not only about being a man with an eating disorder, but a man who was coming to terms with his homosexuality. While some people close to me and in the periphery knew about my struggle, I didn't want to admit it at the level that going to a clinic would have forced me to admit it. I preferred the quiet safety and the anonymity of the one-on-one therapy. Instead of a clinic, I asked Mom if she'd pay for me to go to Katherine twice a week. She agreed, as long as I was getting better. "Maybe Katherine can even help me not be gay," I uttered and then felt sick. I knew it was impossible to change, but part of me maybe wanted my dad to think that I was still trying to change for him. I wondered if that's what Mom told him to keep the checks coming for the therapy. Regardless, I needed help, serious help, and I finally admitted that to myself.

Katherine was a supportive and kind therapist. She worked gently but persistently toward goals and wanted to see the results. After months of gaining my trust and respect through listening to my story, and understanding my past to help me move forward, she introduced me to cognitive behavioral therapy. This approach and other tools she gave me were meant to help me notice the behaviors I was engaging in and stop them. Katherine's goal was to stabilize the flaring symptoms and get me into remission for longer than just a few weeks at a time.

I liked going to visit Katherine. As I moseyed down the sidewalk on Beacon Street to her office, my anxiety dissipated. Just heading there was a relief. Her building was older, so it had one of those old cramped elevators. It would slowly elevate me to the sixth floor where I'd sit in the waiting room until my session began. Part of me felt crazy that I had to go there so often, but another part of me felt a burden lifting. It brought me peace in some way to be in the quiet of her tiny yet comfortable office. The walls were a cool blue warmed by the off-white light of a table lamp. I sat in the same spot of the couch every session, surrounding myself with the plaid throw pillows.

I still felt at times that I wanted to yield to the torment, but in the comfort and safety of Katherine's office, I was gradually gaining the tools to conquer the demons that were plaguing me. I was ready to surrender to a better way of life.

✳

Chapter 17

Holidays on Ice

At the end of second summer session, my grades went directly home to Andover and Mom called to tell me how proud of me she was for getting all As. I asked if Dad had seen my grades, but she said, "No." If it weren't for the B-plus I received in Stagecraft first semester freshman year (hanging lights wasn't my strong suit), I'd have a perfect GPA. I was feeling pretty good about my grades, especially given what else had been going on that summer. I was looking forward to a couple of weeks off before classes would start up again, even though it would be under the blazing Boston summer sun.

Around the same time, my psych professor, Dr. Feinberg, approached and asked if I'd be willing to help Dr. Carbalatto during the fall semester. She said he needed a teaching assistant but also needed someone to help him get in and out of his classroom. It was located on the ground floor of an old bank across from the Cutler Majestic Theater, and Dr. Carbalatto would have to park in the rear of the building and walk all the way around to the front, complete with steps and divots in the sidewalk. I really liked the idea of helping him, especially since he really needed it, but felt hesitant.

"What if he finds out that I'm gay?" I asked Dr. Feinberg. I had confided to her about my homosexuality in a paper I wrote for my second course with her.

"Are you kidding?" she said. "He's only going to ask, 'So what, does he know about psychology?'"

"Are you sure?" I asked, insecure. "It's just that he's part of that older generation, and what if he doesn't like gay people?"

"You don't know Dr. Carbalatto yet," she replied.

Dr. Feinberg offered to talk with him about it first, just so I would feel more comfortable. Sure enough, he didn't care. He said exactly what she'd predicted. "All that mattered to him was whether or not you knew about psychology. And I told him you were brilliant!" *Great, now he's expecting brilliance? I'll really disappoint him,* the self-deprecating me prevailed.

Starting that September, the beginning of my third and final year at Emerson, I met Dr. Carbalatto every Monday, Wednesday, and Friday for his 9 a.m. class. He'd park his old, beat-up blue Datsun and struggle to get out of the driver's seat. I'd take his briefcase and his bagged lunch and guide him to the front of the busy street. Each one of those walks was only about five or seven minutes. Sometimes we talked about important problems or issues, but other times we just walked in silence. These times together were special to me, more than I realized at the time.

I was also taking my own psychology classes, one of them with Dr. Carbalatto, and was still going to therapy with Katherine. Things continued to improve. My symptoms were more under wraps than since they'd surfaced nearly four years prior, but there wasn't a day that went by that I didn't worry to some degree about fat and homosexuality. I just learned how to manage the anxiety better. I was eating more well-rounded meals than ever, but not without guilt and not with the consistency or frequency that Katherine wanted. I was running less, but not that much less. Nonetheless, we were seeing results. For one, I stopped taking laxatives. I also quit fat burners. "This is some major progress, Jon," Katherine assured me. But I was never one to rest on my laurels nor to give myself credit, even when it was due. The voice in my head had quieted, but it was still nagging me, mostly in the form of whispers when I was alone.

Simultaneous and consistent with the ups and downs of my disordered eating, Katherine helped me see what should've been a glaringly obvious and persistent conflict in my life: I repeatedly chased the illusion that my dad would change and accept me. My heart still longed for his approval and love even though my mind came to terms with the notion that he'd never budge. I often questioned, out loud with Katherine, why I even needed his approval at my age. But even as I realized the impossibility of gaining his acceptance, the old obsession, ingrained from childhood, begging for his forgiveness, groveling in my mind to God to make him change, prevailed in moments of weakness or vulnerability. It would still take years of determined self-reflection and self-knowledge to really get past it. Little things helped along the way.

One of those things was a book Dr. Carbalatto assigned in our Advanced Psychology Seminar: *The Secret Language of Eating Disorders* by Peggy Claude-Pierre. She was visiting Emerson to talk about her book, so I read her book cover to cover as quickly as I could. I'd also seen a piece about her clinic in Victoria, Canada, on the TV news program *20/20*. I thought she was a miracle worker. She'd been able to restore good health in girls who weighed next to nothing, and who were on the verge of death with IV feeding tubes keeping them alive, and through just a combination of unconditional love and hugging. Her hugs appeared to be a magic remedy for her patients, but, despite her high rate of success, many in the academic, mental health, and medical communities scoffed at her methods. Some even called her a witch doctor and a fraud.

To me, her philosophy and approach sounded a lot like the "unconditional positive regard" practiced by psychologist Carl Rogers and others in the humanistic movement that Dr. Carballato had been teaching. She removed all judgment and replaced it with love, lots of love. It made sense to me when I thought about it in my own life. When I heard Peggy speak at Emerson, I was mesmerized by her soft, delicate voice. I even got to say hi to her and have her sign my book. She inspired me so much that I suddenly knew for sure exactly what I wanted to do with my life: I wanted to help people, just like she was helping me and so many others.

The next day, I talked to Katherine about Peggy's visit and how I'd briefly met her. "I now know what I want to do," I said. "I want to help others like Peggy does, the way you and Dr. Carballato do. I believe in the healing power of love and unconditional acceptance." It perfectly resonated with me.

"Why don't you call the local branch of the Massachusetts Eating Disorders Association to volunteer," she suggested. And so, I did. While I knew it would be hard to see so many people suffering (most of them were girls), I thought I would be able to empathize and understand people's issues with their weight and self-image because I had experienced them myself. Maybe it could help me have compassion for myself.

Dr. Carballato eventually became more than just a professor to me. I told Dr. Carballato that I wanted to become a psychologist and be like him one day. "You'll make a gifted psychologist, Jon," he said. Dr. Feinberg told me that as well.

My father's clear disdain for me grew even more obvious through the silent treatment I was getting. I hadn't heard a word from him in months. The more my mom reminded him that I couldn't change my sexual orientation, the more distant my father became, if that was even possible. I can't remember the exact moment when he told me I was no longer welcome in his house; I was no longer his son. He didn't have to. The message was clear. In fact, it always had been, not just after I'd returned home from Europe, but from the time I was a little boy. Part of me wonders if deep down he knew from the beginning, even unconsciously, that I was different. Throughout my life, he saw something in me that was so threatening, so scary that he started in on me when I was as young as three or four to try to combat the inevitable: I was gay. Now that I had actually said it, now that it was confirmed that I would never be the "real man" he'd tried to make me with football, baseball, and basketball, I was his greatest disappointment, his greatest failure.

Dr. Carballato and Dr. Feinberg learned more about my upbringing and about what was going on at home. They listened and empathized.

Because I was unwelcome and it felt unsafe to go home, I didn't. Dr. Carballato invited me to have Thanksgiving that year with him, his wife, Dr. Feinberg, and with Dr. Feinberg's best friend. I could have gone to any of my friend's homes—Samantha's, Deborah's, Charlie's, Meredith's, James's, or even Chad's. But I felt like a burden, a pain. I also didn't want to be anywhere near Andover. I became *that scared* of my dad. Even though Boston was only twenty-three miles from Andover, it felt like a world away. I accepted Dr. Carballato's invitation and joined him for Thanksgiving dinner at the Four Seasons on Boylston Street, where he had a long-standing tradition of having turkey and stuffing in the Bristol Lounge.

My family had never been anything vaguely resembling poor, but when I walked into the hotel for the first time, I was stunned by the kind of wealth that clearly existed in Boston. The restaurant was opulent. The tables were draped in pressed linens, and bouquets in crystal vases sat perfectly in the center. Around them in plush chairs were people in fancy suits and dresses, the women dripping with jewels, the men wearing ascots and pocket squares. At first I felt out of place and like a tagalong, but everyone at the table made me feel welcome. I'm sure Dr. Carballato and Dr. Feinberg had given everyone else a heads-up about my situation. I remember two things from that meal vividly. The first was the savory, salty, incredible taste of stuffing hitting my taste buds for the first time in a very long time. The second was the laughter and joy around that table that didn't end in a disaster of screaming and yelling.

Mom was distraught that I hadn't come home. I never heard from my dad that Thanksgiving and wouldn't hear from him on many more to come.

Holidays at our house had gotten worse as we got older. Christmases were harder for me than the others. Most of my friends had more typical Christmases: enjoying family, decorating gingerbread houses, gorging on sugar cookies, and drinking hot chocolate with marshmallows. As a little kid, even with our family tension, I'd looked forward to Christmas, mostly because I believed in Santa longer than most. I was probably twelve by the time I let go of the fantasy of Santa Claus. My cousins would tease me during our annual Christmas Eve feasts at Uncle Tony's house. "Santa is fake, Jon! Stupid kid!" I didn't believe them. On the way home, I would look in the sky, convinced I was seeing Rudolph's ignited red nose. I'd pray on that night sky that the next morning, like a Christmas miracle, my dad would wake up kind and gentle, loving and accepting of all of us.

For a long time when I was younger, Christmas felt like a time of renewed hope, a time when I thought my dad would change. As I got older, though, I realized my Christmas wish would never come true. Instead, our house was more of a mess at Christmas. Dad would start the day by using gifts and money to buy as much of our affection and tolerance as he could for another year.

By the end of most Christmas days in Andover, Dad was ranting and raving about how something was wrong with the meal Mom cooked, or that the table setting wasn't perfect. By the time I was in college, holidays were a source of angst for me.

The Christmas of my third and final year of college was one of the worst I can remember. A bunch of my English Family friends went to Vinny's house on Christmas evening, to spend time together playing cards, joking around, laughing. Earlier that day, I had taken the train from North Station to Andover to spend a few hours with my sister Julie and her family. I wasn't invited to the Christmas Eve feast at my uncle's that year. I wasn't welcome at Crescent Circle either. I don't think I heard from my father at all that year, not even on my birthday in October.

By the time we all left Vinny's house, it was late. Charlie and Chad gave me a lift back to Julie's, but I remember feeling as if I was homeless, and a burden on everyone, because I didn't have a home to return to. As usual, I didn't say anything. When we got to Julie's house, it was dark and no lights were on. In the pitch black, I worried that I'd wake up my baby niece Emma. I didn't have a key. I didn't want to knock and make their German shepherd bark.

I got out of the car and waited for the guys to leave; I didn't want them to worry. I sat on the cold driveway, shivering, ironically wishing I could go home to my own house, to my own bedroom; at least it would be warm there.

Instead, I walked from my sister's house all the way down the hill, past the high school, and toward town to catch the first morning train back to Boston. I didn't want to call my friends. They'd taken me in and taken care of me so many other times. On the night of Christmas, I couldn't ask that of them again and I had nowhere else to go. I walked to Christy's Market, a twenty-four-hour convenience store located right next to the T Commuter Rail stop, and waited. I thought I could make it outside until five in the morning, when the first train would come to take me into Boston. But as the hours passed, I began to freeze. My hands were red and raw from the bitterness in the air, and the discomfort became unbearable.

Finally, in the dark hour at the beginning of the morning, I gave in to the chill and called Samantha. I was embarrassed to ask if she'd come and pick me up at that hour, and to impose on her family's tradition. Samantha had talked fondly about how much they loved their Christmases together and I didn't want them to wake up and find me there the morning after.

I called Samantha's private phone line from a payphone. "Samantha, I'm down at Christy's Market," I said. "I am so sorry. Can you come get me?" The combination of cold air and deep sadness made my voice shake. She didn't even ask what was wrong. She said she'd be there in an instant. As I waited, I thought about wanting to just be loved for who I was, and on that late Christmas night, like on so many other nights, Samantha's family became my family. They hugged me and made me a bed of pillows and blankets on the floor of their finished basement. Despite the hardness of that floor, it was cozy, and I was warm. I lay there in the basement of a house full of love and yet I still hurt: I wanted the love of my own family, of my own father, especially on Christmas.

■ ■ ■

In that final year at Emerson, I applied to master's degree programs in counseling psychology across the country. Jared had moved to Chicago for a job in the finance industry, and my cousins lived there, too, which helped to make Northwestern University one of my top choices. Because I'd done the eight summer courses, I made up for the year I took off and caught up with Samantha and all my friends from the English Family. Having done college in just three years, I would graduate at the same time they did.

Samantha, a human development undergraduate major at Boston College, also wanted to go to Chicago to pursue her doctorate in psychology. It seemed as if we were meant to go to Chicago together. My decision was a bit harder because I had also applied to a couple of master of fine arts programs in theater arts management. I'd stayed involved in the Musical Theatre Society, mostly as a producer, even though I'd changed my major to Writing, Literature, and Publishing. I had gotten into two top programs in each of these disciplines: Columbia University's master's in theater arts management, complete with internships at the Shubert Organization or Jujamcyn Theaters, and the master's in counseling psychology at Northwestern University.

To complicate matters further, I received a call to audition for the musical *Rent* in NYC in front of Bernard Telsey Casting Agency. It was because of a letter I had sent to Kevin McCollum, one of the producers, after I returned home from the Castle program. The musical had moved me so much, in so many ways, that I looked in the playbill and picked out the producer whose photo looked the nicest and kindest and sent him a thank you letter. He called me at my apartment on Beacon Street and left a message that invited me to New York to audition for *Rent*. Still filled with stage fright and a lack of confidence, I didn't think I did very well on the audition, but it couldn't have been that bad because while I was at Northwestern for my psychology program interview, I got a call from Telsey & Company to go to New York to sing for the Off-Broadway part of Hedwig in *Hedwig and the Angry Inch*. I asked the casting agent for more information about the part and she told me. At the moment she called, I was in the car with my mom and brother, heading from Evanston to Chicago after my interview. "What would Dad think if I played a transsexual punk rock girl?" I asked after I hung up. They looked at me like I was crazy. I never went to the audition. And Telsey & Company never called again.

■ ■ ■

When Dad showed up for my graduation from Emerson, one part of me was surprised, and another wasn't. Even though he was rejecting who I was, any time I had any kind of significant achievement to celebrate, he felt the need to show his face and take the credit for what I had done. I was graduating *summa cum laude* and in the top five of my class. He wasn't going to let me keep the recognition for that all to myself. There was another factor behind his presence that day. He was excited that in the fall, I was going to be a "Wildcat." Northwestern was part of the Big 10 football conference, which, in his mind, put it many steps ahead of a "freak" school like Emerson. His son was going to a school with *a real football team,* maybe this would make him a *real man.*

He was so happy he even invited Dr. Carballato and Dr. Feinberg out to the Palm Restaurant for dinner after the graduation ceremonies. He actually thanked them for taking such good care of me the last couple of years at school and especially the times when he wasn't around. I don't know if my dad was actually proud of me that day, or if he put on a good face because my mom made him. It was all about him, really. At dinner he talked about me attending Northwestern and me becoming a Wildcat. He was mostly interested in knowing whether he could go to the football games. He had no clue what I'd been through the past few years, or at least he didn't act as if he cared, or had any regrets about how he'd treated me. He didn't even ask how I was doing. Dr. Carbalatto and Dr. Feinberg, being psychologists, later told me that they saw through the entire charade, but they told me I should be grateful that he showed up at all. I think everyone, especially me, always wanted to believe that my father would come around sooner or later.

Of course, Dad didn't show up when he was really needed—moving day. Mom took me on the thousand-mile trip to Chicago without him.

✳

Chapter 18

Boystown

A few months before grad school, Samantha had gone to Chicago on a trip with her parents and picked an apartment on Roscoe Street at the corner of Halstead, in the heart of Lakeview, "in a great location," Samantha said. It was a nice apartment and well within our price range, but I always wondered whether Samantha picked it with ulterior motives. Our apartment was in the heart of "Boystown," directly across the street from Roscoe's, one of the city's most popular and well-known gay bars. Samantha had seen me suffer at the hands of my own internalized homophobia long enough. I think she thought that if she put me in a place where I'd have no choice but to confront my issues head-on, eventually they would dissolve.

I was uncomfortable with the choice, but I had to admit, at least to myself, that I was also intrigued. I chalked it up to the fact that it was a spacious two-bedroom with a full bathroom, a giant study with space for both of our desks (we were both students after all), a living room, a kitchen, and a back deck. It was bright and airy with high ceilings, and it was perfect for us. I was so excited to be living with Samantha in one of the best cities in the country, and to be starting my program at Northwestern. I also felt safe living near my brother, who was just a cab ride away in Lincoln Park. It was great having some distance from my father, too. I had hope for the future and started to envision a new beginning.

Samantha was also a runner, and oftentimes we'd run together from our apartment heading east toward Lake Michigan. Running along the shores of Lake Michigan was breathtaking in the beginning. As we'd run toward the lake, I'd notice the many gay men who lived in our neighborhood. I'd find myself getting upset at some of them. *How dare that guy sashay down the street in pink sunglasses,* I'd think to myself. It again reminded me of what my father warned me I'd see in San Francisco, and it bothered me. All the other gay men—those who were out, loud and proud, bothered me, too. I'd hear my dad's disapproval in my head still, even being exactly 999 miles away from him.

The problem was, some part of me still held out hope that I could change my sexual orientation. Now that my dad was proud of me for going to Northwestern, that part of me also actually thought there might be a chance he might someday completely accept me, and I didn't want to do anything to interfere with that. He even let me live at home the summer before going to Chicago while I worked on the psychiatric unit of Holy Family Hospital. Dad and I didn't interact much. I often worked double shifts or the graveyard to avoid seeing him. When I wasn't working, he was always at the baseball field, focusing on other young men. *Maybe some miracle will bring us together,* I sometimes prayed. While he didn't interact with me much, I could tell he had hopes for my future now, unlike before, and so I remained celibate that whole summer. I lost the earrings and cut my hair. I didn't even let myself think about other men.

In Boystown, I never made eye contact with any of the many obviously gay men in my midst. I'd hear the "unzt unzt unzt" coming from the dance club across the street, but I didn't dare go explore. I just kept my head down. I studied, and ran, and focused on school and the friends I was making there. We had a two-day-a-week internship in addition to our regular classes, so I was too busy to look for love anyway and pretty much stayed chaste for two years.

It gave me time to focus on my work with my new therapist. At Northwestern, we were required to be in therapy while we were in our training program. The philosophy made sense to me: How can you help others learn about themselves if you don't know yourself as well as you can?

At the beginning of the semester, we each had a meeting with the assistant director of the Counseling Psychology program. She asked us what we were looking for in a therapist, and then she matched us up with the clinicians she thought could help us continue to resolve our unresolved issues. "I want to be able to accept that I'm gay, once and for all; I'm tired of beating myself up for it," is what I said, even as that part of me still hoped I could revert to straight for my dad's sake. But being in Chicago, a thousand miles away from him, gave me the space to consider making peace with my sexuality, with the help of a therapist. It's strange that I didn't ask her for a therapist to help me with my eating disorder. But clearly I knew it was more than that. I wanted to understand the *root* of my eating disorder symptoms and excessive running, which, somewhere in my mind, I knew was my lack of acceptance of my homosexuality. I wanted to understand why I hated myself still for something I couldn't change, something I couldn't control.

"I think I have the perfect match," the assistant director said.

Dr. Robert's office was close to my brother's apartment on the outskirts of Lincoln Park, so I had to drive to get there. I was nervous that first day, almost like my first day of school or my first school dance. *What will he think of me?* I wondered. *Will he be able to help me?* His office waiting room was immaculate. It had comfortable yet sleek Room & Board furniture and beautiful artwork. The place was soothing. On the floor was a white noise machine, designed to eliminate any words coming from under an office door. We learned in class that you could never be too careful when it came to confidentiality. Suddenly one of the two office doors off the waiting room creaked open.

"Hello, you must be Jon," the therapist said. "I'm Dr. Robert, and it's so nice to meet you."

"It's nice to meet you, too," I said.

"Come on in and have a seat anywhere you'd like."

I scanned the room quickly and found the spot on a cushy leather couch that seemed to call to me.

"Is this okay?" I asked.

"Of course. Please sit."

Several diplomas and certificates were displayed on his walls. *God,* I thought, *this guy sure is smart.* It made me feel as if I'd be in good hands.

He sat down in a comfortable chair across from me, crossed one leg over the other, and took in a deep breath. Letting it out he instructed, "So tell me, what brings you here today?"

"Gosh, where do I begin?"

"How about at the beginning? And it may take us a few sessions to get through some of the story, but I really want to hear it. I really want to learn more about you, and I want to help you reach the goals you have for yourself, Jon."

I went to Dr. Robert with a different agenda than I'd had before with therapists. In the past, it was as if I was trying to make myself *not be gay,* or to make the running stop and the starving to lift. But I went to Dr. Robert to really try to understand the demon eating me, eroding me from the inside. I wanted to finally find a way to accept myself for who I was: a young gay man.

I started seeing Dr. Robert once a week, then twice a week, and at one point during my first year at Northwestern, I was seeing him three times a week. Mom got nervous about why I needed so much help, but I assured her I was in professional hands. She even spoke to Dr. Robert a couple of times by phone, and over time she grew to trust him, too. He had a careful, gentle way of helping me, as if he were carefully removing a bandage that had covered a massive wound for years. He didn't tear it off; he pulled back the adhesive slowly but steadily. For so long, I'd been building walls around my heart as a way to keep from falling completely apart. Patiently, session after session, Dr. Robert removed one stone after another of the protective defenses I'd built up since I was that scared little boy in preschool having to make an adult decision. From the time I was a child in such an unsafe household, I'd been putting on layers of emotional fat, thickening myself for years to protect myself from the inevitable truth. I must have been preparing myself for the ultimate rejection I assumed would come from my father, and eventually, everyone else.

"Defense mechanisms are there for a reason," Dr. Robert explained. "We are in the middle of tearing them down and getting to the center of you, the core of who you really are. It's not going to be easy, and at times it is going to feel incredibly painful and depressing. But I know you can handle it. You are a very strong person, Jon."

It *was* painful. Revealing truths and accepting realities were not easy. My anger—at myself for being gay, at my father for his hatred, at my mom for staying with my father—had for so long been turned inward and got expressed as chronic anxiety and obsessive, systematic self-punishment. I had been doing everything I could to be something and someone different from who I was, to be "better" in God's eyes—frantically achieving to prove my worth, yet running and dieting excessively to obliterate the part of me that I believed was unworthy of love.

Bottom line: I was trying to starve the gayness out of me. Dr. Robert also helped me understand that my affair with running and anorexia was a way to keep me preoccupied and away from being homosexual altogether. It kept me chaste and asexual. It allowed me to regress, physically, and therefore mentally, to being a child, when I wasn't sexual at all. My obsessions kept me pure. Maybe God would love me, or my daddy would love me, if I was a "good" boy. It was so much to process, so much to unravel. It took tremendous energy to keep going and it was exhausting.

Over time, most of my anxiety calmed and turned to depression. After about eight months of work with Dr. Robert, my mood deflated. I was fatigued all the time. I was full of sorrow. I'd struggled with melancholia for most of my life; that was obvious. I'd always been sad a lot, mostly because I felt alone with my issues—my dysfunctional family, my sexual orientation. While I'd experienced suicidal ideation in high school and at Emerson, this new depression was more paralyzing, more exhausting. I didn't feel I had any gay role models. I didn't look up to anyone I knew to be gay except for a couple of famous people to whom I didn't relate. I felt completely alone. The depression sucked my energy dry. I was flatlined, defunct, dispirited completely.

I can't imagine how hard it was to witness my pain every day. For Samantha, living with me must have been really tough—agonizing, actually. Nonetheless, she stuck by me. We also had many fun times together and we were excellent roommates. We had our traditions, including Mexican food and margaritas at the Texas Star fajita bar at the end of our street (still followed by an early morning long run). I was beginning to eat more and feel less and less guilty about it. It was a growing year for Samantha, too. She hadn't been more than thirty miles away from home before, and she was exploring what she wanted in her own life, just like any twenty-something would. She was also juggling the breakup of a long-distance relationship and realizing that the love of her life was living in her midst, just a few neighborhoods away in Lincoln Park. While training for the New York City Marathon, she realized that pursuing her doctorate in psychology wasn't what she wanted after all. Kindred spirits since the second grade, we seemed to be still growing and changing in synch with each other.

I knew it was only a matter of time before she'd return to New England. Then, she told me one night over bowls of cereal at our small kitchen table, "Jon, I'm leaving Chicago at the end of spring." I thought about going home with her, but I wanted to finish my program at Northwestern, and more importantly, I knew I needed Dr. Robert, that he was guiding me in the right direction. I would be living completely on my own, but maybe that was the best thing for me.

■ ■ ■

I rented the third floor of an old house in the southeastern part of Evanston. It was small, just four tiny rooms, with barely enough room for a loveseat in the den and barely enough room to stand in some corners. In the bedroom, there wasn't enough space for a bed frame, so I had to rest my mattress directly on the floor. The bathroom didn't even have a stand-up shower. It was just an old cast-iron tub with a hand-held shower. I lived alone in that third-floor apartment in Evanston that entire second year at Northwestern.

Although I'd made some good friends among my counseling program cohorts, I spent a good deal of time by myself. Despite all the studying, reading, and writing I needed to do, I had plenty of time on my hands. I was eating vegan at that point. I was filling my plate more than I ever had, but I was comfortable having limits on what I could fill it with. Veganism provided a good transition for me. I continued to run; I couldn't just quit since it had been such a major part of my life. It was slightly different now. I was enjoying it as more of a release than anything else.

I enjoyed being alone on my runs. In Evanston, I loved running along the water on campus, hitting some of the area's public beaches. My enjoyment of those spectacular sunrise runs was an example of how much more I appreciated life now than I had in the past. Something was changing. I was reflecting on everything I saw. I was pondering everything I heard and smelled and tasted. I noticed things I hadn't seen for many years. I was feverishly writing poetry.

I seemed to have been trying to digest so much at once. I regretted not enjoying life more in my earlier years. I resented how I had given up so much for the approval of just one person. Processing it all, plus a very rigorous second year at school, continued to exhaust me. It probably didn't help that I was living completely alone; it was like a many-months-long solo from Outward Bound in some ways. The depression wouldn't dissipate. Suicidal thoughts even made their way back into my mind. I wondered, *am I a lost cause?*

Dr. Robert tried to convince me to try antidepressants. I was reluctant at first, but after much thought and discussion, I agreed. I didn't want to go back to the consistent lows of the past, and even though I sometimes still prayed to God to bring me peace and maybe even death, I really wanted to get better. I'd worked so hard to get to this point, and if Dr. Robert believed it would help, I was willing to do it. I just wanted to be content.

The Prozac helped. It was a small dosage, about twenty milligrams, but it was just enough to help lift the fog that seemed to hover around me. I still hurt; recalling my past was painful. But it was easier to pull myself out of my bed and out of that apartment.

Eventually I found my way to the 1999 Chicago Marathon. In hindsight, on some level, I believe it was another attempt to win my father's approval. Never mind that contemplating killing myself hadn't drawn his attention. But maybe this would?

While most people eat more when they train, I just kept doing what I had been doing. I didn't eat more, I didn't eat less. Training actually distracted me from my hunger, and from other things. I was eating good foods, lots of fruits and vegetables, and seitan and tempeh, all food that was good for me, and while still not enough, not less than I was burning every day.

I was excited when I learned my father would be joining my mother flying to Chicago for the race. If Jared didn't live in Chicago, too, he may not have come. When I greeted Mom at the Orrington Hotel in Evanston, she hugged me and cried. "Jon, you're so skinny," she said. "I thought you were getting better." She cried and held me. "I'm better, Mom," I promised her.

I'd been training seriously all summer and fall. One of my friends from the counseling program would drive and meet me at different stations along Sheridan Road heading north from Evanston to bring me water or Gatorade. On my twenty-mile runs, my nipples would bleed until they were raw. I ran in the rain. I ran in the heat. It didn't matter, I was going to finish this marathon, and I was going to beat my goal of completing it in four hours.

On the morning of the marathon, my dad arranged for a car service to pick me up in Evanston at four o'clock and drop me off at the starting line, a gesture that moved me. The moon was still out when the car took me from my apartment in Evanston down Lake Shore Drive to Grant Park, where it was all to begin in just a couple of hours. I was by myself, in my head with my headphones on. I was psyched. I was ready.

I had a lot of support. Mom was there to cheer me on. Jared was there, too. Samantha scheduled her trip back to see her new boyfriend so that she could watch the race as well. This was really happening. I had on my lucky white spandex with Umbro shorts over them and I had on two shirts, one long-sleeved with a short-sleeved shirt on top. It was October in Chicago, so it was cold, but the sky was crystal blue. It was the perfect fall day to run twenty-six-point-two miles.

The massive scene of people at the starting line was overwhelming. We were packed in like cigarettes, one lined up next to the other. And we moved slowly, like a mob, toward the starting line. Your time didn't start until you crossed the line, and the chip on my shoe registered the time. I was barely able to move, but the adrenaline in my body was bouncing me up and down. By the time I'd gotten to the starting line, the crowded field separated a bit. Once I crossed it, I was actually able to start jogging. My goal was to start out slow, as I had done so many times during my excessive training. I'd take it easy in the beginning and let many people pass me, but once I hit mile fourteen or so, my autopilot would kick in and I wouldn't feel much. The most I'd run before the marathon was twenty-one miles. But they say if you can do thirteen, you can do twenty-six, so I had a pretty good shot at finishing.

At mile three I heard my mom's voice screaming, "Come on Jon, way to go!" and she gave me a high five. I couldn't believe I saw her. Out of the sea of thousands of people who go to watch the Chicago Marathon, my mom found me! It excited me and boosted my energy. I kicked it up a notch. Then a few miles later at mile marker twelve, I heard her screaming again, "I love you, Jon! You can do it." She gave me the thumbs up. I smiled and kept running. Step by step, stride after stride, like so many of those long runs in Andover, and in Boston, and now in Chicago, it was like clockwork.

At about mile twenty-one, things started to get really hard. I could barely pick up my legs and I was in so much pain at this point. I was dripping in so much sweat, I had removed and dropped one of my shirts, but I had to keep on going.

My brother and Samantha met me around the twenty-four-mile mark and could see that I was struggling. They both jumped in to finish with me.

Jared started yelling at me, "Look at these grown men on the side of the road barfing and look at you! You are amazing! You got this!"

Samantha said, "Just remember your breathing, and imagine that you're just running along the lake. You're almost there."

I kept running, moving one leg after another, pumping one arm after the other with Jared on my right and Samantha on my left. A mile ahead of me I could hear the stands of people cheering. To my right was Lake Michigan; to my left was a sea of people. In the distance were the finish line and a clicking clock. When I looked at my watch, I couldn't believe what it read; I was actually going to finish this close to three hours and thirty minutes, shaving almost a half hour off my goal. While that mattered to me, it was more important simply to finish.

And then the next thing I knew, Jared sprinted in front of me and Samantha stayed by me with her Kodak disposable camera taking pictures and screaming at me, "You did it, you did it!" I was hazy from exhaustion, but I could see the finish line, the crowds of people, and the huge digital clock: 3:29:13 . . . 14 . . . 15, the fluorescent numbers changing by the second.

Then, suddenly, off in the distance, from up in the bleachers at the finish line, in the symphony of screams and cheers and claps, I somehow managed to distinguish my dad's loud, signature whistle, "EEAWEET, EEAWEET!" Elated, shocked, in awe, I breathed it in. *I did it*, I thought. *I finally made him proud!*

The race team wrapped a foil blanket around my shoulders and put a medal around my neck. I could barely stand or walk, yet I took it all in—the sky pastel blue without a cloud in sight, the crowd cheering, the wind blowing off the lake. I had a moment to think about where I had just been—more than twenty-six miles around the amazing city of Chicago.

My brother ran at me, calling out, "Jon, you okay?"

I grabbed him and held him tight and released a series of deep sobs into his chest. "I just can't believe I was strong enough to do this, Jared," I cried. "I just can't believe I did this. And he noticed, Dad noticed." I let go in my brother's arms.

"You're strong enough to do anything you put your mind to, Jon," he said. And for that moment, I believed it.

✳

Chapter 19

An Ocean Away

M y friends always told me love happened when you least expected it, but I'd stopped believing them. I wasn't sure I was interested, anyway. I'd reached a point at which I believed I was meant to be alone. I thought it was easier than being gay.

I certainly wasn't looking for love. I'd jog along Chicago's winding path of Lake Michigan and try to keep my head down so that I wouldn't notice cute guys in great shape also running there. I was afraid of being tempted—tempted to fantasize that I'd actually go on a date with one of them. So if I spotted one, I'd quickly look down or away. I kept looking away and keeping to myself.

After the marathon, running, although I continued to do it every day, was no longer something I did to the point of exhaustion. I continued because running was my best companion, next to Samantha, next to Mom. I promised Dr. Robert I'd keep my runs to a certain number of miles—a realistic number, each day. The general rule was that I didn't allow myself to run longer than an hour.

Dr. Robert's counseling really was helping me. Between that and my serious commitment to getting healthier, I was able to put the running and starving and purging in check. I certainly wasn't eating fatty, highly caloric foods like pizza, even though I would have dreams about it. But I was consciously trying to eat three meals a day. Sometimes I failed, but most days I would do the things I had been taught by Katherine and Dr. Robert. I'd have a piece of wheat toast with a tablespoon of peanut butter in the morning with my black coffee. I'd have a salad with a vegan protein like seitan or tempeh for lunch. I'd even have a little pasta with broccoli and a sprinkling of lowfat soy cheese for dinner. I ate more fruits and veggies than I ever had as a kid.

I was on my way, but tempering my obsessions made room for me to think and feel different things about myself. I was coming to believe that I'd never find a man with whom I'd be able to have a long-term relationship. And even if I could find such a man, I didn't think I'd ever allow myself to *fall in love* with him, because there was too high a price to pay.

Feeling terribly lonely at the end of my first quarter at Northwestern, I decided to spend part of the two-week holiday break in Europe, revisiting Emerson's Castle and spending time with Helga, our resident director there, to whom I'd since gotten even closer through letters and email and the occasional phone call. With some of the savings I had from my job at the hospital that summer, I booked a Lufthansa flight from Chicago to Dusseldorf, Germany. There, I'd be greeted by Helga and she'd drive me back to the Castle so she could finish up her duties for the remaining days of the semester. After, we'd travel together to Bruges, Belgium, and Garmisch-Partenkirchen, Germany, places I didn't get to on my first trip to Europe.

I hadn't expected to return to the Castle so soon. When I was there the first time, three falls prior, I felt something I hadn't felt before, or since: a freedom created by the distance from the realities of my day-to-day life, an ocean away. For some reason, the Castle felt more like home than anything else I'd ever known.

After a two-hour drive on the autobahn, and through the winding, tree-lined roads of Holland, we turned left onto Kastellaan Street at the Vink. The sounds of Helga's red '89 Saab were muffled as we reminisced about the laughter, music, and dancing during my semester there in '96. As we pulled up around dusk, the Castle looked to me like an oversized jack-o-lantern, with its many windows illuminated.

I was happy to see the main tower stretching toward the sky. The weeping willow still hung on the front lawn, dropping its branches to sip the water and to touch the lily pads in the moat. As we drove over the driveway's brittle and bumpy bricks, my body pulsated as if it were being shaken alive. The Castle's splendor was just as impressive as I remembered.

When we stopped, I pulled myself out of the car and immediately took in the smells—rotting tulips, cow manure from the nearby farms along the river. The grass was soggy from all the fall rain. Swirling steam rose from the moat. Mozart was playing from my favorite room, Sophie's Lounge. Sophie, one of the Castle's storied spirits, must have known I was back.

Being back in the Castle's hallways and walking from room to room was disorienting for me. Every time I passed a bedroom, I expected to see someone I knew from my last visit. Each time I heard a voice, I'd turn my head to see who it was, only to find an unfamiliar face. It was just as much this class's Castle as it was ours back in 1996, and that of all the other students who'd come and gone before us. We all shared something in common. We'd discovered majesty on a continent thousands of miles away from home. I said to myself, *it's still magical.*

I believed that Castle Well indeed had a power. It made everyone feel sharp and brilliant and free to create. It inspired new thoughts and sensations. I wanted someone to sit with me until three in the morning and talk about Shakespeare or to sing or dance or read a poem. I wanted to hear a lecture about the painting strokes of Van Gogh and his tragic lust for life. I wanted to call my friends and the people I loved back in America to tell them how alive I felt again and for them to feel that way, too—most of all, my mom.

Helga introduced me to some of the students, and they were gracious and interested in hearing about my experiences at the Castle. They wanted to hear my travel suggestions for their long weekends.

As we were leaving Sophie's Lounge to head to dinner in the Castle's dungeon, a tall guy wearing a light blue American postal carrier's shirt on top of a white long-sleeved T-shirt approached me, forcing his way through the small crowd with his hand out as if he were hailing a taxi. Once in front of me, he offered his hand and introduced himself, as if we'd met before. "Loren. Loren Theodore!" *Loren?* I tried digging for it in my brain. Hearing his name sent me back to my Beacon Street apartment in Boston, where I suddenly recalled meeting him only one time before, at a party my second roommate Tom (and roommate from the Castle) and I had thrown. It was the night before my graduation from Emerson and the summer before I would leave for graduate school in Chicago. I'd forgotten how handsome his face was with those blue-green eyes, that once-blond hair underneath a haphazardly brown dye job someone must have done with a bottle. That smile, those cheekbones, that slender build, and that voice. "Remember me?" he asked. *I remember that voice,* I said to myself. He had an amazing singing voice. "I do," I said. "Of course I remember you."

Helga continued out the doorway and I continued behind her, causally looking back over my shoulder at Loren, who was now sitting by the piano. He was looking at me. I turned away. I smiled and caught my breath.

A few nights later, Helga decided we'd skip the Castle's cafeteria food and go to one of the quaint restaurants in the village. Since I couldn't speak the language, Helga ordered our meals. Before my trip, I'd resigned that while away, I was going to eat what I was served. Eating vegan in Europe seemed impossible. I felt freer to eat in Holland than in the States, although I still kept track of the fat grams I consumed. I'd been making progress at home in the United States, but for some reason, in the Netherlands I even worried less. Somehow, there, I felt more assured that one indulgent meal wouldn't make me fat. But then again, I was also distracted: during the entire dinner I was wondering what Loren was up to.

After we returned to the Castle and Helga had gone to bed, I wandered down to the lounge. Sophie's Lounge was especially beautiful when it was empty, devoid of the chaos of all of the students. I put on Beethoven and dimmed the lights so there was a soft glow in the expansive room. I wrote in my journal about feeling different in Holland, feeling at peace there, and wondered why that was.

Suddenly I heard laughter and footsteps creaking on the lounge's wide-plank floors. It was Loren and two friends, Chris and Cassidy, giggling as they entered the lounge. They didn't notice me at first, sitting quietly by myself at the long dining-room-style table in the corner. Undetected, I studied Loren from afar. He sat in one of the large overstuffed chairs hugging his knees to his chest, his chin resting on the right knee. At once, in his face I saw both innocence and intensity. I hoped his attention would at some point turn in my direction.

And then it did. "Jon," he called out to me, "I didn't see you over there!" He came over and gave me a hug. *That was nice,* I thought. "Come on over and sit with us," he said sweetly. I was nervous to engage, but took him up on his offer.

Loren, Chris, Cassidy, and I exchanged travel stories for hours into the night. We talked about hidden treasures of sidewalk art and sculptures from Copenhagen to Prague, Budapest to Salzburg.

As the hands on the grandfather clock reached 3:30, Chris said he was exhausted and was going to bed. His eyes were bloodshot from the pot smoking he'd done earlier, and from being up late the last two nights. Sleep was a rare thing at the Castle. I certainly don't remember sleeping much when I was there. Cassidy said she was going to follow Chris to bed. I wasn't sure if they were together or not, but I could tell that they were going to sleep together. Loren smiled at me, as if he was happy that they were leaving us alone.

Loren's fidgeting knee made a loud sound hitting the coffee table. I hoped it was louder than the pounding from my chest. "Can I play you something?" he asked. He jumped up and sat down at the piano, hunching over the ivory keys. Softly, he played the chords of something familiar. He began to sing. It was Sarah McLachlan's version of Tom Waits's tune, "Ol' 55." He kept it low, since it was so late, but even then his enchanting voice mesmerized me. When he stopped, the silence was jarring.

"Hey," he asked, "what was the name of that song you wrote and sang at the orientation show my freshman year? I loved it. Can you play it for me?"

"Right now, like, right here, right now?" I asked. I hadn't realized that I'd left an impression on Loren so long ago.

Fittingly, I'd written the song when I was at the Castle the first time. "I'll play it for you some other time," I said bashfully. "Right now, I've got to get to bed; I'm exhausted."

I really didn't want my singing to prevent me from remembering the sound of his voice. "Good night, Loren," I said. "It's been good to see you again." I walked out of the room floating so high I don't think I even made a creak on the floor.

I couldn't sleep that night. It's tough enough to fall asleep when you're in a medieval castle with energy from centuries past abounding through the halls. It was even harder now, because I was so taken by Loren. I couldn't stop thinking about him. I tossed and turned, haunted, not by ghosts, but by the song Loren had sung just a couple of hours before.

I only managed to sleep about forty minutes before Helga knocked on my door. Her "Time to get up!" startled me. My eyelids were heavy and I felt bloated from eating too much the night before at dinner. *I wish I could go running.* And then, *I wish I hadn't eaten that last bite.* I started to obsess.

Then I remembered Loren. He seemed to think I was cute. So maybe the cheese I ate hadn't made my face fat just yet. I showered and got ready quickly so that Helga and I could get on the road. We were going to visit her family near Eindhoven.

When we arrived in Helga's hometown, she gave me a tour of her childhood school and her favorite shops downtown. Then we went to the house she grew up in. It was a pretty little row house on a quiet little street. Her family was welcoming and generous. We sat down at their kitchen table for lunch, and they passed me casserole dish after dish with cheese and vegetables, cheese and breads, cheese and meats. Everything in Holland was made with cheese. I thought to myself, *Couldn't something here be made without fattening cheese?* I did my best to stop obsessing about fat, and avoid being rude, by not eating. I took small spoonfuls from the dishes. I was hoping no one noticed my discomfort. It was hard, but I swallowed everything down, as if it were like cough syrup, and did my best not to worry.

I couldn't converse much with everyone without Helga's translation. But it was clear we had something special in common: Helga. Helga's dimples were deeper around her family. She seemed at ease there. Her sister had a three-year-old son who was running all around the house. If you have a picture in your mind of a little Dutch boy, Arnold would have matched it perfectly. He had big, bright blue eyes beneath an abundance of light red hair. He was chubby and happy. He was especially happy being around his Aunt Helga. She was really good with him, and it was clear how much she loved him. I thought at that moment, *One day she's going to make a great mother.*

Then I wondered if I'd ever make a great father. *I can't be a dad if I'm gay,* I thought, remembering what my dad had said about it being wrong that some kids had to grow up with two dads or two moms. I often worried that I'd be like my father if I were to have kids: mostly absent, and angry when present. For the first time in my life, I wondered if a woman would ever carry my baby. I fantasized about letting go of the self-acceptance as a gay man that I had been coming to. *Maybe I just have to trade in the gay in me for a chance at a normal life?* Was it even possible? I still hadn't ever been with a woman; maybe I just didn't know what I was missing.

Then I wondered if Helga liked me more like a boyfriend than like a brother, as I'd assumed. I got that impression from time to time, but it was just an impression. Perhaps I wanted her to think of me in that way and that a part of me still held out for the life of "a real man" that my father wanted for me. I'd hear my father's voice in my head: "Real men have babies and work to support them."

I left Helga's family's house feeling sad and confused. I was quiet the entire way back to the Castle and spent most of the time gazing out the window of the car at the beautiful, flat green land. I saw a windmill in the distance with the sun setting behind it, and asked Helga if we could pull over so I could get a picture. I was feeling tension in my neck, my shoulders, my head, and just needed to get out of that car.

I wondered whether I could purposefully deny my sexual orientation—suppress it and marry a woman, a woman like Helga. *Maybe I could have a baby and the normal life I was supposed to have,* I thought, desperately promising myself I'd once again try to stifle my feelings for men. And yet, even though my brain really wanted to, my heart was still fixated on Loren, and as much as I wanted to deny it, to stifle it, I couldn't.

■ ■ ■

Not long after this, I had gone to the Vink, the café and bar in the village, one evening to have a drink when I spotted Loren sitting at the counter, smoking a cigarette. I was already a little tipsy on wine and so walked toward him more eagerly than I normally would have. "Do you need another drink?" he asked. He bought me a glass of cheap red and lit another cigarette. When I sat down next to him, he moved his leg closer to mine, as if to make sure they were touching. I smiled. Then he grabbed my left hand—the one resting on the thigh touching his—and squeezed it hard. *Wow, that's amazing,* I said to myself. I didn't want him to loosen the grip, so I squeezed back.

I looked down and realized we were holding hands in a public place, in a bar in a small village in the southeastern corner of the Netherlands. And for the first time, I didn't look around to see if someone was looking at us. Or maybe I didn't look to see if my father was watching. Instead, I thought of being with Loren, kissing him, and it didn't make me feel guilty or gross. *This is different,* I noticed. His touch, his eyes, his voice—the whole experience was different. And despite my burning desire to understand why it was different, I just let it be. *Just go with it, Jon,* I told myself. *Don't overthink this for once.*

I allowed myself to feel the softness of his hand as his fingers rubbed the center of my palm and noticed my heart beating faster, not out of fear, but out of pleasure.

We drank, talked, and laughed for hours until Ravel's "Bolero" began to play in the background. This was the Vink owner's traditional way of closing down his bar and sending all the Americans back to the Castle for the night. As the saxophone played the melody and the drums rolled behind it, everyone started to drink their glasses dry.

"Can I walk you back to the Castle?" Loren offered.

"Sure, I'd like that," I accepted.

It was a cold night, drizzling and foggy. Loren held on to my arm as if it were a crutch to help him walk upright. He was slurring his words, perhaps words he'd forget the next morning.

"You know, I was so drawn to you when I saw you sing in Boston a few years ago," he said. "I couldn't believe it when you showed up here." He started to go on, but I put my finger on his lips and told him, "Later." I wanted him to tell me those things when he was sober. I wanted to know he was telling me the truth and that it wouldn't be something he would regret later. So, we just kept walking, arm in arm, in a peaceful silence, down the street to the Castle.

It was one of the most exhilarating moments of my life: walking down an open street, linked arm in arm with another man, nobody there to make me ashamed or to question our motives and our attraction to one another. My father was thirty-five hundred miles away, with an ocean between us. He couldn't break down my dormroom door and berate me for being a faggot. It gave me the freedom to want Loren even more.

I walked Loren into Sophie's Lounge, pulling him by his hand, and laid him down on the couch. I fixed the pillow so it was just right under his head. I was going to leave him there to sleep, but he whispered, "Stay." So I did.

I stayed and watched him sleep, his chest moving up and down peacefully. I sat beside him on the hardwood floor, ignoring the discomfort so I wouldn't miss a thing. I watched him all night long. There were moments when I hoped he'd wake up so I could kiss his lips. Occasionally I did kiss the fingers of the hand that held mine, but other than that it was just my longing, my fondness for Loren turning to something more as the sweet pain in my chest lingered.

Tears came to my eyes more than once that night. I didn't know why I was so emotional at the time. Maybe I was reminded of Chad, and watching him sleep in Ocean City but not being able to have him. Perhaps I was cutting through layers of emotional insulation I'd held onto my entire life. I knew the moment was bigger than what I was actually experiencing. I was allowing myself to feel this for another man, without guilt or shame.

In the middle of the night, I placed Loren's hand on top of his chest, kissed his head, and quietly left Sophie's Lounge for my own room. It was too hard to stay there and think of all of the possibilities before us. The reality was that we'd just met, and he was headed back to the States in two days. I was filled with emotion and I needed to be alone the rest of the morning. I had such an intense longing, and a sense of loss, despite the fact that we hadn't had more than one evening of talking and holding hands. I'd never hurt inside like this, and I knew what pain was. It was a different kind of hurt, the kind I'd started to feel with Chad but never allowed to blossom.

■ ■ ■

On his last full day at the Castle, I went to Loren's room in the fortress tower, where I knew I would find him packing for his journey back to the States. He was alone, folding shirts and jeans, khakis and sweaters. There were piles of clothes everywhere, and on the walls were drawings he'd sketched on his travels. Beside his bed was his guitar. I wanted him to play it and sing to me, but I didn't have the courage to ask. I handed him a bag I'd brought for dirty laundry, but had used it to wrap his gift, my favorite brown roll-neck sweater.

"What's this for?" he asked, smirking.

"It's just for being you," I said.

He hugged me and rubbed my back, making circles around my spine. His touch made me shiver. He leaned his head back and stared into my eyes, then at my cheeks, my nose, my hair, and finally, my lips. It was almost as if he was studying everything about my face, everything he was seeing in that moment. He closed his eyes and leaned in. He brought his lips down to touch my lips and we kissed. Slowly and softly, the sensual movements of his mouth, combined with the stubble on his face, nearly moved me to the ground. He held me up with his arms and continued to maneuver his mouth in rhythm with mine. It was as if our lips were dancing.

We *were* dancing. We were dancing as if we had danced together before, maybe in some other lifetime, some other place, but it was all too familiar and too natural to have been my first time. My head fell upon his chest. He tilted his head and nuzzled mine. The feel of his body, the tickling of his hair on my neck, and the heat of his hands open on my back were all sensations I'd dreamed about feeling. I wondered how anyone in the world could argue that what I was feeling, what we were feeling in this moment, was anything but natural. For the first time, I thought, *God didn't make a mistake in making me like this.* There was no other explanation to the instinctive way that I was magnetically drawn to Loren's body, touch, and smell.

In that moment, I came to terms with the notion that I'd fallen for someone who had fallen for me, too, something I'd missed out on the first time I'd been in this magical place. But I also knew that once you left the Castle and Europe, once you were back in the United States, something snaps you back into reality—practicality. I began to wonder if what we had was doomed. Was it going to be trampled by the rhythms of everyday life, by the distractions of school, work, money, food and weight, family, friends—all of the things that don't exist at the Castle? Our bond had been planted in one of the most precious places to me on earth, and it had all the ingredients to bloom—but maybe only in this fantasy land. Could it exist in real life, too?

"Play me that song?" Loren asked. I had hoped he'd forgotten, but since I'd promised, I obliged. We walked down to Sophie's Lounge hand in hand, and I sat at the piano and looked down at the keys.

Cautiously I placed my fingers on the ivory and began to play the simple chords. My voice resonated as I sang the words I'd written years before in that very room:

Take my hand and hold it tight
and we'll walk to that place where it's all right.

Listen now, the chaos is gone,
the talking has stopped, so I'll sing you this song.

If we keep walking, we'll be sure to find,
this place which lives in the hope of our minds,

so hold my hand, hold my heart, and hold my love,
in this place we're dreaming of.

There's no need to pretend or hide,
this place isn't afraid of what you hold inside.

Lay down your head, I promise to care,
don't be afraid, here, we're allowed to share.

Together we can live our lives as one,
like no other two have ever done.

Hold me.
Hold me.

Take my hand and hold it tight,
love me in this place where it's all right.

I'd written the song hoping I would one day be able to love some-body freely and openly. I sang that song for Loren still thinking it might never come true, even as it seemed to be coming true with him.

That night at the Vink, in line with tradition, the students were allowed underneath the beer taps. It was messy. It was a mixture of drunken happiness and sadness. I held Loren's hand all night long. I couldn't take my eyes off of his face, his lips. We laughed together, we danced, we drank, we hugged, and we kissed. Everyone could see the energy that we had together, and they smiled at us with approval. "Look at you guys," one friend said. "It's amazing." It was everything I'd ever imagined and hoped for, and it happened in less than five days.

On our way home to the Castle we walked in blissful silence, still holding hands. We stopped every few feet to make out. We kissed on the bike path, in the apple orchard, on the banks of the outer moat, on the bridge, in the courtyard, at the main gate, at the front doors, on the first-floor staircase, in Sophie's Lounge, in the library, on the third-floor staircase, on the fourth floor, in my room, behind the closed door, on my bed, beneath the sheets, without shirts, without pants, without underwear. Flesh upon flesh, we created a blanket of woven arms and legs, and in that warmth and glow of sexual freedom, I never closed my eyes. I didn't want to miss one thing. It was my first time; my first time truly making love and I actually loved making it, even the morning after. Lying there with Loren, I didn't ever want to get out of bed.

■ ■ ■

Loren didn't leave my side at the Brussels airport. Sitting on the floor, he had his backpack snug to his body. His legs were crossed and he held both of my hands in his. He began to say things to me that I had been waiting to hear from a guy since pulling away from Chad so many years ago. "This shouldn't be sad, Jon," he said. "This isn't the end, it's just the beginning. No matter where we are, we can make this work. I'll come to Chicago and you can come to Boston. This is too good, too real to let distance get in the way."

I didn't want us to part. I knew it was an ending of some kind. Even if we had a future, it would never be the same. Loren didn't realize how hard the culture shock of returning home was going to be. He didn't know yet what I'd already learned about being an ocean away.

Loren looked at me and then looked away. He reached out and pulled me into his body and we kissed for what seemed to be forever. I wondered, *Am I really doing this in the middle of an airport?* We kept holding, kissing, as if we'd never kiss again. "I. Love. You," he said with conviction. And I knew he meant it at that moment. I heard what he said, and I heard it in my mind for a long, long time to come.

He followed the line of passengers waiting to get their passports stamped at customs. Slowly, he began to fade away from me. After he passed the customs agent, he stood behind the glass wall and waved me toward him. In between us was a thick wall of glass. He put his hands up against it and I followed. I didn't feeling anything but the cold glass. Suddenly I couldn't remember what his fingers felt like, what his skin against mine felt like. I couldn't even make it up in my mind any longer. He blew me a kiss, but it never got through the partition.

He walked away and looked back several times. I think he was trying to capture what I looked like, but each time he turned around, his face blurred more and more. I thought of how mine must have been doing the same, until he was no longer in sight, no longer able to turn to remind himself that I'd still be in Belgium when he landed in Boston, where things would never be the way they'd been at the Castle.

✳

Chapter 20

Risking It All

ew Year's Eve.

"Where are you going, Jon?" my mom asked as my father eyed the overnight bag over my shoulder.

"I'm going to the First Night festivities in Boston with my friends," I said, a little nervously. I've never been very good at lying. "You know, they have a bunch of different events around the city all night. I figured I'd stay with Samantha or somebody. I hate to drive on New Year's."

Whew, I thought as I got out the door. I'd flown back to Boston from Europe to spend a few days with Mom and Julie, and to rendezvous with Loren.

The truth? I was headed for the Copley Plaza Hotel, where Loren and I booked a room together. What I told my mom wasn't a complete lie, because Loren and I planned to take part in some of the First Night events.

When I got to the hotel, Loren was standing in the grand lobby amid the holiday trees, decorations, and colorful flower arrangements in massive vases. I took a deep breath when I saw him. *He is striking,* I whispered to myself, unable to hold it in. He was a little bit more dressed up than I'd ever seen him at the Castle—khakis, button-down shirt, tweed blazer, black scarf, with a black hat and black leather gloves to match. He looked more sophisticated than I expected. He fit into the scene well.

When he saw me, he beamed. He ran to me and embraced me, engulfing me. It felt so good to be there in his arms again. Well, at least for a few seconds. I abruptly broke our hold. "Not here, in public," I said, looking away. Loren appeared surprised. The last time we'd held each other was in the middle of the airport in Dusseldorf, where we ended up kissing for minutes at a time.

When we got to the room, closed the door, and turned the lock, I felt free again. It was a small room but cozy with elegant linens and pillows and table lamps letting off a warm glow. We started to kiss and I wanted to stay there all night with him.

"Let's get room service and stay in," I begged. "It'll be romantic." I wanted to dine alone together, and maybe make love and recapture the magic of our feelings at the Castle.

"What?" Loren asked. "You don't want to go outside and take in all the festivities? I want to!" Loren was so enthusiastic, as if he'd never seen a ball drop before.

"Seriously?" I complained. "Why can't we just stay here and watch it on TV?"

"Because I came all the way here to be with you on First Night and to experience it all," Loren explained. "I don't want to just stay inside the whole time. Come on, it'll be awesome!"

"It's like twenty degrees outside, Loren," I said, having a hard time hiding my irritation. "I really don't want to freeze my ass off. Besides, it's the same thing every year. I thought you wanted to come to Boston to just be with me."

I wasn't honest with Loren about what my real concern was: that if we went outside, I'd get caught in the lie I'd told my parents, and my father would flip. What if a news camera caught us holding hands? Who knew what Dad would do? Being caught would set me back in all the headway I'd made with him. Since going to Northwestern, he'd been talking to me more than he had in years—maybe even since I'd left Bates. It wasn't much, but I took what I could get. Suddenly, I had tremendous empathy for my mother and understood her staying with him. Despite being terribly afraid of my father, despite loathing him most of the time, like Mom, I still wanted Dad's love and affection. He made all of us feel that way; somehow we always wanted his acceptance. Now I seemed to be getting something for which I'd been waiting years. But it came at a cost.

I hadn't talked about a guy or being gay in months. I'd learned that if I kept my sexual orientation to myself, no longer pretending not to be gay, but just not talking with him about it, Dad would remain at least on the margins of my life. I wasn't going to risk losing that affection by going out in the middle of First Night and possibly being spotted by someone from Andover who could report back to Dad that I was with another guy.

I was torn, because I also wanted to please Loren and make the most of this little bit of time we'd have together. So I got dressed in my warm clothes again, and we went outside. We crossed St. James Avenue and onto the plaza where Trinity Church has stood since the late 1800s. Suddenly, I was as frozen as the dozens of ice sculptures. Overcome with fear, I stopped in my tracks.

"I gotta go back," I said. "I'm freezing. I can't be out here." But it was really my paranoia, not the cold, that blew it for me.

I returned to the hotel room without Loren, who stayed outside by himself for some time. A couple of hours later, when he finally knocked on the hotel door, he looked cold, but more obviously sad and disappointed. I tried to explain to him what I was feeling, but I think he felt as though I was embarrassed by him or ashamed of our relationship. Understanding my fears, whether rational or irrational, was hard for the men in my life up to that point to really comprehend.

Loren and I lay on opposite sides of the bed that night, chilly from a draft in the old windows and from the emotional distance between us.

When we said good-bye in the morning, my heart was heavy with remorse and sadness. I chided myself. *Why can't I just risk it all for Loren?* I'm sure he wondered the same thing.

We saw each other a few more times after that, but it was never the same as it had been at the Castle. We remained in touch, but Loren wasn't really interested in me after what happened New Year's Eve. I knew it was best for me to let him go. It was an experience that changed me forever and laid the groundwork for what was to come. My heart ached for him for a long time, longer than I expected.

■ ■ ■

For the last year of my master's program in Chicago, I didn't get romantically involved with anyone. Sometimes I'd find myself still thinking about Loren, but mostly I put my focus on my coursework, and I excelled.

After graduation from Northwestern, my parents threw me a huge party back home in Andover, with more than one hundred guests. My dad seemed excited about it. As far as I could tell, he was genuinely proud of me. I even heard him gloating to some of my friends and their parents about my achievement. Sure, it was always in the wake of achievement when Dad swooped in, but I didn't care; he was noticing me. I was the first in our family to earn a master's degree, which reflected well on him. That year, I gave Dad multiple reasons to feel proud, or at least less ashamed of me. I was visibly getting healthier and stronger, in his mind kicking the "girl disease" once and for all. I'd completed the Chicago Marathon. To his knowledge, I wasn't "actively gay"—he certainly didn't know what had happened at the Castle. And the icing on the cake: after my next course of study, I was going to be a doctor. Neither of my parents could stop talking about it. It appeared as if it made it easier for him to feel proud of me. *There it is again,* I thought, *it's about what I do and not who I am.* I knew his pride wouldn't last long.

The coming fall, I was set to start a Ph.D. program in human development with a concentration in clinical psychology at the University of Chicago. Before starting the doctoral program, I'd study Spanish in a summer-long certificate program in Granada, Spain. There, I'd live with a family and take classes at the university. I'd studied Spanish since seventh grade, but I wanted to study more, to become truly fluent. I'd been told that living in a Spanish-speaking country was the best way to start dreaming in the language.

Just a few days before I was to leave for Spain, Sophia called me from Manhattan, where she was now living and working. "I've got this roommate," she said. "He's struggling with his sexual orientation, too, and I think it would help him—maybe both of you—if you talked. Would you be open to meeting him, or just talking on the phone about your own experience?"

"Sure," I said, although not confident I was the best person to talk to, considering how much I still was struggling. She gave me his email. "You should reach out to him," she said. "He's probably too nervous to begin the dialogue, so you may have to break the ice."

"It's getting late here in Andover," my email began. I told Stephen my story. I knew that if I was honest and open, I could encourage him to be the same. The next day we spoke on the phone for the first time. I noticed that his voice was like velvet, like Loren's. It was no surprise that he was part of the a cappella singing group on his college campus. He loved theater and music. He was raised in Massachusetts. He was having a hard time coming out. We had a lot in common. Our connection seemed strong right off the bat, especially having such a special friend in common in Sophia.

We talked a few times on the phone, and I could tell Stephen felt connected to me.

"I'm so disappointed you're leaving for the summer," he said. "I wish we could have the opportunity to meet in person before you leave."

Then we learned that we'd both be at Logan Airport on the same day, at the same time. He'd be flying in from New York for business just as I'd be leaving for Barcelona.

Cut to scene of me, in the middle of the international terminal at Logan, looking for a guy with short brown spiky hair and green eyes. "Jon?" I heard.

"Stephen?" I responded.

"Hi, it's so nice to finally meet you in person!" We hugged for an awkward moment. But it felt good, too. When we separated and looked at one another, we both smiled.

■ ■ ■

It was hot in the south of Spain. It was dry heat, like the kind in Palm Desert or Scottsdale. It was the perfect running weather. My obsession with fat grams had eased over the two years I'd seen Dr. Robert. I didn't realize it at the time, but as my internal self-hatred started to lift, so did my obsessive and compulsive thoughts and behaviors. I had been learning, through lots of therapy, and even Outward Bound, that food was fuel that was good for me and not an enemy. What hadn't stopped, though, was my love of running, and maybe that was a good thing. It helped clear my mind and became a sort of meditation for me. It was also a way of assuring that as I became less rigid about what I was eating, even if I ate a little more than I was comfortable with, that I'd still be able to maintain my weight.

But in Granada there was something about the hot sun and the dusty roads along winding mountain paths that enticed me to run more and more—even break the rule that I'd established with Dr. Robert not to exceed an hour. I had a lot of time on my hands, because classes were held in the mornings and the students I was with were mostly college kids. While they were out getting drunk on sangria at noon, I focused on my long runs and other exercise, and searching for phone booths from which to call Stephen.

It had started by trading emails. We began in the morning and continued at night, long emails through which we shared our life stories. I'd be writing while sipping café solo in an Internet café tucked away off some obscure city street. I'd imagine him in his fancy office atop the Chrysler Building writing and thinking. Soon the correspondence turned romantic. I don't remember who made the first move. Maybe it was me, because the distance between us allowed me to find the nerve. Emails turned to phone calls. I could barely wait the duration of my two-hour class to call him from a phone booth in the middle of the square outside of my classroom building. Our noon was his six in the morning; I knew he had to be dedicated to want to take my call at that hour.

Eventually, there were three calls a day. We became ritualistic with talking to one another. He even started to make calls to the flat where I was staying. Marian, the woman in whose home I lived, who took in international students to supplement her income, would hand me the phone and smile. "Es Stephen, Juan," she'd say. I'm sure I grinned.

It seemed that once again, while far away from my father, it was easier for me to allow myself to fall for someone. I was liberated with the Atlantic between us, able to be more of myself than I had anywhere else. Perhaps it wasn't just Holland or the Castle, or being in Europe; it was being so far away. Whatever it was, I allowed the seeds of my feelings for Stephen to plant themselves and grow. My love for him was budding.

About four weeks into my stay in Granada, Marian asked me out for a drink one night after one of her amazing dinners that she made for my roommate and me. "Yo conozco. Y esta bien." *She knows*, she was saying, *and it's okay.* Here was this Catholic, Spanish woman in her seventies telling me she knew I was gay, and that she was okay with it. "You're mi bebe." She had called me her baby in an English-Spanish mix just after a few days of being there. Maybe she could sense I was a bit of a mama's boy? Marian reminded me of Mom. She loved to smoke cigarettes, and her olive skin was wrinkled like Mom's. She looked tough, but she was warm and kind. She even invited me to her beach apartment at the Costa Del Sol, where we went to a jazz concert by the sea. She told me that she hadn't developed a bond like ours in the many years that she'd been taking in students. It meant a lot to me that she cared for me that deeply, even if I was gay.

After two months of talking by cordless phone in the wee hours of the night in Marian's apartment under the covers of my single bed, or in phone booths all over Granada, I was ready to see if the love I felt an ocean away could actually be real. Since it never worked out with Loren, or anyone else for that matter, I owed it to myself to fly back to the States and try. For Stephen, I was ready to let myself go.

■ ■ ■

When I got off the plane and passed through Newark's customs, I worried I might not recognize Stephen since I'd only met him that one other time at a different airport. All my other memories were based on photos he sent me in care packages to Spain and the images I made up of him when I'd talk to him from phone booths in Granada. But I immediately spotted his glowing face and huge smile gleaming in the crowd.

I ran to him and hugged him long and tight. It felt like we belonged there together. He hired a car service to take us from Newark to the city, and we kissed for the first time in the backseat of the car. I just kept kissing him and wanting to kiss him more. We couldn't get enough of one another. I didn't even care what the driver thought of me. I wondered, *Has Dr. Robert's therapy really taken hold of me? In some timed-released way?* Whatever it was, it didn't matter. I just enjoyed it. I enjoyed Stephen.

It was like that every day for weeks. There were weekend mornings when we wouldn't come out of his bedroom. Some days I didn't even feel the heavy air of downtown New York City, just the cool air-conditioning on my hair and the warmth of Stephen's body under the sheets.

We went to see Broadway shows. We shopped near the South Street Seaport. We ate out at fancy restaurants in Union Square. The whole thing seemed like a fantasy, like a surreal scenario that knew no bounds. We made love and I didn't feel remorse. I even walked down the streets of New York *holding his hand* from time to time. I felt invincible, like when I would run for miles upon miles in Andover or Chicago or even Granada.

When I arrived in New York, I was in incredibly good shape. I was lean, but stronger than I'd been in years. I actually had muscles visible in my arms, and there was the faintest sign of a six-pack coming. It helped that I'd been eating healthy meals that Marian had made me, a Mediterranean diet of lots of fish, lean meats, olives, and nuts, and lots of fruits and veggies. While I ran in Granada, I did lots of sit-ups and push-ups. I didn't drink a lot of alcohol; I barely went out, afraid to miss Stephen's call. I was focused on being at my best when I got back to see Stephen. In the sea of beautiful men all over Spain, I never got tempted by any of them.

In the whirlwind of the love affair with Stephen, I stopped running so much. I stopped worrying so much about fat; it was as if I forgot to. Just as the intimacy with Stephen wasn't bringing about guilt in me, by some miracle neither was allowing a reasonable amount of food to enter my body. Where I'd normally hide away at meal time, I was instead joining Stephen across the table. I rarely ran; in the mornings and evenings, when I'd normally run, I chose to be by Stephen's side instead. Perhaps I didn't know how long things with Stephen would last, and that shifted my priorities. It was more important to me to be with him. I chose him over running and starving.

After being with Stephen for about two months, I asked him if he'd move to Chicago with me. I remember making it a romantic night out—making dinner reservations, sitting at a candlelit table. I probably even prepared a poem. I asked him to move to Chicago with me the way you'd ask someone to marry you.

"Stephen," I said, looking into his eyes, "will you move to Chicago with me, and live with me there?"

It was a big moment for me. He said yes. He was able to secure a transfer to one of his company's offices in Chicago.

■ ■ ■

Before returning to Chicago, I had one more thing to do: I needed to go home to Andover to tell my parents that I'd fallen in love with someone. I wanted them to be happy for me, but mainly I just needed them to know. I rehearsed my speech to my parents in front of Stephen and in front of Sophia, who I saw frequently now, and they told me it would be fine. The last time I'd seen my dad was at the graduation party, when he'd been so proud of me. I knew this happier, easier period with my dad was about to end.

When I finally got the courage to call my parents to the family room for a discussion, I was shaking. Prior to Stephen, I hadn't met anyone other than Chad or Loren who I would've wanted to bring home to them. But Stephen was the guy you'd want to bring home to your parents. He was handsome and sweet and had a great job. He came from a wonderful family and had shown American saddle-bred horses. He was an all-American guy who happened to be gay . . . and who happened to love their son. I wondered, *how could they not understand this?*

I thought my mom would be fine, if not at that moment, then eventually. She'd always come around and I trusted that she would again. However, I knew that it was likely my dad wouldn't understand. Yet I felt compelled to tell them both at the same time. My happiness, the excitement of finding the first real and reciprocal love of my life, was something I wanted to share with my parents the way any young adult would.

"Mom? Dad?" I said. "I need to tell you something." *Deep breath.* "I've fallen in love. With a man. His name is Stephen. And he's moving with me to Chicago. He loves me so much, he's moving his whole life to be with me."

My mom looked down and away, as if in fear. She didn't want me to see the look on her face, a look of sadness and fear for me, because I think she knew what would come next.

"You come into my house and tell me this?" my father exploded. "I thought you had gotten over that phase? I didn't think you were . . . uh . . . anymore . . . I mean, I don't believe it. What a disappointment. After all the good news this year. Do you do this on purpose to me? I can't believe you are *my* son!" As he spewed his anger, he reddened and inflated. He came toward me aggressively. I got up quickly; I knew better than to stick around. I feared he'd run after me with the belt. It's amazing how quickly you can regress, no matter how old you are. But then I turned around and stuck out my chest.

"You'll never love me for who I am!" I screamed. "And I can't change! This is how God made me. What I feel is normal and is NOT disgusting. The love I feel for Stephen is not disgusting . . . it's not." I couldn't speak anymore and broke into tears. My mother came to my side and said, "I love you, Jon. We'll get through this. I promise."

I left my parents' house in tears after my father screamed that he wasn't going to be lectured in his own house. I stayed at Samantha's that night. She was bewildered; like me, she thought my dad had been coming around. I really had hoped it was going to be different, that the long struggle was going to be over. I actually had imagined Dad standing up and hugging me and saying, "I love you, Jon, no matter what. I'm happy you are happy." But that was just a dream.

When I woke the next morning, I drove home after I knew Dad was out of the house. My mom helped me pack my car and kissed me good-bye. I didn't see my dad. I headed west on the Massachusetts Turnpike toward Stephen's hometown to pick him up for our drive to Chicago. My father's disapproving image hung in the distance, in the rearview mirror of my mind. He was not to be heard from for over a year and on a day none of us will ever forget.

■ ■ ■

Everyone remembers where they were on September 11, 2001. As I was finishing my breakfast and preparing to leave for my workday, I got a call from my boss. I had ended up leaving the University of Chicago for a job at an HR consulting firm, mainly so I could spend my nights with Stephen instead of with books. "Turn on the news," my boss said, and then told me to stay home. Our office tower was evacuated because it stood in the shadow of the Sears Tower, a likely terrorist target.

Stephen and I sat on the couch alternately looking at the beautiful blue sky outside our twenty-first-story windows as F-16s passed by above Lake Michigan, and at the news, wondering how this could be happening in America.

I spent the morning calling Jared, Julie, Samantha, and Mom, Sophia, and other friends in New York, and friends in Massachusetts. When our phone rang later that day, I expected it to be one of our friends, or Mom, or Stephen's parents, checking in on us. But on the other end, I heard, "Jon, it's Dad, are you okay? I got your number from Mom and I am just so worried about all you kids." I didn't know what to say. I hadn't talked to him since he had rejected me for loving Stephen. He was, honestly, the last person I wanted to hear from and I just remained silent. "I'm stuck outside of Chicago at a meeting," he continued. "I wanted to see you. Maybe you could come out here and meet me for some pizza and a beer?" I don't know what came over me, but suddenly I was strong and unwilling to be manipulated by him.

"I'm sorry, Dad," I said. "I really appreciate you calling me and reaching out, and I'm glad you're okay, but there are so many other people that I need to find and talk to who care about me and know about me and have been in my life. I really don't want to see you right now. Good-bye."

I was like a different person. Maybe it was the severity of the loss and destruction that day. Part of me wondered, *Did I just tell him how I felt and do what was right for me instead of what I thought was right for him?* After desperately wanting his unconditional love, at any cost for so long, it was empowering to say no to him. And, it was true, what I had said to him; there were too many other people whose voices I needed to hear that day. They were my priority. I'd never been my father's priority, not at any time. He had banished me not only to my room, but at times from our home, and he hadn't helped me when I clearly had needed his help most.

Just three months before, at my brother's July wedding, my father wouldn't even say hello to me, or to Stephen. He didn't acknowledge we were there over the course of the entire two-day event. It was just another instance in which, as far as my father was concerned, I didn't exist. I'll never forget the pain on Mom's face, because her husband wouldn't look at his youngest son, not even on a day like Jared's wedding. It was moments like these that I knew her heart kept being whittled away, little by little.

Recalling times like Jared's wedding reminded me of why I didn't need my father at this tragic time; I needed people who loved me and whom I loved. Maybe his heart was cracking now that he was alone in the middle of Illinois on that horrible day, but my heart had been broken many times over. And what about my mom's heart, and my sister's, and my brother's? What about how he had turned around the framed photo I'd given Mom of Stephen and me so he didn't have to look at his gay son? Why would I want to look at him now? Why would I need him now, or more yet, why would I *want* him now, at this moment of enormity, this moment of national grief that would remain branded in our minds forever? Even though I knew he was trying to reach out to me, I didn't care.

■ ■ ■

I'd been seeing Dr. Robert since 1998. Mom made sure whatever wasn't covered by insurance, she'd take care of. Dr. Robert was making a major difference in my life. The work he and I did together, in my view, freed me from much of my own internalized homophobia infused in me by my father. After he had earned my trust, he challenged me and never let me off easy. I liked that he pushed me.

I'd always wondered about Dr. Robert's sexual orientation. It was hard to tell whether he was gay or not, kind of like the first time I'd gone to Emerson and wasn't sure about Paul. Dr. Robert didn't match the stereotypes I'd been taught, either. I admired him, especially since, at the time, I thought I wanted to be a clinical psychologist. I fantasized about having a thriving practice like his, in a tall high-rise tower in downtown Chicago.

Then one day, seemingly out of the blue (but now I know Dr. Robert didn't do anything without thinking about it first), he said, "Jon, you know I'm gay, right?" I didn't know how to answer. Truthfully, I *didn't* really know. I mean, it was something I thought about. And maybe I wished he were, but not because I had a crazy patient-therapist crush or anything. "You are?" I said. "I mean, you *are*. That's great."

"And you need to know," he continued, "that I'm a happy, healthy, whole person."

That moment has stuck with me. Dr. Robert was the first older gay role model I'd ever had. I'd had other positive male figures in my life, whom I'd needed desperately, like Jared and Matt, Samantha's dad, and Dr. Carbalatto. But it was such a powerful, significant thing for Dr. Robert to let me know his sexual orientation. It mattered to me in that moment, and the effect on me would be profound. For the first time since coming out, I believed that because of Dr. Robert—not just what he'd done for me but who he was—I was going to make it. I was going to make it in the world not despite being gay, but *because* I was gay—because of all the tumultuous and painful things I'd been through. That's how I had become the man I was. Through hours and hours of "unconditional positive regard," and what I considered to be very good therapy, I saw for the first time that I was not a burden to the world, but rather an asset.

The love and respect Dr. Robert showed me in therapy, and the love and respect I was receiving from Stephen every single day, were changing my life. I found more balance than I ever had before. I'd allowed myself to gain weight, and while it was hard to see myself rounder and plumper, I was happy. I still ran along Lake Shore Drive next to Lake Michigan on some mornings, not for the sake of burning fat, but to nourish my soul. Sometimes as I ran when the sun was rising, I would be inspired by the red sun, the vast lake that seemed like an ocean, the seagulls flying, the smell of the crisp air, and I would write emails to my friends in awe. I felt alive. I felt like living. I laughed more and noticed things that I'd taken for granted for so long. Dr. Robert found a way, over time, to get my father's image, which had haunted me ever since I was a child, to move first to the side of my mind, and then behind me. It's almost as if Dr. Robert's therapy relocated my father permanently into the rearview mirror. To say that he wasn't around or still in my view would be a lie, but he was behind me now. Despite his not being much of a part of my life since I had told him I was gay in that letter he said he'd never read—and even though he continued to pretend that it wasn't true or real, and acted as if I didn't exist when I insisted it was real—still, he was always in my mind. But Dr. Robert helped me move him into the background, so I could get on with my life.

When Mom visited Stephen and me in Chicago alone a few times, she could see that I was learning how to be content. She knew that Stephen had found something deep down inside of me that even she hadn't been able to awaken. In embracing and loving Stephen and having him love me back, I was embracing and loving myself. With Dr. Robert's steady voice and hand and with Stephen's loving heart, my journey to recover myself had reached a point that I had never imagined possible. Mom told me, "I love seeing you happy, Jon."

■ ■ ■

After September 11, Stephen and I wanted to move back to Boston so we could be around the people we loved the most. Even though it brought me in closer proximity to my father and all of the painful memories I had associated with Boston and Andover, we felt life was too short to almost never see loved ones. I applied for my doctorate at a few places and picked Boston University, where I received a fellowship. To help pay the bills, I got a job at Emerson College. I did both full-time.

Stephen and I rented a teeny, run-down apartment on Marlborough Street, in between Emerson and Boston University, so I could walk to both. We were broke, but we made the most of it. Disagreements about finances, which we'd completely co-mingled, crept in and eroded the seemingly unbreakable bond we had together. Stephen spent money we didn't have, mostly with romantic, thoughtful gifts, trying to make me happy. I'd get upset, wondering how we'd pay off the mounting credit card balances. His good intentions were backfiring. The intended romance of his surprises became only price tags and debt for me to worry about.

Eventually, I got a second job at New England Medical Center, working odd weekend shifts on the psych unit, to try to pay off the credit card debt that racked up. Then there were Stephen's endless parking tickets. For some reason, he refused to obey the Back Bay parking rules. When he got the boot, first for not paying the tickets he'd received on time, and then again for not paying them at all,

I nearly lost it. I did lose it when the car was towed and I discovered how much it was to bail it out (the number included all of the unpaid parking tickets). He promised me it would stop, and I wanted to believe him.

Even with these problems, Stephen and I continued to enjoy a good relationship, for the most part. We were each other's first live-in boyfriends. The fact that I was living with a man in an intimate relationship and feeling little shame about it was a huge feat. We had fun and traveled to great places together. We loved going out with friends. We had a good life, and it was really the first time that I traded my anorexia and running completely for my love for another man.

Stephen's reckless spending didn't stop, but we managed to stay together for four years, moving from one town and apartment to another. We both wanted our relationship to work—we wanted it to last forever. We had settled in at a condo on the outskirts of Boston, and that's where things really crumbled. As a surprise for me, Stephen purchased a second, very expensive dog. We could hardly take care of the golden retriever he'd adopted just a few months before because of the hours we both kept at work and school. I was flabbergasted.

Then, a couple of months later, as spring turned to summer in June 2004, four years to almost the day from when we became a couple, I returned home from a two-day business trip. In the two days I was gone, Stephen managed to turn our compact, concrete back porch into an overgrown greenhouse. He'd gone to the local nursery and bought so many flowers, hanging plants, bubbling fountains, and stone tables to hold even more plants and flowers that I couldn't open the door and step onto the patio.

I didn't dare look at the bill on the credit card and called and cancelled the account. I knew his spending wouldn't end, and in that moment I knew that if I stayed with Stephen, the issues we had with finances, which were probably a symptom of larger issues, would persist and make us resent one another more and more. A few days later I ended it. I called my sister Julie and her husband Matt. They helped me load what few things I wanted to take with me into the back of their minivan and I left most of the furniture for Stephen. It was devastating to walk out the door and close it behind me. I was walking away from a passionate love affair that had once seemed like a fairy tale, and I desperately wanted it to continue—but it couldn't. I knew it was over, and it was wrong to stay in something that wasn't working. If I did that, I feared I'd be too much like Mom.

The breakup was hard on both of us. We cried to one another on the phone many nights after we separated. We'd had experienced so many "firsts" together. Living and loving someone for that many years makes you have to reprogram yourself and your routine. I wasn't looking forward to remembering how it was to be alone again. And I was sad for Stephen, too.

When Dad learned that Stephen and I had broken up, suddenly he was willing to let me come back home. I received the invitation through Mom. He hadn't spoken to me almost the entire time I was with Stephen. It was almost as if now, because I wasn't actively in a gay relationship, he would now acknowledge my existence. But I knew, as did everyone close to me, that living with him would have been the worst thing for me. Samantha invited me to move in with her and her husband, Tim. "Why don't you come live with us for a while?" she offered. "You're not going back to your father's house, not if I have anything to say about it."

I was starting over this time, at least theoretically, from a stronger foundation. And yet, things shifted a bit—in reverse. In the solitude, unable to focus on the love I had for Stephen, I turned my focus on eating less again and running more. I tried my best to hide it from Samantha, which wasn't easy. She watched me like a mother bear. I didn't want her worrying. I traveled on weekends so that she and Tim could have alone time. While I always felt welcome there, I was very conscious of the fact that they were newlyweds, and I didn't want to be a burden to them.

I didn't want to be a burden to anyone, and in the difficulty of the breakup with Stephen, I again started to think of myself as a burden. So I just kept my head down while running, kept my head down while studying, kept my head down while working—kept my head down while living. Only this time I hoped, and even believed at times, that when I lifted my head at some point, there would be something waiting for me.

✳

Chapter 21

The Guy in the Photo

The year 2004 was intense. I was working at Boston University while also completing my doctorate there, still both full-time. Following my breakup with Stephen, I was still living with Samantha and her husband. I was in a messy place emotionally, so it was good to have their company on a regular basis—and good to be busy with work and school. I didn't much feel like going out and socializing, but every once in a while I'd force myself to go see one friend or another, if not so that I wouldn't become a complete hermit, then to get out of Samantha and Tim's way.

One night I paid a visit to an old friend named Noah. He was in a new relationship and couldn't wait to tell me all about it. "I'm really happy," Noah said. I liked hearing about it—it made me feel less pessimistic about love.

At first when he handed me the creased, glossy photo of him and his boyfriend from his weathered wallet, I thought nothing of it. "This is Justin," he said. And then I took a good look at the picture in my hand. *Oh my God,* I thought, *he's stunning!* When I looked up, I gasped. "That's such a nice picture; how'd the two of you meet?" I quickly asked, hoping Noah hadn't noticed my reaction—visceral and heart-stopping. Still mesmerized by the photo, I tuned out his answer.

I pulled the photo up to my face for a closer look. *Who is this guy?* "You guys are so cute together," I said enthusiastically, overcompensating. Justin's eyes were large green saucers. His smile was bright and beaming straight at me. There was warmth in his face, in his expression, that was very genuine and sincere.

On my drive back to Samantha's house in Winchester, I couldn't concentrate on anything but the guy in the photo. Despite the cars zipping by me on 93 South, I was fixated, fantasizing. Not of dating my friend Noah's boyfriend—but of *marrying him.*

I burst in after Samantha opened the front door. "You're not going to believe this," I said, "but I think I met my future husband today."

"Oh my God," she said, "who is it? Are you serious? Tell me, tell me!" she demanded.

"Okay, but you have to take me seriously," I said. "You promise?" She nodded yes. "Okay, so I saw this guy in a photo today that Noah showed me. It's actually his new boyfriend."

Samantha was silent, with her mouth agape.

"I know. I know. I'm crazy, right?"

"I'm just processing this."

"There was something about this guy's face," I explained. "It's hard to describe, but I could feel empathy radiating from him, right through the photo. I've never felt anything like this. But, tell me the truth, is this crazy?"

"I don't know, Jon," she said. "It sort of *sounds* crazy. If anyone else were telling me this, I would say they were crazy."

She paused for a moment, and I held my breath. "But, you . . . you have these gut instincts that always seem to be pretty right."

Whew. Samantha was on my side. She'd always been supportive of me—my crazy hopes and dreams, my fantasies around being a person who creates change and helps make the world a better place. But I could also pretty much always rely on her for a reality check. She would've told me I was nuts if she'd thought so; she hadn't been shy about telling me the truth in the past.

"Who knows, I'll probably never see him again," I lamented. We were sitting at Samantha's kitchen table, the one we'd had with us in our apartment in Chicago, the one at which, on so many nights, we'd talked about searching for and finding love. This night was no different, except that I was actually imagining, out loud, spending the rest of my life with another man.

■ ■ ■

A few weeks after seeing that incredible photo, as I was driving home on a Friday night, my friend Kathleen called my cell phone and invited me to a small party at her North End apartment. I thought about it for a moment, but I was still reeling from the fallout after the breakup with Stephen, and I was tired from work and school. "I don't know, Kathleen," I said, "I'm not really in a partying mood."

"Come on, Jon," she begged. "Just for one drink? There are so many people I want you to meet." But I was determined not to go. I was in a shitty mood. I started to explain about that sad state of my heart. Then, just as I was about to make the left-hand turn that would take me to the Zakim Bridge toward Winchester, Kathleen interrupted me. "Hold on!" she said.

"Jon?" said an unfamiliar but pleasing deep voice on the other end.

"Um, yeah," I said. "Who's this?"

"This is Justin, Kathleen's friend," the voice replied. "She's told me so much about you. Don't be depressed about your breakup. Just come on over. Just for a half hour. I bet you'll feel better. We're a fun bunch!"

When the light turned green, I suddenly found myself making a right instead of the left turn I made every day. "Ok, fine," I said to Justin. "I'll be there as soon as I can."

It was a warm end-of-June night, humid and sticky with the Boston Harbor salt air. When I got to Kathleen's, I hit the buzzer. From the intercom, I could make out Kathleen's voice in the midst of the music and laughter, "Jon, is that you?"

"Yup, I'm here. Buzz me in!" A loud click followed by a buzz, and I pulled the door. I ran up the several flights of stairs, following the noise. I banged on the door and it was opened—by the guy in that photo!

"Hey, I'm Justin," he said, putting his hand out. "Good to meet you, man!"

Holy shit, I thought, *it's Justin! The Justin.*

I didn't say a word to anyone. What was I going to say? *Um, hi, I'm Jon, it's nice to meet you and by the way, I'm going to marry your friend Justin. Oh and yeah, we've never met before; prior to this I've only seen him in a photo.* Instead, I didn't take my eyes off him. I just observed.

Everyone in the room was drawn to him—men and women alike. The women hung all over him and the guys joked with him. He was drinking a Corona with a lime in it, chugging it like a man, but holding it like a lady. He was thin, but fit, like a cross-country runner. His hair was light and tightly cropped to his head, spiked in the front, just as it had been in the photo. He had on a slim-fitting pair of jeans and a white, blue, and red checked button-down shirt. The sleeves were folded up above his strong-looking forearms, sprinkled with blond wispy hairs. He was masculine but in a gentle way. I could tell watching him interact with others that he was a loving person—*a good soul,* I vividly remember thinking to myself.

I met a lot of Kathleen's friends that night, all of whom were welcoming and fun. I ended up staying for more than that one drink. I didn't want to leave, actually, since Justin was there. By midnight, buzzed on alcohol and happiness, a bunch of us, including Justin, bought tickets for the Ben Folds and Guster concert coming up at the Pavilion on the Boston Harbor. A couple of hours later, Justin said he had to get back to his new apartment in Salem, the one he shared with Noah, to get a few more things unpacked before Noah got home from his overnight shift at the hospital. Before he left, he got my cell phone number and put it in his. I did the same. "Until the next time, Jon," he said and looked over his shoulder as he closed the door.

I crashed on Kathleen's couch that night, probably sleeping only a couple of hours before the sun streamed in through the one window in the teeny kitchen of the apartment and woke me. I instantly re-membered Justin's face, his warm handshake, his great laugh. I left a note for Kathleen thanking her for a great evening, slipped out of the apartment and walked down to my car. I drove back to Samantha's, barely able to contain myself until I got home.

Over the next few weeks, Justin and I had a few friendly phone conversations, and also crossed paths at another party or two. When the weekend of the Ben Folds concert arrived, I invited him to park his car at Samantha's house—which I just happened to have all to myself, as Samantha and Tim went to the Vineyard that weekend. "We can take the train together, from here, to the concert," I suggested.

It was one of those gorgeous, warm summer nights in the city. We had great seats under the tent and close to the stage. The breeze off the ocean carried Justin's scent right to me. *God,* I thought, *he smells amazing.* I wanted to grab him and make out with him right there.

My crush had matured over those several weeks. I'd been thinking about Justin and writing about him in my journal, perhaps in line with so many of my unrequited loves from across oceans, or across sexual orientations. In this case, a different boundary separated us: his status as my friend's boyfriend.

Standing beside him, I had a strange feeling in my stomach, although it was familiar. It wasn't a reaction I'd ever had to another person. Instead, it reminded me of the feeling I had when I was especially obsessed with starving and running. Since breaking up with Stephen and moving in with Samantha and Tim, I'd been doing okay, although I was sad a lot of the time, and to comfort myself, I sometimes allowed familiar thoughts of self-loathing to creep in. At times, they prevailed and made me believe I was meant to be alone so that I once again had reverted to running more and eating less. But this time I wasn't trying to disappear, at least not consciously, like before. Perhaps I was holding on to something familiar at a time that was transitional and challenging. To the eye of a doctor or therapist, it might have looked like a relapse, but I was convinced I wasn't that bad.

It helped to have Samantha right there, under the same roof, keeping a watchful eye. She made healthy, square meals that would have been difficult for me to refuse. It would have been nearly impossible to starve myself even if I wanted to. That was just it, though—I *didn't* want to starve myself anymore. Sure, I thought about my weight and always believed that when I was thin I looked better. But I was past wanting to die. Even though Justin was taken and I wasn't going to do anything about that, my feelings for him gave me hope that finding real love with a man was possible. Maybe not with Justin, but with someone. My feelings for him felt more like that kind of love than anything else I'd experienced.

At one point in the concert, the rest of the band cleared the stage, and Ben Folds sat at his piano alone. He played a song I'd never heard before—"The Luckiest." *And in a wide sea of eyes I see one pair that I recognize. And I know that I am the luckiest.* It was one of the most beautiful songs I'd heard in a long time. I wanted to hold Justin's hand, but I knew I couldn't; I wouldn't do that to Noah *or* Justin.

At the end of the concert, as we were leaving the pavilion, it began to pour. We ran with our friends down the streets of the Boston Waterfront to try to get a taxi to North Station. By the time we got on the train, we were soaked. We laughed as our clothes stuck to our bodies.

When the conductor yelled, "Winchester Center," it was torrentially raining, with thunder and lightning. We didn't have anyone to call to come get us from the station, so we just ran. We ran through town, and across the track and football field near Samantha's house. We jumped in the puddles, splashing like two young kids, unafraid of being struck by lightning or catching a cold from being soaked through. "It's just water!" Justin screamed out loud, spinning with his arms wide and his mouth open to let the drops of rain quench his thirst.

When we got up on the front porch of Samantha's house, I asked Justin if he needed a change of clothes for his ride home. "That's probably a good idea, thanks." He came in and I got him my favorite running jacket and a pair of sweatpants. He went upstairs to change in the spare room, where I'd been staying. For a moment, I considered running upstairs and catching him in the middle of his changing, but, of course, I didn't. Instead I poured some water into a glass and waited for him to come down the stairs. "Thanks," he said, "this is so much better." He looked handsome with his hair starting to dry. It wasn't styled—there was no "product." This was how I imagined he'd look after a shower. He drank the glass of water and kind of just looked at me. It was awkward for a moment, mostly because I wanted him to stay and maybe he did, too. "I should get going," he said.

"Yes, right," I said. "You've got to get home."

My heart panged as the taillights of his car grew fainter down Samantha's street. I wanted him to stay with me, all night. Instead I stayed up alone that night, writing a letter to Justin in my journal—one I never sent. I fell asleep alone with that journal in my arms.

■ ■ ■

I kept quiet all summer. My heart ached for Justin as my yearning for him grew, but there was nothing I could do about it. I could only be his friend, and that way, I got to know him quite well. I discovered I admired so much about him. His exterior beauty was matched by inner beauty. He was kind and thoughtful. I'd learned that he spent two days each week with an intellectually disabled adult, helping him do his shopping and manage his bills. Justin had real friendships that endured, just as I did. His character was solid, built with loyalty and trustworthiness passed on to him by his loving parents, who also happened to be in love with one another, providing Justin with the example of a happy relationship. He came from a close-knit family full of goodhearted people. He was smart and curious about everything. He had a great sense of humor, and—the icing on the cake—he thought *I* was hilarious. Being able to reveal my funny side to Justin was a huge indication that I trusted him. Only a few good friends had ever seen the zany side of me—the Jon who'd put on impromptu, silly lip-synching shows to music, replete with spontaneous choreographed dances and faux-serious faces.

No matter how hard I tried, it was hard to find anything about

Justin *not* to like, which was unfortunate for me, because there were no signs of him breaking up with Noah.

Not any that I could see, anyway.

■ ■ ■

In the early fall, some of Justin's friends, who had become my friends now, told me they were really worried about Justin. He'd lost a lot of weight since he started dating Noah. Some said he became quiet and distant, insecure even. Others said he'd turned inward and wasn't himself. "He's only himself when he's around you, Jon," one of his friends said. *Oh, dear.* "No one understands what Justin sees in Noah," another friend said. Maybe their relationship wasn't as solid as I'd initially thought. Noah did work long and off hours as an overnight nurse, and so Justin spent a lot more time with his friends and family than he did with Noah. And when they were together, Noah seemed to be always criticizing Justin.

One night, I got to see what our friends were talking about. We were all at Noah and Justin's apartment for dinner. Justin was making coffee to go with dessert and accidentally spilled coffee grounds all over the counter. A few of us laughed until Noah snapped. "Ugh, look at the mess you made!" he sighed impatiently, rolling his eyes, "I'll just do it myself." Justin walked away ashamed and silent into the bedroom. It took every ounce of self-restraint for me to not run in after him to give him a hug.

It was hard not to fantasize about them breaking up, and sometimes I believed it was coming, even though I cared about both of them. I could do nothing, though. If they broke up, it couldn't be because of something I had done if I was going to seem honorable in Justin's eyes. I wanted to be honorable to myself, too. If I felt as strongly for Justin as I thought I did, I wanted to protect the relationship at all costs. If it meant that I had to do what was best for him, and if that meant that he loved Noah, then so be it.

I remained intent on not telling anyone other than Samantha about my feelings for Justin, as I knew deep down that I had to let his relationship with Noah run its course. A part of me worried they'd stay together forever, either out of convenience since they shared an apartment, or because they were actually in love. Another part of me knew that if Justin and I were meant to be together, then we would be.

After a while, I wasn't able to see Justin without feeling sad. Then, I got a call about an open position from a university with a campus on the West Coast. I'd finished with my doctoral classes in June and had only my dissertation left and had gotten a big chunk of it done over the summer. I thought, *what the hell? I have nothing to lose.* Justin and Noah were still going strong and I couldn't wait forever. I was sure I wasn't helping Samantha and Tim's dreams of starting a new family by cramping their style on most weeknights. Maybe it would be running away, like I'd been doing—literally and figuratively—for so long, but I decided to go for it, no matter what the reasons. *Here goes nothing,* I thought. I was offered the job and took it. It was one of the most spontaneous things I've ever done. I just packed up and went.

After two weeks in San Francisco, with over three thousand miles between us, I could still think only of Justin. I was in the middle of one of my favorite places in the world. I was a single man in one of the gayest cities in the United States, as my father had made a point to tell me when I was a teen. And all I could do was obsess about Justin. He and I would talk on the phone and I'd tell him I was lonely, but kept to myself how much I missed him and wanted to be with him. Justin learned a lot about me during those long-distance phone calls. He listened intently as I told him about my struggles with my sexual orientation, and I confided about my eating disorder. Even though his coming out experience was the exact opposite to mine—his parents basically said, "So what? We love you. What's your boyfriend's name?"—his empathy was as deep as I thought it would be from my first glimpse of that photograph.

Cut off from my friends and my mom, and in desperate, unrequited love, my old liaisons of running and starving tried to move in on me more permanently. Part of me wondered if I became thinner and had less body fat (and I didn't have much to begin with), would

Justin find me attractive enough to leave Noah? It was irrational thinking, but it was easy for me to go there when I was by myself so much. I fought against it, but it wasn't easy. I had bad days.

I'd run every morning along the Embarcadero toward the Golden Gate Bridge, in the chilly fall of the season, thinking about Justin. Everything I saw, every sound I heard brought me back to thoughts of him. I wondered, *what am I doing here?* I'd spent my entire life looking for love and acceptance, and here I was across the country, running again, day after day, away from the very thing I longed for. After work, I'd walk the streets of the Financial District toward my temporary apartment with temporary furniture. I couldn't find a place I liked enough to put down a deposit. Something was blocking me. Everything felt, well, temporary, and even though I knew why, I couldn't admit it.

My friend James, now a musician, had some gigs in San Francisco and crashed in my apartment for a few days. I broke down and told him about Justin. "What are you doing here, then?" he asked. "What are you waiting for? You've been looking for something like this your whole life. Why don't you go after it?"

■ ■ ■

I quit my job and packed my things and flew back to Boston. I needed to finish my dissertation, and having the time to write and prepare for my defense was probably a good thing. That's what I told everyone. I didn't tell them that I was really returning to be near Justin, even though he wasn't mine, and maybe he'd never be.

Back in Boston, a couple of months went by and Justin's relationship status didn't change. I kept my mouth shut and simply did all I could to be the best friend to him. I'd listen to him lament about his boring job as an insurance clerk, and I'd help him brainstorm about other career paths he could take. I saw more in him than he may have seen in himself professionally. I noticed that he seemed to be more forlorn than when I'd first met him, but he didn't say anything to me about his relationship with Noah. We'd see each other at parties and talk on the phone. Our bond grew stronger and stronger. I even dog-sat for Justin and Noah at their apartment when they went to Savannah, Georgia, for New Year's.

I thought it was odd when Noah asked me if I wanted to move into his apartment when they got back.

"What do you mean?" I asked, perplexed.

"I just think it's coming to an end, me and Justin, and I'll need a roommate," Noah said.

Part of me wanted to warn Justin and protect him, but I knew I couldn't. Then one day, right after New Year's, I got a call from Justin. He was distraught and hysterical.

"He broke up with me," he wailed. "He wouldn't tell me why. Can you call him and ask him why? I just don't get it!" It was hard to hear Justin so heartbroken over someone else, but I was his friend, and I'd vowed to myself I'd be a true friend and be there for him. "I need to move home to my parents' house," he added. "Can you help me?"

I consoled him as best I could. I called Noah just as Justin asked me, looking for answers, but it didn't do any good. Noah just said it was over and seemed cold about it. Justin was devastated. I knew what he was going through since I'd been through it with Stephen. As I listened to him talk about how painful the breakup had been day after day, week after week, it was hard for me not to tell him the way I felt, but I knew the timing wasn't right. Just as I'd promised myself that I would never cross the line while he was with Noah, I promised that I wouldn't confide in him about my feelings until I knew he was ready to hear it. I needed everything to be right because I knew it was all or nothing. I'd either have him—or lose him—forever.

I ended up waiting three weeks after Justin and Noah broke up, and finally, I couldn't bear it any longer.

Justin was working at an insurance company in Andover (of all places!) at the time, and I asked him to meet me at a florist downtown. I stayed in the car and watched him go in. A dozen peach roses were waiting for him, with a card that read, "Thank you for Blue Skies. Look outside." Justin had been my blue skies for a long time, getting me through the final phases of my dissertation, helping me deal with my breakup with Stephen, listening to me as I talked about my strained relationship with my father. It was the title of a song he and I had grown to like together as our friendship developed. He was surprised, and he was smiling so broadly, I could see his teeth from the car outside the shop's window. When he came outside, he asked me, "What is this for?"

And I declared, "I've been waiting for you for a long time and I am willing to risk our friendship on taking you out on a date because I'm that certain we're meant to be. Are you coming with me?" Justin opened the door and got in the car.

I took him to Casa Romero, a quaint, authentic Mexican restaurant in an alley off Newbury Street. It was romantic and beautiful. We had a quiet table in a corner, and even though I was nervous, it seemed very natural. Everything flowed: the laughter, the food and drinks, the smiles. It was everything I had hoped.

After dinner, we walked to Symphony Hall, where I got us two mezzanine seats for the Boston Symphony Orchestra. We held hands as we listened to the music and afterward, we walked the streets of Boston back toward Casa Romero, where we had left the car. When we got there, the restaurant was vacant and we were cold. We had to wait for our valet parking attendant to retrieve the car, so we stood in the doorway of the restaurant, huddling close together. Justin held me to keep me from shivering. I looked into his face close to mine and before I even had a moment to wish for it, he leaned in and kissed me. It was one of the most tender, romantic, loving kisses I had ever experienced. And I didn't care one bit who was or was not watching. I was completely lost in the moment.

When we got back to Andover, it was after midnight, and Justin's car was the only one in the parking lot behind the Old Town Hall. I pulled my car next to his and put the parking brake on and left the car running so we wouldn't freeze. We talked about how enchanting the night was. "I always knew you were a romantic, but I had no idea how romantic," Justin said. "Thank you for an amazing night."

He leaned in to kiss me again. At first, I wondered, for just a second, *could my dad be out and about in Andover? At this late hour?* But then something took over, maybe the intense connection that had so long to build, the emotions I had for Justin, and I simply let it flow. We made out in my car for what seemed to be an hour, in the middle of Andover, the street lights shining down on us like spots, in my hometown, the same town where my father still lived, where I'd once thought that finding someone like Justin was impossible. *I don't care if he sees me,* I thought. *I'm in love with Justin and I'm not giving this up for anyone.*

☀

Chapter 22

Finding Home

n March 2005, Justin and I moved to Pittsburgh, both for new jobs at Carnegie Mellon University, and bought our first house together.

For the next few years, we made a home out of a 1937 Craftsman bungalow just off Regent Square. We spent days and nights fixing it up, stripping the old wallpaper, painting, pulling up old carpeting, and refinishing the original pine wood floors that had been hidden underneath. We hung photos and paintings we'd find on our adventures around the world together. We'd make lovely dinners together and we'd enjoy meals out—and I ate, mostly like a normal person, without obsessing too much about the fat content of what I put in my mouth.

We adopted Kelsey, a gorgeous black Labrador retriever. Our home was simple and welcoming, a symbol of the love and friendship that Justin and I shared together. We filled it with people we loved and who loved us as we built a foundation for what we hoped would be a lifelong love affair. We were best friends, travel buddies, lovers, partners, and confidants. It was everything I'd ever imagined a real love to be and one that I never thought I deserved or would revel in. I was wrong about that, because this was *it* this time, the real thing, even if my father disapproved.

Dad never visited. He was staunch in remaining distant, and very uneasy about my relationship with Justin. Still, he was showing small signs of progress, like attending my doctoral hooding ceremony, which we flew back to Boston for, and where I had Justin by my side the whole time. Afterward Dad took me and all my closest friends out to an Italian dinner in Samantha's town. He took me aside before we sat down at the long table. "You're the first doctor in our family, Jon. I'm proud of you, son." He even patted my back. Everyone thought maybe he was getting better, even though I'd pretty much given up hope.

As often as she could manage, Mom would come down to Pittsburgh and stay for a week at a time. She helped us get the house in order when we first moved in, and she came down when I converted from Dad's Catholic religion to Episcopalian, the religion of Mom's family and Justin's, too, and a church in which I felt more welcomed as a gay man of faith.

After one of her visits, she sent us a letter telling us how happy she was to spend time with us and how happy she was for us. She wrote, "Your home, your puppy, and your life together are great and you are so lucky to have found each other. I love you. Mom."

My obsession with staying thin and running miles and miles faded farther into the background, just as my dad did. My father's image, which was always in the forefront of my mind or his voice in the inner most part of my ear, had faded into the background, too. The time and energy that it took me to run miles and miles I preferred spending with Justin: at the movies, at a play, at a bar or restaurant. The focus and concentration that anorexia required from me was now overtaken by my love affair with Justin. I believed the love I was forging with him was something that could and would sustain me.

Just as I was getting over needing my dad's acceptance, he surprised all of us and invited Justin and me on a family cruise to the Caribbean as a Christmas gift. He got each of his kids and their spouses their own cabin. I was uneasy about going, but just like the rest of my family, I longed for us to be a happy, "normal" one.

It was a pretty decent trip. We had a blast with my sister and her family, and my brother and his. I thought—we all thought—that Dad had come around. I never felt fully comfortable around him, and made sure Justin and I weren't affectionate anywhere near him. But it was progress that I'd never thought would come. Our family was moving forward and forgiving all the things that had happened in the past.

Dad was okay to be around, as long as Justin and I acted as buddies and not as lovers. We mostly stayed out of his way, but enjoyed a couple of big meals as a family. On New Year's Eve, Dad even rented out a karaoke room for us. I grabbed the microphone, a bit intoxicated on the champagne bubbles from ringing in 2006, when Julie and Jared played Donna Summer's "MacArthur Park" in my honor. He didn't watch me sing with disgust; he actually seemed to enjoy it. He reached out for Mom and danced with her, twirling her around as she smiled. My heart warmed even more. I wondered if old age was indeed mellowing him, as everyone had promised it would. I thought it was the beginning of a new era. But then one night Dad cornered me on his balcony when Mom was getting ready in their bathroom. "It seems like you and Justin are really serious," he said.

"Yes, we are," I responded. I wondered where he was going with this. I didn't trust that he was going to say something supportive, and I was right.

"I hope you aren't going to be one of those types who goes out and gets married," he said. "It just isn't right. And I really hope you aren't thinking about having children. Do you know how much damage you'd do to your kids? It's hard enough being a kid today let alone having two dads."

I was instantly crushed. I didn't remember asking him for his opinion and I probably wouldn't have, knowing he'd probably say something exactly like what he did. I was filled with rage. But then in my mind, I switched to rationalizing for him. *He's ignorant,* I told myself. *He was raised in a generation that just couldn't—wouldn't—ever understand. Isn't it enough, Jon, that you're here, on this boat with the rest of your family, as one? Leave it alone.*

"Thanks for your thoughts, Dad," I said. "I've got to go get ready for dinner." I didn't tell Justin or anyone else what he said at the time. I didn't want to start a war. Mom was so content seeing all of us together, getting along, for the first time in a decade. I didn't want to ruin it.

Mom radiated in a way that I hadn't seen in a long time. On New Year's Eve she wore a "2006" silver and gold tiara to dinner and smiled bigger than I'd seen her do in the prior ten years. Things seemed different, better, maybe even complete. Even if he was against the idea of me marrying, maybe Dad had softened and he learned that love didn't discriminate. People close to me had always been hopeful that he would finally come to see it that way. Could this be the shot at the real family, the functional family that we all had prayed to God to for so long?

■ ■ ■

When my grandmother, Mom's mom, died at ninety-six that following July, Dad wanted Justin and me to stay at their house. I was stunned. It was one thing for him to deal with us staying together in our own cabin on a cruise; it was another, entirely, for him to deal with us staying together, sharing a room, under his roof.

"Your mother needs you," he told us, "and I'm okay with you being here. I can handle it."

I was nervous about staying at the house. It had been years since I'd been there even just by myself, and I'd never brought Justin home before. "We can just stay at a hotel," I said. "It's no big deal, Dad. Maybe that would be easier?" But he insisted. And I would've done anything for my mother.

After the funeral, my parents had several guests to their home for sandwiches and other finger food. When the majority of the people left, some of us gathered in the family room to sit and relax for the first time that day. I was particularly weary because at the request of my mom, I had stayed up late the night before to write and practice the eulogy.

Our ten-year-old niece cuddled between Justin and me on the couch. As I turned to reposition myself, my arm barely brushed up against Justin's shoulder. That was it.

"Jon, enough is enough!" my father shouted before I could even figure out what had set him off. He forcefully encouraged our niece to join him in the kitchen.

An hour later, Jared told me that Dad said he felt that my cuddling together with Justin and our niece would damage her and his other grandchildren, sitting nearby. It wasn't right, he said. That set off something inside me. I felt violated and immediately regressed, doubting myself and my relationship with Justin. I was instantly filled with the all-too-familiar self-loathing. Then, I learned that Dad told my sister that he couldn't have "that disgusting crap" in his house.

I completely snapped. Instead of pouting and feeling sorry for myself, I puffed up and became protective of Justin. Faced once again by my father's repugnance, but this time with Justin, the love of my life, witnessing it, I couldn't hold back and went to find and confront him.

"I've heard what you said to Jared and Julie," I said. "This is who I am, Dad." I couldn't believe I was scolding my father, with my mother by his side, but I couldn't stop myself. "I am *not* disgusting and I am *not* damaging your grandchildren. They love their Uncle Justin and their Uncle Jon. I've given you so many years to get over this. What is wrong with you?"

That question enraged him and appeared to raise his blood pressure, as the red veins began bursting in his eyes. "You ARE damaging my grandchildren!" he screamed, lunging toward me, pointing his finger. His face was swollen, his eyes wild with fury. "You are not going to lecture me in my home, Mister. Get out of my house!"

"I am not the one damaging these kids, nor our entire family," I fired back. That set him off even more. He ran after me, full of wrath, with his finger flying at my face. "Get out of my house, Mister. I'm not going to have this disgusting shit in my house!" he screamed. "This is my house!" he screamed. "This is *my* house!"

Justin and I ran upstairs and quickly grabbed our belongings. With our loosely packed bags, we waited at the end of Crescent Circle for my sister to take us to Samantha's house a few towns away. There, we gathered ourselves and our emotions for the night.

The next day we went to Justin's parents' home, where we were always embraced and welcomed. In the car, I looked at Justin, whose upbringing had been far from all of this. You could still see the horror in his eyes. For me it was nothing new, my father had cast me out, more times than I could remember. But Justin was mortified. He'd heard the stories, but had never seen my dad in action since Dad had been, for nearly all of my two-year relationship with Justin, barely talking to me.

"He's scary, isn't he?" I said. "Especially when faced with anything he perceives as threatening to his manhood. And that is me, a threat. I am the biggest failure, the biggest threat to what he's created for his life."

■ ■ ■

That summer, after this incident, I cut off contact with Dad. When Justin and I got back to our home in Pittsburgh and we walked across the threshold, I was greeted by the memories we had already created there. As I took in the familiar scenery and breathed in the familiar scents, I was overtaken by a sense of peace and quiet. *This,* I thought, *is a safe place. This is a home.* I was reminded of the journey that had brought us there, the journey that had gotten *me* there. I had allowed myself to be loved by a wonderful man, who was loyal and kind. And I loved him unconditionally and wholeheartedly back. In that moment, something deep inside me was profoundly altered. After years of putting up with rejection, verbal abuse, and the threat of violence because I so craved my father's love, I could no longer take it. Being chased out of my childhood home with the man I loved on the day of my nana's funeral made me realize that I needed to protect Justin from my father. I needed to protect him the way my mom had not been capable of protecting me. I did what she couldn't: I left and never looked back.

Now, returning to my new, my real home was an epiphany, an alignment of shifting plates that I had been moving since I fell for Chad in high school. By willingly and completely accepting the love between Justin and me, I was able to accept who I was. In that acceptance and surrender, I knew I needed to fully let go of desperately wanting to be loved by the most rejecting and abusive figure in my life. Being chased out of my home as an adult changed everything.

I embraced Justin and held onto him for several minutes. "I need to write my dad an email, and include Julie, Jared, and Mom on it," I told him. "He can't pretend to not get another one of my letters. He needs to hear what I have to say this time."

The subject line read: "Basketball." I chose that because I knew my father would open the email if it seemed to have something to do with sports. It was probably the only way to get his attention.

"The ball is in my court and I'm never passing it back to you," I wrote, addressing him in his own terms. *"I've made the best decision: to stay far away from you. I'm done dribbling in your court of ups and downs."*

My heart raced as my fingers frantically typed the words flowing from my head.

"I feared, every single day of my life, telling you who I was. I wanted to kill myself to avoid the truth just to protect you. I tried starving myself to make it easier for you, but it was never enough. I was never good enough for you.

"I quit the hardest habit of my life: running back to you for your unattainable acceptance; grasping for love from my father, a love you never had the capability to give. I finally realized that I deserved so much better, and my addiction was killing me inside, so I quit. You will never have the opportunity to push me down again. You will never have the chance to tell me I'm not worth it ever again. I never wanted to play basketball in the first place."

Relief came over me as if a stream of toxins seemed to gush from my body. *I'm ready,* I thought. I clicked SEND and closed my laptop. I was done for good.

Or so I thought.

■ ■ ■

It felt unreal to find myself standing on the Woolvenstraat Bridge in the middle of Amsterdam two Januarys after our first date about to propose to the true love of my life. With lights shimmering off the canal, I felt like we were the only two people in the city. We brought rings from the United States with us in little ring bags. I wanted Justin to see Holland and to see Castle Well, where I'd done so much growing. I believed that what I'd been through was my journey to find my way to him; all of it to be ready for Justin.

We both got onto one knee, giddy with happiness and love, and we each asked the other for his hand in marriage. It was one of the most unbelievable moments of my life. I thought, *have I really traveled this far? Here I am standing in the middle of a city, in front of passing bikers and walkers, kissing my future husband in public, without a care in the world.* We planned to marry, nine months later, on September 8, 2007—9/8/7.

The next several months were a blur of planning and preparation. Justin and I were to be married outside under a pergola in the "systematic gardens" at Tower Hill Botanic Garden. I couldn't wait.

Finally, the day arrived. It was the hottest, most humid September day Massachusetts had seen in years. If you closed your eyes, you might think you were in a dense jungle in Costa Rica instead of the Boylston sanctuary.

It hadn't been that stifling the evening before, at Justin's parents' home, where our people of honor, those who were standing up in our wedding, gathered for our rehearsal dinner. Tears flowed as our family and closest friends toasted our future and talked about the struggles we had endured to get to this very special day. We felt a lot of love that evening and had tremendous hope for our future.

The weather turned just before our ceremony, and we were forced inside. With flashes of lightning, crashes of thunder, and huge raindrops pelting the roof of the "great hall," Justin and I recited our vows and exchanged rings in front of our guests.

"With this ring I gave you and that is blessed today, never abandon the notion that I am devoted to you, that I am truly in love with you. Wear it as a symbol of our bond and our undying commitment to one another; for you are the love of my life." At that moment, the Rev. Dr. Peter, Justin's childhood Episcopal priest, introduced us as "loving spouses." The room erupted in applause and cheers. I thought, *I can't believe I'm married to a man, this man!* Flooded with emotions and flashbacks of all I'd been through, I hugged Justin, burying my face into his shoulder to try to stop the flood of tears.

Mom came without Dad. He and I hadn't spoken since Nana's funeral. Justin and I had made the very conscious decision to only have people at our wedding who had loved us unconditionally through the years and who supported our union. My father was not one of those people.

In the middle of the reception, in the glass structure called the Orangerie, Mom pulled Justin and me aside. The rain had stopped and the ground was wet and steaming from the heat. She brought us to a private cocktail table and handed us a card. In it were two checks. One check was from her, made out to Jon and Justin Croteau. The other check was for more money, and signed by my dad. It was made out only to me, and with my former last name. Mom said, "You choose which one you want." We hugged her and thanked her, and returned to her the check with my father's signature. She took it back with her.

My gut told me, as it had before, to keep doing whatever it took to ensure my financial freedom from my father. In the times when Dad wouldn't speak to me, Mom never let me suffer financially and wanted to give me gifts the way she did my brother and sister. She had to be stealthy about it—never using the credit card she shared with Dad to buy me things, writing checks at the local family-owned grocery store, for which they'd give her cash in exchange. She'd save the cash up until she'd see me, and then use it to go shopping with Justin and me for things we needed.

I knew she was conflicted about buying things in cash so my father wouldn't find out. Looking back, I'm even more aware of how very difficult it must have been for her to deceive my father. That she did it anyway is a testament to how much she loved me.

After the ceremony, people couldn't stop dancing and singing and holding on to one another in group circles. Even though there was food everywhere, Justin and I didn't have one drink or one nibble; we were locked hand in hand most of the evening.

Embracing my mother in a dance, I whispered in her ear, "I adore you, Mom." I had forgiven her years ago, about the time I was in graduate school at Northwestern, for not leaving my father. I empathized with why she stayed, struggling with her own insecurities and limitations. Because she had accepted everything about me, I always believed she deserved the same.

"I am so proud of you, Jon," she replied with a quivering, deep, raspy voice, the result of her many years of heavy smoking. "This ceremony, this wedding was gorgeous. You are such a wonderful, loving man, and Justin is lucky to have you. Remember that. And don't forget how lucky you are to have him, too. What you share together is more of a love than I ever had with your father, and don't let anyone ever tell you that it is wrong."

I had learned in my counseling program that children and teens were resilient as long as they had one adult consistently loving them throughout their life. I knew that I was dancing with more than just my mother; I was dancing with my greatest champion.

✳

Chapter 23

Saying Good-bye

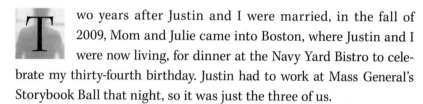wo years after Justin and I were married, in the fall of 2009, Mom and Julie came into Boston, where Justin and I were now living, for dinner at the Navy Yard Bistro to celebrate my thirty-fourth birthday. Justin had to work at Mass General's Storybook Ball that night, so it was just the three of us.

Despite the pain that had come more often to her legs when she walked, she insisted she was up for the walk from my house near the Bunker Hill Monument, all the way down to the Navy Yard. We had learned from specialists at Mass General through a sophisticated body scan that her arteries had been hardened by the multiple-pack-a-day-habit she'd just given up almost a year before. The scan lit up like a constellation map. Atherosclerosis was serious, but doctors assured us that with Mom getting off "the butts," she'd live many years longer, at least long enough to see many of her grandchildren grow up and maybe even get married to whomever they loved. Though not immediately life-threatening, the hardening stopped blood flow and caused immense pain for her. But she insisted. "It's a gorgeous night, let's enjoy it!"

To look at her that night, you'd never know she was suffering. She was especially glowing that evening. That summer, she'd started wearing a slightly longer variation of the Dorothy Hamill hairstyle she'd worn in the 1980s, the years I remembered her being most vivacious. Even though it was nearly thirty years later, her hair was thick, full, and highlighted, with not a touch of gray despite her having celebrated her sixty-seventh birthday that previous Independence Day.

She didn't look nearly her age on that windy, chilly October evening by the Boston Harbor.

The night was perfect. The three of us laughed and enjoyed a great meal with endless discussion. "BBs said to wish you a happy birthday," Mom said. "I told him to call you himself and to fuck off." We all laughed hysterically. "BBs" stood for "Big Balls," a name she'd given my dad in my early twenties, not necessarily referring to the size of his anatomy, but rather as a reflection of how he always saw himself: big man on campus, in charge. Her sarcastic sense of humor, which had become even drier with age, was legendary. As she grew older and more tired of my father's antics, she was known to not only give him names, but also give him the middle finger (in front of him and behind his back).

Even though I was laughing about my mother's comment, it still stung, realizing that this year marked yet another in which my father wouldn't call to wish me a happy birthday. The last time I'd seen his face was when he was charging at me out of his house. In the meantime, he'd missed many family gatherings. Mom, Jared, and Julie had taken a stand after Nana's funeral that if he couldn't come around about my sexual orientation, that it would be he who would be left alone on holidays and vacations. Earlier that year, in February, we all went to Disney World: Julie, Jared, their spouses and their children, me, Justin, and Mom. Dad was left at home by himself because he still couldn't handle seeing me and Justin together.

As we walked back along the winding, gas-lit Charlestown streets, even heading uphill toward the Bunker Hill Monument, Mom didn't complain once about the aches and pains in her legs, and continued at a faster clip than normal. She seemed noticeably happier that night than usual. The years of living with my father had made her jaded and depressed most of the time. On this night, she was lighter, freer.

I walked Mom and Julie to Mom's car. We said our good-byes. When I got back to my house, I went upstairs to the bathroom to wash my face; on my cheek, I noticed that she had left me a maroon lipstick kiss.

When she got back to Andover, she called my house to tell me she was safe and sound. She laughed, saying that Julie was the worst "side-seat driver!" We giggled, and then she said, "I always have so much fun with you, Jon. I hope you had a happy birthday dinner. I love you so much."

"I love you, too, Mom," I said. "Talk to you tomorrow."

■ ■ ■

It was the morning of my actual birthday when I got the call.

Justin had asked my birthday wishes weeks before. "I just want to have breakfast out with you on a 'school day,'" I had said. That had always been my favorite thing—what Mom and I often did together starting back when I attended Hudson Country Day in Ohio.

Justin and I were sitting in a small neighborhood breakfast café; the sky was a crisp October blue and the sun was bright. Leaves cascaded to the ground as passersby, bundled in their New England layers, rushed to get to work on time. It was the perfect birthday morning.

Julie's number kept making my cell phone buzz, and I kept ignoring it. I was enjoying talking with Justin over omelets and pancakes, and I was wondering why my sister wouldn't stop trying to interrupt. Since moving back to Boston to be closer to family and friends, Justin and I hadn't enjoyed many quiet moments alone, so I wanted to savor this one. I figured Julie wanted to wish me a happy birthday or reminisce about the great night we'd just had with Mom at the Bistro.

Finally, Julie texted, "9-1-1, Julie." When I called her back and she picked up the phone, she was panic-stricken. I couldn't understand a word she screamed, but still, I knew. I begged her not to say anymore. "We'll be there as fast as we can," I assured her. "Just tell me where you are!"

When we arrived at Lawrence General Hospital, Julie lunged at me. She wrapped her arms around me and cried, "She's gone, Jon!"

What? No! I screamed inside. At first, silenced by the shock, I buckled at the knees and Justin had to hold me up from behind. There was no way Mom was *actually gone*, that I hadn't been there to catch and hold her, that I'd never get to say good-bye. It was too late for all that. I sobbed, then wailed, "She's gone?"

Suddenly I noticed a loud banging. I looked up to see my father kicking the wall.

"All she wanted was for me to love you and accept you and now it's too late," he exclaimed. "And it's your birthday, too! How can this be happening on your birthday?" He went on and on, yelling in my direction, crying what looked to me to be false tears.

At this time, my father and I had not been speaking for three years, except for what minimal interactions were called for, for the sake of civility. I had become content to never speak to him again. I tried my best to keep my view of him blurry, out-of-focus. I was occupied, trying to comprehend how it was possible that my mom was here yesterday and the day before, and the day before that, in the flesh, hugging me, and now what turned out to be a pulmonary embolism had stolen her in an instant. I was dazed, in shock, and my father's narcissistic, childish antics were annoying background noise. He hadn't been in my focus for a long time, so it had become normal to ignore him.

But then he began complaining of chest pains, at the hospital and over the next day or so. The next thing I knew, he was being transferred by ambulance from the Lawrence General ER to Beth Israel Hospital in Boston. He had a massive coronary and was going to Boston for bypass surgery. I no longer had the luxury of pretending he didn't exist. I couldn't, in good conscience, continue stonewalling.

Instead, in the jumble of tragedy and emergency, I suddenly found myself feeling sorry for him. It was confusing because he'd been such a monster to me for so much of my life, but what kind of monster would *I* have to be to keep my back turned to him under such extenuating circumstances? The man had become a widower and had a heart attack at the same time. Was it the result of Catholic guilt for the way he'd treated his wife and kids? Was this Mom trying to teach him a lesson from above? Or was she trying to orchestrate a situation in which my father and I would discover each other's humanity, and bond? I chose to see it as the latter.

I went with Justin to Dad's hospital bedside at Beth Israel. There, he was almost unrecognizable to me. He looked feeble with the oxygen tubes in his nose and IV needles in his arm. His eyes were filled with a fear and humility I'd never seen. He knew he'd been spared so far, but still risked seeing the face of God. More surprising was his apparent remorse, which seemed genuine.

"I wasn't good to her," he cried, "and now she's gone." Deep in my own grief, angry for the way he'd treated Mom, I didn't know how to respond. He'd been just awful to her, humiliating her in public, criticizing her for being too thin, for smoking too much, or for being too wrinkled—he cut her down for anything he could think of.

"She hated how hard I was on all you kids, but especially you," he went on. "I was so hard on you!" he said, his voice now cracking, and real tears flowing out of his red, swollen eyes. Standing at my father's bedside as he mourned my mother, my heart went out to him. I couldn't help it. What unpleasant behavior to have to look back on, to have to live with.

"We'll be here for you," I promised him. "We'll get you through this."

■ ■ ■

On the day of my mother's funeral, my father had quadruple bypass surgery. It was an odd blessing for my siblings and me. While we were concerned about him, we were also glad to have him out of the way. He couldn't ruin our tribute to our mother. We could make it about her and not him. And I wouldn't have to worry about him flying off the handle when I held Justin's hand for support.

As hundreds of people flooded West Parish Church for her wake the evening before, I introduced every single person to Justin, including all of Dad's colleagues from his career as a traveling housewares executive, and the guys who'd recently had my father as a baseball, basketball, or football coach, the volunteer jobs he continued to be most passionate about. Half of them seemed shocked, not because I said that Justin was my husband, but because many of them hadn't even known my father had a third child. He had never spoken of me.

As we entered the packed New England stone and white West Parish Church, the polished mahogany wood casket in front of the altar caught my eye and shook me into reality. The melancholy sounds of the bagpipes made me crumble. Barely able to walk down the aisle, I needed Jared and Justin to hold me up, each one holding one of my arms. I was in a state of deep disbelief: it all seemed unreal, like I was in a play or a movie. I had just told my mom, a few days before, that I'd "talk to her tomorrow."

Taking my seat in the pew, with Justin on my right, and my siblings and their families on my left, I couldn't stop crying. Jared had agreed to eulogize Mom since Julie and I felt incapable of holding it together long enough to get through it. He was magnificent. He honored our mother beautifully and spoke with poise and love, without pretense. With my father on a surgical table at Beth Israel Hospital, Jared was free to be himself and say what he wanted to say. I couldn't catch my breath as my friend James sang "You Light Up My Life." My arm clasped Justin's arm on my right, and my head fell on Jared's shoulder on my left. Mom had been fond of that song, and she had loved when I sang it as a child.

As Mom's body was lowered into the ground in West Parish Cemetery, adjacent to the church, the finality of it all petrified me. That death could be among so much life—the autumn trees, the cooling earth's grass, the pond in the distance teeming with lilies and cattails and frogs, all of us around her—was so confusing to me. None of it made sense. *Why?* I asked God silently. *How is it possible that there will be no more tomorrows with my mother?* I couldn't stay there any longer. I placed my single, long-stem rose on her casket, now in its final place, and walked away and into the limousine.

Justin followed me, as did Samantha. They sat with me as I stared out the window onto the picturesque fall day, the colors vibrant and her resting place beautifully peaceful. I put my hand to my cheek, wishing out loud that I hadn't washed off the lipstick kiss from our last night together. I would've done anything for another. And with that, looking at her casket in the grave, I said, "Bye, Mom."

■ ■ ■

My father made it out of surgery successfully. Justin and I made many trips to the hospital to visit him. A couple of days after his operation, he asked for some time alone with me.

When I got to the hospital, I found him still in a remorseful state. "I'm so sorry for what I've put you through," he said. "I feel like a horrible person." I was speechless. Maybe he finally had changed. Maybe this had been my mother's doing—her greatest sacrifice, to bring us together.

But days later when he was released from the hospital and back in his own bed, my real father emerged once again.

"I just don't understand," he began, "why you and Justin couldn't have just had a commitment ceremony instead of a wedding," his anger visibly rising. "And in front of all those people. And why did you have to take his last name?" He sounded paranoid. "You did this to spite me, I know it! Why did you do that to me?" I worried he was going to have another coronary, so I held my tongue. "We'll talk more another time," I said, and then got the visiting nurse to come and attend to him.

As Dad got stronger, Justin and I went out to dinner with him a few times, but the conversations were never nice. Back to his pre-heart-attack self, he talked badly about my brother and sister, trying to pit me against them. I think he always feared that if the three of us were too closely aligned, he'd be the one on the outside. He criticized my hair for being too long and my outfit for being too tight. He said that my sending fundraising letters to mutual friends and family seeking support for the foundation I created in my early twenties to help gay youth was done purposefully to hurt him. *He's back,* I said to myself. I could see he had no compunction, no real remorse.

I started to have a sick feeling when we got together, and then even when I wasn't with him. I began regressing, emotionally, to the insecurity that plagued me through my teens and early twenties. With my father back in everyday view, I started to obsess and be compulsive about things I had let go of years before. Prior to this most recent and seemingly forced reconciliation, I'd come to accept that I'd never have a father who accepted me. After years of hard work in therapy and time with him out of my life, I earned a freedom that I noticed my mother, sister, and brother did not enjoy. I wondered, why had I allowed this unchanged, disingenuous man back into my life?

Mom's sudden death had thrown me way off course. Without my greatest ally, I felt unmoored, completely lost, and once again craved the strange but familiar comfort of my old, destructive customs.

Somehow my mind tricked me into believing that I deserved this nonsensical turn of events. Intellectually, I knew I had no business going back to this way of thinking and doing. I now had the love of my husband and knew this wasn't fair to either of us, but I couldn't stop myself.

It wasn't long before Justin noticed the changes in me. I was isolating myself, running more and more, and eating less, sometimes skipping meals all together. I dropped five pounds, then seven, then ten.

"I know what you're doing," he finally said to me one day. We were sitting at the kitchen counter in our Charlestown home, as I made yet another excuse about why I didn't want breakfast. "I see where you're heading, and you need to stop now."

"I'm *grieving*, Justin," I snapped, rolling my eyes like the teenager I was when the addictions began.

"No, you're starving yourself," he replied. "And I'm not going to let you do that again."

He took me in his arms, and I bristled. The pain of losing my mother reminded me of how deeply afraid I'd been of being so close to someone. It reminded me that real people can desert you, their absence leaving a void that couldn't be filled. Justin kept holding me, though, until I finally warmed and relaxed into him. And yet, emotionally and psychologically, I still couldn't overcome the return of the flood of chemicals in my brain and body taking control of me. I kept acting out, punishing myself.

My runs around the Charlestown neighborhood Justin and I lived in started to extend to the Navy Yard, past the Bistro where we dined before Mom's death. I started to cut back on portions and began adhering to the Paleo Diet—another popular diet I'd discovered months before—more strictly. I was getting scared of carbohydrates the way I used to fear fat. Then, I started running even longer. It had been years since I'd run so many miles for such a long period of time. One day I even asked Justin to bring me water halfway through a run from Charlestown to Watertown and back. *It's back,* I thought. That voice in my head returned. Those miles on an empty belly felt strangely painful, but good. I was making excuses on a regular basis to Justin why I didn't want to go to our favorite pizza place on Main Street anymore.

I rejected his accusations at first, but then admitted I'd become overwhelmed with the obsessions and the compulsions again, albeit not to the degree I had when they took over my life a decade and a half before. Still, I knew in my heart that I was regressing to a Jon that felt much like the childhood or adolescent Jon I had shed so long ago. I was angry and I was turning that anger inward, like I had in the past. But this time I realized that I was angry. I was angry at *him.*

I resented that I was spending time with my father and could no longer see my mother. Visiting his house made me sick to my stomach. The eggshells I had walked on all throughout my life were still all around him. He hadn't changed, criticizing me for one thing after another. He didn't like my pink tie. He thought my untucked shirt was sloppy. He bitched about my sister not taking good enough care of him, and he complained that he had to send Jared money to replace a broken furnace and wondered how he couldn't afford it on his own. The toxicity in my father's veins never left after they removed the clogs in his heart. His own hurt was pumping stronger than ever through his recently restored heart, "the heart of a thirty-year-old," he egotistically declared. Given another chance, my siblings and I had imagined Dad would change. Instead, Dad had started in on all of us, again.

"You know, I am sorry for what I've done to you in the past, but I just don't get it," he said again one day. "Why did you have to call your ceremony to Justin a wedding? Gay marriage isn't what God had in mind. And remember when you created that foundation?" he continued. "That was really embarrassing that you sent letters to people I know, to my family." I couldn't just silently walk away any longer.

"Dad, I created the foundation to help save lives," I said. "I'm not sure how that is embarrassing to you. And I married Justin because I love him and I want to spend the rest of my life with him. Why did you call your wedding to Mom a wedding?"

Then he puffed up, like he used to. "Don't give me a lecture in my house, Mister."

That's when I knew: I had to leave his house altogether.

One day, sitting at my kitchen counter by myself, my iPod shuffled "Keep Holding On" to the play position. I began to cry. I remembered showing Mom the song sung by the *Glee* cast on the television that night we celebrated my birthday. I listened to the words and heard the many voices. Instead of just hearing my mom's voice singing to me, "Keep Holding On," I heard the chorus of my friends Samantha, James, Charlie, Deborah, and Meredith telling me to hold on so many times in the past. I imagined Julie that night she intervened when I was planning to kill myself, Jared at Rollins and at the Chicago Marathon telling me he loved me no matter what, Justin's family loving me like one of their own, and Justin telling me and showing me each and every day that I was the best thing that happened to him. Did I really need my father telling me the opposite, still, in my thirties? Was this really what my mom would have wanted our relationship to be?

I didn't want my father in my life. He was bringing me back to a Jon I didn't want to be again. I didn't want to go back to those doldrums, those self-loathing behaviors. I wanted to be the man my mom danced with at my wedding. And, in that instant, I knew that I had to get back on the path of letting my dad go for good. I needed to say good-bye forever. *I know what I have to do,* I thought. And I did.

■ ■ ■

I was told it's never a good idea to make major life decisions within six months of losing a loved one. But Justin and I didn't listen. Three months after Mom died, in the winter of 2010, we moved from Boston to upstate New York. Justin had gotten a great job offer from the University of Rochester, which he couldn't refuse. "Are you sure it's okay to do this?" he asked. "I mean considering how soon it is after we've lost your mom."

It was sweet of him to consider this. I decided to overlook the timing, though. Justin had supported me and my career so selflessly over the years. It was my turn to be supportive of him. "Let's get out of here," I said. "We have to do this for you."

My dad tried to get in touch, but I knew I couldn't talk to him. He called again and again, and left messages, and all I could bring myself to do was ignore them, or hit delete. If only he'd been this persistent in trying to connect with me for the past thirty-four years of my life, when I needed him. But I knew that by being passive, I wasn't being true to myself. And in a way, I was just stooping to my dad's level—ignoring him as he'd once done to me, back in the days when he regularly acted as if I didn't exist. This was lame. I had to deal with it more directly.

On my parents' wedding anniversary that April, I sent him a letter. In it, I let him know that for the sake of my well-being and Justin's, I just couldn't let him back into my life again, but that still, I forgave him. I explained that after Mom had died, I'd let him back into my life for his sake, because he was suffering. I'd gotten confused, and thought it would be what Mom had wanted. But in fact that's not what she had wanted. What she had wanted was for my dad to accept me, unconditionally, and that still was not happening.

I knew Mom wouldn't want me to do anything that didn't feel right to me, and, I explained to my dad in the letter, that talking to him and having dinners with him as if nothing was the matter didn't feel right to me. I didn't know how to have him back in my life without all the fears and anxieties flooding back in. I couldn't be myself around him and would always worry about him freaking out if I were to touch Justin's hand in front of him, or gain a pound, or drop a ball, or hold my hand "like a fag." I told him that I'd felt liberated before letting him back in my life after Mom's death and I wanted to feel liberated again.

He never responded to the letter. He didn't even acknowledge he'd received it, and to this day, I still don't know if he ever read it.

■ ■ ■

Since Mom died, there had only been a few occasions when I felt her presence nearby—only a couple of those magic moments when my heart actually believed something that my mind did not. The first time, on the day of our third anniversary, Justin and I were in Hawaii and we saw three shooting stars race across the sky, one after another, as we awaited the sunrise atop the Haleakala volcano in Maui. Then, a year later again on our anniversary, while hiking Stratton Mountain in Vermont, we noticed that a heart-shaped rock appeared on the ground before us. Mom had come to visit me in my dreams, too. The dreams felt so real that it was hard to believe she hadn't really come back to life. I'd wake up, sobbing, when I realized it was just a dream.

The third time was during the summer of our fifth wedding anniversary. Instead of one long vacation, Justin and I decided to take five long-weekend trips in its honor. One of the places we traveled to was Pittsburgh, the place where we had begun our life together, the place where we'd bought our first house and turned it into a home. It was the place where we'd built our solid foundation. We hadn't been back as a couple since we'd left.

Pittsburgh was a place Mom had visited often. She loved coming not only because it meant visiting us, but also because it meant escaping from my father for at least a short while. When she'd visit, she'd go to church with us at Calvary Episcopal Church, where I had been received into the Episcopal faith. It was important for me to be part of a faith that, for the most part, believed I was a worthy, loving, and good member of the world, no matter whom I loved.

That summer weekend when we returned, Justin and I sat in Calvary Episcopal Church once again, surrounded by its beauty, which had always moved Mom, too. The rector spoke brilliantly of forgiveness that Sunday. As he went on I heard something whispering in my mind: *Let it go.* Was this Mom? Regardless, I suddenly knew I needed to make sure my father knew I had forgiven him. As I'd done in so many other moments throughout my life when I was moved, or questioning, or pondering, I wrote another letter, in email form, and sent it. This one I know he read. Jared said he saw it marked as read in his BlackBerry. That's how I have been able to let him go and say good-bye. Once again, I wrote to him letting him know that even though I could never forget all that he'd done, and all that he hadn't, I forgave him. "And, even though you will never be a part of my life to understand it, I needed you to know that I forgive you. I have forgiven you."

✳

epilogue

As of this writing, it was four years ago that I first told my father I'd forgiven him. In that complete letting go, and in that forgiveness without qualification, I have felt freer and lighter. Far from perfect, but no longer seeking perfection, I now strive for acceptance: acceptance of myself, acceptance of all those around me.

While a distorted self and body image will always be a part of my life, I've learned how to realign myself. When I hear my father's voice, albeit way off in the distance in my head now, telling me I'm not good enough, I let it go.

I've learned to let go of the things I used to hold on to for dear life, things that aren't necessarily good for me, although sometimes I need to remind myself. It's something I keep looking at and working on. I'm feeling very liberated and very balanced.

I don't know if I'll ever stop thinking about what goes into my body and the consequences. But I try to remind myself to accept that my body will never be the perfect specimen that my father wanted it to be. Now, when I say to Justin that "I feel fat" after eating several slices of pizza, or a half pint of my favorite Ben & Jerry's ice cream, I remember that *I feel fat* but *I'm not fat*. I'm thankful that I actually ate it and I enjoyed it with less shame and guilt than ever. Afterward, Justin and I usually have a moment together: he smiles and tells me that I'm beautiful. I acknowledge, accept, and move on. More often than not, I'm able to think about food as fuel and not as fat or calories or carbohydrates. But even when I'm not, food is no longer my nemesis.

And while I still think about and believe in the importance of exercising to stay healthy, I haven't obsessed about it in a long time.

Maybe I'm just too tired from running all of those miles, all those years. Justin and I still enjoy staying active, whether jogging around our neighborhood or along a river, or climbing a mountain, or hiking a path, or kayaking in the ocean. Nature is still a place of solace for me, and as long as I can be outside and surrender to its magnificence, then I realize I have to make the most of every moment as often as I can. Maybe that's why we've made our permanent home in the mountains.

Dr. Carbalatto, my beloved psychology professor from Emerson, believed that gravity, the energy that keeps us all grounded to earth and bound to one another, was actually love. Gravity is a power that none of us can conquer. You can try, but you'd drain yourself of all your power. You have no choice but to surrender. And like surrendering to gravity, surrendering to love gave me the power to embrace myself once and for all. Dr. Carbalatto said consistent and unconditional love could heal most things. I wanted to believe him. And so I tried.

Despite everything, I opened my heart and allowed the love of others, especially my mother, my sister, my brother, my dear friends and their families, and Justin's family flow into me. And more so than with any other man in my life, I've accepted Justin's love, and it has, indeed, helped to heal me. In return I am able to love him more than anything else I have loved in my life. I found him at the right time. If I'd seen his photo any sooner, it never would have worked. I was ready to accept his love because I was ready, finally, to accept myself, and ready to heal.

While being with Justin these many years, I've filled out a bit, as many of us do when we find true love and give in to its weight. We cook meals, dine out, and spend holidays together with our families and friends. We travel and try new foods all over the world. I accept Justin's consistent, nonjudgmental love. It makes me feel as if I deserve the nourishment of food, and the everyday pleasures that life with him has to offer. Sure, there's more of me to love now, but it's all Justin's.

Looking back on when I met him, I now realize it was the warmth and the benevolence in his face that I believed could fill me up. By letting in all of that love, I learned how to truly love and accept *myself.*

The greatest love of all indeed.

※

acknowledgments

No endeavor like self-actualization or writing a memoir comes by working alone. I am who I am because of the village of people who believed in me, many of whom have helped make this book a reality as well. I know that on my own imperfect journey, I inadvertently hurt people along the way, and I'm sorry.

I'm grateful to my family, best friends, best friends' families, teachers, professors, boyfriends, therapists, and professional colleagues who did not give up on me and pushed me to strive on. Thank you to my sister and her husband, my brother and his wife, my very best girl and her husband, my godchildren, my nieces, my nephews, and my husband's family, who have loved me, embraced me, and welcomed me as one of their own.

For my goddess-of-an-agent, Rayhané Sanders at WSK Management, I'm eternally grateful. She is much more than an agent to me; she is a talented literary manager and a wonderful friend.

Thank you to my friend, accomplished writer, and talented editor, Sari Botton. Without her dedicated mentoring, encouragement, and brilliant editing of my manuscript, I would've gotten lost in the pages.

To Sid Farrar and the team at Hazelden Publishing for their commitment to this story, and for believing that it could help others. Thanks to Sid for taking time to give me thoughtful feedback on the manuscript and working with me every step of the way.

Thank you to James, Dr. Feinberg, Sophia, Samantha, Jared, Julie, Justin's mom, and Justin for reading drafts, giving wonderful feedback, and for encouraging me to be brave when I didn't think I could be.

I'm grateful to Emerson College, especially "the Castle," and to Outward Bound, which gave me more than an education; they set my life on an altered course. Thank you to Bianca for encouraging me to look at a college that would accept me for who I was.

To all of those who pioneered before me and all those who had it and have it worse than I ever did, to the kids, teenagers, young adults, and adults out there struggling: Don't give up.

To my father, whom I have wholeheartedly forgiven: Letting go has allowed me to flourish into the man I was always meant to be. I wish you peace.

I am grateful for my late mother, whose laughter, beauty, and wit I now get to see in my dreams.

Finally, to Justin Paul Croteau, thank you for laughing with me, holding me when I cry, forgiving me my many flaws, and supporting me in this undertaking until it was done. I am "the luckiest."

＊

resources

Every day, **The Trevor Project** saves young lives through its accredited, free, and confidential phone, instant message, and text-messaging crisis intervention services. The Trevor Project offers the largest safe social networking community for LGBTQ youth, best-practice suicide prevention educational trainings, resources for youth and adults, and advocacy initiatives. If you or someone you know is thinking about suicide, call the Trevor Lifeline at 1-866-488-7386.

www.thetrevorproject.org

Point Foundation (Point) is the nation's largest scholarship-granting organization for lesbian, gay, bisexual, transgender, and queer (LGBTQ) students of merit. Point Foundation empowers promising LGBTQ students to achieve their full academic and leadership potential—despite the obstacles often put before them—to make a significant impact on society. Point promotes change through scholarship funding, mentorship, leadership development, and community service training.

www.pointfoundation.org

Eating Disorder Hope™ offers education, support, and inspiration to eating disorder sufferers, their loved ones, and eating disorders treatment providers. Eating Disorder Hope resources include articles on eating disorder treatment options, support groups, recovery tools, and more. Whether an individual struggles with bulimia, anorexia, body image distortion, or binge-eating disorders, Eating Disorder Hope can help.

www.eatingdisorderhope.com

Outward Bound U.S.A. is the leading provider of experiential and outdoor education programs for youth and adults. Regardless of who you are or where you are from, there is an Outward Bound U.S.A. course at an Outward Bound School that is right for you. Outward Bound U.S.A. teaches to and works by these values: compassion, integrity, excellence, inclusion, and diversity.

www.outwardbound.org

The Human Rights Campaign Foundation works to enhance the lives of LGBT youth in their homes, schools, churches, communities, and beyond. HRC's youth and campus engagement program provides tools to foster safe campuses and to empower LGBT youth. Its children, youth, and families program provides innovative training and direct consultation with schools, child welfare agencies, and other service providers. The HRC Foundation is focused on creating a better today and tomorrow for LGBT youth, wherever they may be.

www.hrc.org

about the author

Jon Derek Croteau, Ed.D. (www.jonderekcroteau.com) is a consultant, educator, speaker, and writer. *A Huffington Post* contributor, he is the author of three books on leadership and numerous journal and periodical articles, as well as poetry, essays, and short stories. He is also executive producer of singer-songwriter Will Dailey's fourth studio album, *National Throat.*

Jon is a sought-after speaker on resilience, eating disorders and recovery, leadership and talent management, and LGBTQ issues. He has served on boards, committees, and councils for Emerson College, Point Foundation, The Home for Little Wanderers, Boston University, and The Trevor Project.

In 2007, Jon married his husband, Justin, and they enjoy theater, traveling, home design, gardening, skiing, and the outdoors. They reside in Vermont.

suggested discussion questions for book groups

1. What was the significance of the role that Jon's experience at Hudson Country Day had on the rest of his life and how does it foreshadow the rest of the story?

2. Why is Chad a significant character in the story? Do you think Chad understood how powerful of a role he played in Jon's life?

3. Why do you think Jon develops an eating disorder? Discuss the contributing factors that led him to this path.

4. What role do friends play in Jon's life? How are they able to help him on his journey?

5. Discuss two or three of the pivotal moments in Jon's journey that led him to recovery. What are they and how do they contribute to his healing?

6. How does Jon's father portray what a "real man" should be and how does Jon struggle with that notion throughout the story? Identify and discuss the times when Jon rebels against that notion.

7. Can you identify some times when Jon is able to let go of the past and move forward more freely?

8. Why was the campfire after the solo during Outward Bound so meaningful for Jon?

9. How does our society's need for perfection and appearing perfect play into Jon's struggles?

10. What was it about Dr. Robert's approach in therapy that worked for Jon? What did they focus on in therapy that seemed to work for him?

11. Why was Loren so important to Jon's development of his true self? What was it about that relationship that transformed things for Jon?

12. What does forgiveness mean to Jon? How is he able to forgive and move on?

13. Can you describe a moment where Jon's self-hatred begins turning to self-love and acceptance?

14. Jon didn't have many positive male role models in his life. Can you identify one or two who made a difference in his life and how?

15. Discuss Jon's relationship with his mother. What were her strengths and weaknesses and how does he gain from both?

16. Jon's siblings play a significant role in his life. How do they help him toward acceptance of himself?

Other titles that may interest you:

Almost Anorexic
Is My (or My Loved One's) Relationship with Food a Problem?
JENNIFER J. THOMAS, PH.D., AND JENNI SCHAEFER

Determine if your relationship with food is a problem, develop scientifically based strategies to change unhealthy patterns, and learn when and how to get professional help when needed with this inviting, hopeful guide.

Order No. 4389 (softcover)
Also available as an e-book.

Gay Men and Substance Abuse
A Basic Guide for Addicts and Those Who Care for Them
MICHAEL SHELTON, M.S., C.A.C.

By exploring the social and psychological factors that play into homosexual men's addictions, nationally certified treatment counselor Michael Shelton presents a timely, comprehensive look at best practices in meeting the unique needs of gay men in recovery.

Order No. 7934 (softcover)
Also available as an e-book.

Mind without a Home
A Memoir of Schizophrenia
KRISTINA MORGAN

Experience the inner world of a woman with schizophrenia in this brutally honest, lyrical memoir.

Order No. 2698 (softcover)
Also available as an e-book.

Hazelden books are available at fine bookstores everywhere.
To order from Hazelden, call **800-328-9000** or visit
hazelden.org/bookstore.